Chaucer's Native Heritage

American University Studies

Series IV
English Language and Literature

Vol. 11

PETER LANG
New York · Berne · Frankfurt am Main

Alexander Weiss

Chaucer's Native Heritage

PETER LANG
New York · Berne · Frankfurt am Main

Library of Congress Cataloging in Publication Data

Weiss, Alexander, 1944-
    Chaucer's Native Heritage.

    (American University Studies.   Series IV, English
Language and Literature; vol. 11)
        Bibliography: p.
        Includes index.
        1. Chaucer, Geoffrey, d. 1400 – Sources.   2. English
Poetry – Middle English, 1100–1500 – History and Criticism.
I. Title.   II. Series.
PR1912.A3W45   1985   821'.1   84-47695
ISBN 0-8204-0128-5
ISSN 0741-0700

CIP-Kurztitelaufnahme der Deutschen Bibliothek

Weiss, Alexander:
Chaucer's Native Heritage / Alexander Weiss. –
New York; Berne; Frankfurt am Main: Lang, 1985.
    (American University Studies: Ser. 4, English
    Language and Literature; Vol. 11)
    ISBN 0-8204-0128-5

NE: American University Studies / 04

© Peter Lang Publishing, Inc., New York 1985

All rights reserved.
Reprint or reproduction, even partially, in all forms such as
microfilm, xerography, microfiche, microcard, offset prohibited.

Printed by Lang Druck, Inc., Liebefeld/Berne (Switzerland)

For Sam and Pam

PREFACE

The study of medieval literature, particularly for the non-specialist, has often been hampered by the difficulty of obtaining reliable texts, even when these texts existed. During recent years, however, the appearance of excellent new editions, relatively inexpensive, has done much to alleviate the problem. The poetry upon which the present study is based is a case in point. Consequently, in selecting the texts from which poems quoted either in part or in whole have been reproduced, I have been guided by two principles: first, that the texts are reliable, in many cases those by common consent of the scholarly community accepted as "standard" editions; second, and equally important, that they be readily available.

To this end, Provençal and northern French lyrics have been reproduced from Frederick Goldin's Lyrics of the Troubadours and Trouveres. Old English and Middle English poetry has been reproduced from the excellent "standard" editions that have been available for some time now--Beowulf from Fr. Klaeber's Beowulf and the Fight at Finnsburg, 3rd ed.; other Old English poetry from The Anglo-Saxon Poetic Records, edited by George Phillip Krapp and Elliot Van Kirk Dobbie; and Chaucer's works from F. N. Robinson's The Works of Geoffrey Chaucer, 2nd ed. Exceptions to these general practices are indicated in the notes.

The Middle English lyrics pose a special problem, not only because they are too numerous to be conveniently collected in a single volume but also because many are so similar that it is sometimes difficult to determine whether we are dealing with different poems or different versions of the same poem. Many of the lyrics have been reprinted in one or another of the anthologies of Middle English verse that have appeared in recent years, and anyone interested in pursuing further the study of these lyrics should have no difficulty gaining access to them. However, the best and most comprehensive editions, although no longer all in print, remain those of Carleton Brown (English Lyrics of the XIIIth Century, Religious Lyrics of the XIVth Century, Religious Lyrics of the XVth Century) and Rossell Hope Robbins (Secular Lyrics of the XIVth and XVth Centuries, Historical Poems of the XIVth and XVth Centuries), and these are the ones from which selections here have been reproduced. The reason for this choice is largely pragmatic--to facilitate identification and to distinguish between those lyrics where more than one version has survived. Each lyric is identified by its first line, by the editor's last name and the volume in which it appears, and by the particular number assigned to it in that volume.

I would like to express my deep gratitude and great indebtedness to Professor Franklin Cooley, with whom I first studied Chaucer and who instilled in me not only a student's curiosity about medieval literature but also a genuine love for it; Professor Charles Muscatine, who fostered that love and encouraged

the curiosity until it matured into scholarly inquiry; but most
of all to my wife, Frannie, who never lost faith in me, and
whose constant good humor, patience, understanding, and encourage-
ment through the years made this book possible.

CONTENTS

INTRODUCTION

CHAUCER AND THE CRITICAL TRADITION

Geoffrey Chaucer occupies a crucial place in the history of
English literature. He is our first major poet. His poetry
has survived both the linguistic changes and the changes in
literary taste and fashion wrought by time. From his day to
our own, poet and scholar, literary critic and historian,
casual reader and conscientious student--virtually all have
been unanimous in their praise. It is not surprising then
that Chaucer has come to be commonly regarded as "the father
of our splendid English poetry."

For many literary historians modern English poetry begins
with Chaucer.[1] This view is supported by the underlying
assumption that Chaucer's greatest achievement was to "civil-
ize," so to speak, English poetry by introducing into it and
naturalizing many of the forms and modes of continental literature, thereby laying the foundation for future generations of
English poets.[2] Particularly emphasized is the importance of
French poetry for Chaucer in this regard. Albert C. Baugh's
comments are fairly typical: "Others had translated and
adapted French works before, but nobody else, either in his
[Chaucer's] day or before or after his day, so completely
transferred to English the whole spirit of polite literature in
Europe."[3] Consequently, the tendency has been to depict Chaucer
as a poetic genius, gifted with a natural talent, who, nourished
first by French literature, then by Italian literature, produced
his earlier poetry under their respective influences. Then,
during his later years, having fully digested these foreign
sources, he created his masterpiece, The Canterbury Tales.

For many years the standard textbook approach for dealing
with the development of Chaucer's art was to consider his literary career as falling into three major periods--his French period, his Italian period, and his English period. Because
Chaucer's earlier poetry--many of his extant lyrics, The Book
of the Duchess, The House of Fame, The Parliament of Fowls--is
so very much indebted to French sources, it was convenient to

think of these works, written sometime between the mid 1360's and the very early 1380's, as constituting Chaucer's French period. But in the 1370's Chaucer made at least two voyages to Italy. It is most probably during these visits that he became acquainted with the works of the great Italian writers of the thirteenth and fourteenth centuries, primarily Dante, Boccaccio, and Petrarch. And much of the poetry that Chaucer wrote during the 1380's--Troilus and Criseyde, The Legend of Good Women, The Knight's Tale--is so indebted to these Italian writers that it becomes readily apparent why this period of Chaucer's literary activity came to be thought of as his Italian period. Then, in the late 1380's, Chaucer began work on The Canterbury Tales, a work which was to occupy him for the rest of his life. Although virtually every tale in this collection has a source or an analogue in some other literature, and while the framed collection is not uncommon in the Middle Ages, no precise model is known that corresponds to Chaucer's total conception. Furthermore, because the setting is localized in the English countryside, travelled by pilgrims, most of whom have English names, on their way from an English inn to an English martyr's shrine, The Canterbury Tales is Chaucer's most obviously "English" creation. And so this final period of Chaucer's literary career was designated his English period.

While such a scheme has some merit--it provides us with a simple, chronological perspective against which we can view the complex development of Chaucer's art and emphasizes the very significant influences exerted by French and Italian literature upon this development--it also has severe limitations.[4] In the first place there is considerable overlapping between the periods. The House of Fame and The Parliament of Fowls can more accurately be described as transitional poems than as belonging to the French period, since both already show signs of Italian influence; French influence is still clearly evident in Troilus and Criseyde, The Legend of Good Women, and The Knight's Tale; and both French and Italian influence persist in the works assigned to the English period. Nor does the so-called English period in any way constitute a distinct period of particular influence in the same sense that the French and Italian periods are presumed to. Rather, it is the time in his literary career during which Chaucer, having fully assimilated all the influences that had helped to shape his art, produces some of his greatest and most distinctive work.

Not only does this three period scheme represent a too simplistic approach to the complex question of the development of Chaucer's art, more important it is also misleading, for it ignores Chaucer's relationship to the native English poetic tradition he inherited and the role this tradition played in the shaping of his art.

In the prefatory note to A Critical History of English Poetry Grierson and Smith write, "No doubt every poet is the child of his age and the heir of a particular tradition; but the

great poet helps to create the spirit of his age and to mould
the tradition he has inherited." Surely this is a sound observation and is particularly apropos with reference to Chaucer.
However, the prevailing assumption heretofore has been that the
tradition to which Chaucer was heir was that of continental
Europe, the tradition represented primarily by Latin, French,
and Italian literature. Thus, John Speirs writes,

> It is evident from his [Chaucer's] poetry it-
> self that he had French and Italian prede-
> cessors and contemporaries and that in some
> ways they formed the community of poets to
> which he belonged and knew himself to belong.
> But it does not appear to have been so much a
> matter for his conscious consideration that
> there was a contemporary poetry in English.[5]

Baugh at least places Chaucer at home in England, but he expresses
essentially the same view as Speirs: "Of course he [Chaucer] was
the heir of previous centuries of English civilization and of a
language adequate for his purpose, but what he owes to previous
English writers is slight in comparison with his debt to French
and Latin and Italian books" (262-263).
      Such a view functions as a point of departure for the many
studies that examine the effects of Chaucer's poetic genius working upon these literatures. And until recently Chaucerian criticism has focused primarily upon Chaucer's relationship to these
foreign traditions.
      A very great deal of work, much of it both necessary and
useful, has been done by generations of scholars to discover in
these foreign literatures not only the sources of Chaucer's plots
and of particular individual lines, but also those elements that
contributed to his style. Fansler has shown the pervasive influence exerted by the Roman de la Rose on Chaucer's work; Cummings
has pointed out Chaucer's indebtedness to Boccaccio, while Fyler
has analyzed in detail his indebtedness to Ovid; Jefferson has
demonstrated how Chaucer employed Boethius' Consolation of
Philosophy; Schaar has shown to what extent Chaucer's descriptive
technique derives from a common medieval tradition; Muscatine has
shown how Chaucer's different styles derive from the French tradition; and Landrum has pointed out Chaucer's use of the Vulgate,
to mention just a few.[6] And a host of scholars, too numerous to
mention by name, have pointed out Chaucer's indebtedness to Virgil,
to Dante and Petrarch, to Machaut, Froissart, Deschamps, Graunson,
and others.
      In any discussion of Chaucer's poetry we must certainly
acknowledge the important contributions made by French and
Italian, as well as Latin, literature and the traditions that
these represent. But we must be careful to maintain a sense of
proportion and not to overstate the case, especially since this
emphasis on foreign influence has, in the past, tended to exclude the native tradition from the consideration due it and

has led to much confusion and certain misconceptions about the nature of Chaucer's poetry, misconceptions which, sanctioned by the acquiescence of generations of scholars, have become so firmly established that they have attained the status of generally accepted critical commonplaces. The result has been to create a partially distorted, if not erroneous, picture not only of Chaucer's poetry, but also of the early history of English literature and Chaucer's place in that history.[7]

Literary historians and critics have commonly viewed English literature during the three centuries following the Norman Conquest as little more than a barren wasteland until, in the middle of the fourteenth century, Chaucer came along, planted in it the seeds obtained from France and Italy, and fertilized it with his genius. Then, after some years of toil and cultivation and careful pruning, Chaucer's labors bore fruit, and English literature burst into full bloom in the form of The Canterbury Tales.[8] J.A. Burrow, for example, remarks, "Collections such as the Auchinleck MS., despite their great bulk, offered little work of sufficient distinction to command the respect of sophisticated London readers. If that was their [Chaucer's and Gower's] native heritage (and where else are we to look for it?) then it was a poor thing."[9] Others have imposed their assessment of English poetry prior to Chaucer on Chaucer himself. Norman Eliason writes, "As best we can tell from his few references to English poetry...and his almost scrupulous avoidance of it as a source for his own work, he [Chaucer] must have regarded most of it with disdain."[10] In a similar vein Derek Pearsall, referring to Middle English romances of the type parodied by "Sir Thopas," asserts, "The only debt, in fact, which Chaucer can be proved to owe to earlier English poetry is one which he thought worth paying with withering scorn."[11]

Such disparaging views of English poetry prior to Chaucer, implying that the poetic tradition he inherited from his English predecessors was totally inadequate for the purposes of an aspiring poet, seem to me far too extreme to be accurate, as does the concomitant notion that Chaucer's poetry was the product of a continental marriage, born in France and reared in the continental tradition. That English poetry before Chaucer was less refined, less sophisticated, less rich than the poetry of France and Italy is immediately evident even to the beginning student of the literature of the Middle Ages. Chaucer himself, on more than one occasion, refers to the limitations of the English of his day for the purpose of writing poetry, in the envoy to the "Complaint of Venus," for example:

> And eke to me it ys a gret penaunce, Syth rym
> in Englissh hath such skarsete, To folowe word
> by word the curiosite Of Graunson....(79-82)[12]

But if this poetry was indeed such a "poor thing," and if Chaucer's attitude toward it was one of "withering scorn," why then did he choose to write in English? Clearly, the choice of French would have been an equally viable option, perhaps even a more natural one.[13] For despite the fact that English was reasserting itself during the second half of the fourteenth century, the aristocratic household in which Chaucer grew up and the court circles through which he moved in later years were still essentially French in character. But whether the courts of Edward III and Richard II were French-speaking, as Rossell Hope Robbins maintains in his valiant attempt to convince us that Chaucer's now lost "many a song and many a lecherous lay" were actually "court love lyrics written in French,"[14] or whether the court of Edward III was already undergoing the transition to English, as seems more likely,[15] one incontrovertible fact remains--that while French poetry written by Englishmen contemporary with Chaucer but of lesser status as poets has survived, no single line of verse written in French has as yet been discovered that can with any kind of certainty be ascribed to Chaucer.

Chaucer's decision to write in English must have been a very carefully calculated one, involving no small degree of risk. What could have prompted him to take this risk? At the very least, he must have recognized the potential of English as a literary language capable of equalling and perhaps even surpassing the French with which he was so intimately familiar. And what possible evidence could he have had to suggest such potential if not the poetry of his English predecessors? As Patricia Kean so well observes, "It would hardly be conceivable that he should thus choose to write in English without any reference to the fact that a long established tradition of the use of the vernacular for poetry lay behind him; and, in fact, he does show obvious knowledge of the work of some of his predecessors, especially in the fields of romance and lyric."[16]

But what may be even more significant, Chaucer must have been aware that the perimeters of a literary tradition are, at its core, more fully circumscribed by its language than by considerations of subject matter or any set of artificial conventions cutting across linguistic boundaries; that whatever affinities, for example, French poetry--its lyrics, romances, epics--may have had with the poetry of classical antiquity, these were secondary to the fundamental fact that comprising the French tradition were those works written in French. Chaucer's decision to compose in English can best be regarded not simply as a fortuitous, experimental venture into new and unexplored realms of poetic expression, but as a carefully considered commitment to the tradition, still in its infancy, of his English predecessors, linking his poetic endeavors to theirs, and a clear and unequivocal declaration of his intention to carry on in that tradition.

It may well have been Chaucer's purpose, at least in part, "to give the idiom of English poetry the entrée to the court, to ennoble it after the French pattern,"[17] but this does not mean that Chaucer wrote French poetry in English, as Grierson and Smith contend (24). Nor does it necessarily mean, as W.J. Courthope maintains, that "Chaucer resolved...to look exclusively to France for his...models" (252), metrical or otherwise. Kean's judgment, more temperate and more balanced, also seems to ring more true: "Modern critics of Chaucer have, I think, sometimes shown a less accurate understanding of the situation, in that they have tended to concentrate on the newness [of Chaucer's poetry] and to deny the way in which the poet's Englishness links him to what has gone before"(3).

Others too have linked Chaucer to what had gone before. H.S. Bennett, for example, comments, "Not only French poetry, but English poetry, was also known to Chaucer and was not without merit." And he goes on to warn against overemphasizing Chaucer's dependence on French models: "This is to ignore the abundant evidence of a living body of verse which was in circulation when Chaucer began to write" (9-11).[18] R.T. Davies remarks in this regard, "It is also true that Chaucer's own poetry probably derived fundamentally far more from the native tradition than appears on the surface."[19] Even Wolfgang Clemen concedes that Chaucer was "conversant with the complex development of his own literary tradition..." (3).

Both J.A. Burrow and D.S. Brewer suggest that Chaucer's style is indebted to this native tradition. Burrow writes, "Even Chaucer, whose knowledge not only of French and Latin but also of the insufficiencies of Guy of Warwick and Sir Orfeo, cultivated an English style which is much more traditional than many people realize" (12). And Brewer asserts, "The truth is that Chaucer inherited a particular English style, which he enriched by his borrowings from French and Italian and Latin."[20] Ian Robinson perhaps best summarizes the case: "Chaucer's individuality survives and shapes a great many traditions and does so, moreover, in English, which means that whatever rules he was following they could not have been simply transferred from another language."[21]

But it is what these scholars do not say that is also significant here. If there was a native tradition and if Chaucer was "conversant" with it, there is every reason to suppose that the audience to whom Chaucer's poetry was addressed was also to some extent familiar with it. Nor is there any reason to suppose that this native tradition was not a matter for Chaucer's "conscious consideration" or that he was not aware of "continuing in it." In fact, Chaucer's very decision to compose even his earliest poems in English would seem to suggest just the opposite. What Chaucerian scholarship has not then clearly defined is the nature of this tradition, nor how it is reflected in Chaucer's poetry.

An interesting paradox, if we may call it such, emerges from an examination of Chaucerian scholarship. While many scholars have gone to great pains to find continental sources for Chaucer's poetry and to demonstrate at great length various influences, sometimes obvious and sometimes very subtle, which helped to shape his poetry, virtually all agree that there is a certain quality which marks it as distinctly Chaucerian and which is, perhaps, the very essence of Chaucer's greatness, a quality most often referred to or described as "English."[22]

This quality should not, however, be confused with the conventional notion of Chaucer's English period. Certainly, The Canterbury Tales is Chaucer's most distinctly "English" work, but it is not The Canterbury Tales alone which bears a distinctly recognizable Chaucerian stamp. Nor is it his only work characterized by this English quality, which, as Wolfgang Clemen has noted, is discernible in Chaucer's earliest poetry, even that most dominated by the influence of French models(2-8). Clemen's opinion that Chaucer's "English period" begins with his first poem is eminently sensible, and to regard the whole corpus of Chaucer's works, his entire literary career, as constituting his English period is more accurate and less distorted than the traditional scheme of a French, Italian, and English period and, on the whole, preferable to it.[23]

Most discussions of this English quality have been limited to Chaucer's success in depicting the people, customs, and manners of the England of his day, or to his "good ear," his ability to reproduce in his poetry the idiom and colloquial mannerisms of the English of his day. Dorothy Everett, for example, suggests that Chaucer is able to capture and reproduce not only the rhythms of the spoken language in his poetry, but also the idiosyncratic speech traits of different people and different dialects.[24] Margaret Schlauch reaches much the same conclusions in her study of the structural traits of Chaucer's Colloquial English:

> Chaucer shows an ear attuned to people's idioms according to character, circumstance, and social level. It is not only a matter of choosing words fitting to subject matter...but of choosing linguistic structures fitting to the speakers' personalities--their characteristic ways of organizing experience....[25]

John Speirs declares, "His [Chaucer's] genius owes more perhaps to the English language of which he is a master, the English that was spoken around him, than to the French and Italian poets from whom he occasionally borrowed and to whom he certainly owes much."[26] A similar view underlies Paull Baum's study of Chaucer's prosody:

> The language which Chaucer used, which he
> spoke and heard, was a Germanic language with
> definite lexical accent; and when he composed
> in verse his language was still the same.
> When he read his poems to himself and when he
> recited them aloud to others, it was still the
> language of his normal speech adapted to met-
> rical patterns as he understood them.(9)[27]

Such a view, while rightly emphasizing the importance of the
spoken language in helping to shape Chaucer's art, still essentially ignores the native literary tradition, for, as Emerson
Brown pointedly reminds us, "Chaucer is an English poet in more
than the language of his verse."[28] There is a distinction to
be made between a language as it is spoken and that same language as it is used for the purpose of writing poetry. The spoken
language provides the poet with his raw material, but it is how
the poet uses this raw material, the form he gives it that determines the poetic tradition. To say, then, that the spoken English of Chaucer's day was instrumental in the shaping of his art
is to say only that it provided him with the raw material for
his poetry. But this tells us very little about that poetry itself or the tradition to which it belongs, particularly since we
have no way of knowing with any certainty what exactly the
spoken English of Chaucer's day was like. Consequently, it would
seem that we can arrive only at a very limited understanding of
Chaucer's relationship to the native poetic tradition from this
direction.

A poetic tradition may exert an influence quite independent
of the spoken language. Robert O. Payne provides a useful summary of the ways in which tradition may operate upon a poet:

> First, we may mean by "tradition" simply the
> series of linguistic, substantive, and per-
> ceptual habits--largely inherited from the
> past--which a poet necessarily acquires if he
> is to write at all. In this sense, "tradition"
> is roughly equal to "language." Second, "tra-
> dition" may mean those particular literary acts,
> in the past, to which the poet turns in the
> attempt either to create or to justify his
> creation; that is, "tradition" as model or
> specific source. Finally, it may indicate
> the total continuity of the past, contem-
> plated by the poet as a process, in the at-
> tempt to establish its significance in toto and
> relate himself and his art to it--approximately
> the sense in which Eliot uses the term in his
> Tradition and the Individual Talent. It should

be noted that all three of these distinctions
are phrased in terms of a possible significance of the past to the poet, and also that
the first indicates a much less conscious
relationship between the poet and his past
than the others do.[29]

It is primarily in this second sense of tradition that
Chaucerian scholars have pointed out affinities between Chaucer's
poetry and the considerable body of extant Middle English poetry
other than Chaucer's, much of which he was himself no doubt
familiar with. James G. Southworth, in his studies of Chaucer's
prosody,[30] focuses on the conversational quality of Chaucer's
verse and attributes this quality to a native prosodic tradition
to which belonged not only the poetry of Chaucer but also the
northern alliterative poetry:

> I think it can be said with a great measure of
> truth that the native tradition is found un-
> checked in Piers Plowman, checked and altered
> in the poetry of Chaucer. In both it is a
> rhythmical rather than a metrical tradition.
> (Cadence, 1)

Southworth describes Chaucer's rhythms in terms of this tradition:
"The movement of Chaucer's verse is that of Piers Plowman, Sir
Gawayn, Gower, and others--it is the movement of a highly developed English speech" (Cadence, 91).[31] Ian Robinson also suggests
a relationship between Chaucer's poetry and the alliterative
poetry in this regard:

> Chaucer's racy conversations almost anywhere
> in the endlinks give the modern reader the
> illusion of hearing what fourteenth century
> speech was really like...Here Chaucer is in
> an obvious way working with the pieces of
> speech of the alliterative tradition and
> here, above all, the function of the metre
> is to point the speech and suggest its
> shades of tone without turning it into some-
> thing that is not speech. These "pieces of
> speech" are, just as in Sir Gawain or Piers
> Plowman, the half-line phrases. (Prosody, 167)[32]

Other similarities between Chaucer's poetry and that of his
northern contemporaries are noted by J.A. Burrow, who argues
pursuasively that too much critical emphasis has, in the past,
been placed on the differences between these. Burrow finds both
to be characterized by a "story-telling" quality, and he points

out certain features, such as the direct face-to-face relationship between narrator and audience, the repetition of stock
phrases, and the simplicity of diction that they have in common.
He further suggests that these features derive from the verse
romances of the native minstrel tradition, a tradition which,
according to Burrow, was particularly influential with regard
to Chaucer. Thus, he concludes, "The narrative manner of these
romances, which Chaucer must have learned both from hearing
minstrels in London and Westminster and from reading books,
especially anthologies such as the Auchinleck MS., formed an
important part of his native poetic inheritance...(14).[33]

   Burrow is not the first to have noticed similarities between Chaucer's poetry and the verse romances. Caroline Strong
in 1908 pointed out that Chaucer's Sir Thopas was indebted to
Guy of Warwick in certain particulars of phrasing and detail,[34]
and in 1940 Laura H. Loomis demonstrated conclusively that the
version of Guy of Warwick used by Chaucer was the one contained
in the Auchinleck MS.[35] Chaucer must, then, have been acquainted
at first hand with this collection of Middle English verse, which
includes not only a number of romances but also several Breton
lays and some lyrics.

   That Chaucer was indebted to the Middle English verse romances has been suggested by others as well. Ruth Crosby, for
example, describes a number of characteristics of Chaucer's
narrative poetry--the narrator's direct address to the audience,
repetition, especially of stock phrases, religious beginnings
and endings, and clear and simple transitional phrases--and
emphasizes the similarity between his use of these devices and
their use in the Middle English romances.[36] She sums up her
findings as follows:

> Of course it is undoubtedly true that many of
> the phrases used in common by Chaucer and the
> romance writers were popular colloquialisms.
> Chaucer must have heard and used such expres-
> sions in every day speech as frequently as we
> do similar ones today. But in using such popu-
> lar phrases in literature, he was following an
> example set by the Middle English romance poets.
> It is in his style, then, rather than in his
> subject matter that the influence of Chaucer's
> English reading is most apparent. For his
> materials he often went far afield; but in the
> manner of telling his story, he combined with
> the devices of the classical rhetoricians
> those characteristics which had their origin
> in the technique developed through the centu-
> ries by the professional minstrels, and which
> were distinct marks of the English popular
> literature which he had read, or heard. (431-432)[37]

E.T. Donaldson argues persuasively that Chaucer's diction derives, at least in part, from the romances,[38] and D.S. Brewer points to the romances as a primary source for the characteristic tone of the particular style he maintains Chaucer inherited from the native tradition: "This tone resides in the language as it had been spoken and evolved in the country for nearly a thousand years, and in that artistic formalization of the language which is found in what may be called the Middle English rhyming romances"(34).[39] Similarly, Patricia Kean contends that Chaucer's style owes much to these romances. According to Kean, "The main contribution of the earlier English narrative style is, obviously, to the formation of the kind of neutral, unemphatic language which is so necessary to the poet who sets out to tell tales in verse" (Love Vision, 11).[40]

D.W. Robertson approaches the question of the relationship between Chaucer's style and the native tradition from the broader perspective of late medieval Gothic art, and suggests that Chaucer's "Englishness" resides in stylistic features that his poetry has in common with the distinctive form English art in general, but principally as reflected in manuscript illuminations and architecture, took during the late Middle Ages. Among the characteristically English features of this style Robertson includes its "conservatism"; its "sense of detachment" and "emphasis on ideas rather than on feelings"; its exuberance and vivid exemplification"; its "tendency to compartmentalize, to prefer a juxtaposition of discrete forms to a lineally integrated whole"; its preference for structural simplicity; and a general rejection of the heroic.[41]

Finally, Carter Revard has argued that there is a relationship between the techniques of the links and prologues of The Canterbury Tales and a group of Middle English satirical lyrics.[42] Revard suggests that lyrics such as "The Papelard Priest," "A Satire on the Consistory Courts," and "The Man in the Moon" are part of a native English genre which he calls "Confessional Satire." He remarks, concerning these lyrics, "They are survivors proving the existence of a native comic genre...whose later and greater achievements include the links and prologues to the Canterbury Tales..."(57).[43] He further suggests that Chaucer, in creating certain characters like the Host, the Reeve, the Pardoner, and the Wife of Bath, used the techniques he learned from this native genre.

Even if no poet has better claim to the title "Father of English Poetry" than does Chaucer, whatever else his achievements may have been, it is clear that Chaucer neither invented nor created English poetry, nor were his literary ancestors solely the poets of continental traditions. Chaucer's poetry, in fact, represents not so much the beginning of a new English poetic tradition as the culmination of an existing native tradition, a varied and in many ways rich tradition that he inherited from his English predecessors and that in part reaches as far back

as the earliest English poetry itself. This native tradition
provided Chaucer with a sound foundation, and it was upon this
foundation that he built. But despite the fine work of the
many Chaucerian scholars who have established beyond question
that Chaucer not only was familiar with but made use of native
sources, the precise nature of Chaucer's Englishness has continued to remain elusive.

To illustrate, let us turn for a moment to last things
first, to The Canterbury Tales, which readers have always identified as Chaucer's most distinctively English work, in large part,
no doubt, because its surface presents us with such a vivid and
seemingly genuine panorama of England in the fourteenth century--
its places, its customs, its manners and above all else its
people speaking its language.[44] To be sure, the setting for the
pilgrimage framework is identifiably English, but whatever
Englishness derives from the setting exists only at a surface
level, serving little more than to impart to the work as a whole
a bit of local coloring. If we look more closely below this
surface, we actually find surprisingly little that is characteristically, much less uniquely, English. Of the tales themselves, only five--the Miller's, the Reeve's, the Cook's, the
Friar's and the Summoner's--are explicitly set in fourteenth
century England, all, interestingly enough, fabliaux, a genre
itself more native to France than to England. To these we
could add the Wife of Bath's tale, though Arthur's kingdom is
far removed in time from the fourteenth century, and both the
Canon Yeoman's account of his master and the Parson's sermon,
neither of which, however, is properly a "tale." Even so, there
remain sixteen tales set in places ranging from Flanders to Asia,
from France and Italy to Greece and Syria, and in times ranging
from the fourteenth century to classical antiquity. Nor is
there, with the possible exception of what Revard has termed
"confessional satire," anything more distinctively English about
literary genres other than fabliaux represented by these tales.
Romances, beast fables, saints' lives, legends, miracles of the
Virgin, tragedies, exempla, sermons--all are commonplace, the
staple forms as much of continental as of English medieval literature.

Moreover, it need hardly be pointed out that the pilgrimage
itself, either as a literary device or as a fact of life, is no
more exclusively English than are the types of individuals
gathered together for this particular pilgrimage to Canterbury.
Knights and their squires, monks, friars, pardoners and summoners,
parsons and nuns, merchants and cooks populate the literary and
real worlds of the whole of medieval Christian Europe, and on
the continent they stop at inns very much like the Tabard and
make their way to shrines very much like the one at Canterbury.
Nor is there anything more notably English about the attitudes
and values, the ethics and morals, the politics and religion,
the hopes and aspirations, the concerns and fears, in sum, the

philosophy of life expressed throughout the tales either by the
tellers themselves or those they tell about. Rather, the
weltanschauung of the Canterbury pilgrims, including the narrator, and so, it would seem, ultimately of Chaucer himself is
typically that of the medieval Christian "Everyman."

What, then, is so English about The Canterbury Tales or,
for that matter, about any of Chaucer's works? In one sense,
the answer is perfectly obvious--they sound English. That an
English poet working in the English language would quite naturally produce poetry that sounds English hardly seems startling.
But this simple fact, so commonly acknowledged that it is often
taken for granted, has implications beyond the recognition of
Chaucer's "good ear" or his colloquial and idiomatic use of
language, and raises more problematic questions, many of which
have gone largely unexplored. Most basically, what does "sounding" English mean, especially with reference to the composition
of verse in Chaucer's day, and how did Chaucer succeed in doing
so? To what extent did the native tradition influence Chaucer's
decision to compose in English, and in what ways did it contribute to the sound of his verse?

Speirs' succinct and perceptive observation that "He
[Chaucer] has in common with the English poetry...all that is
implied in the fact that he is an English poet"(18) serves also
to underscore the problem. The question is, of course, just
what precisely is "implied" in the fact that Chaucer is an
English poet. The fundamental intention of this study is to
attempt at least a partial answer. Its aims include to ascer-
tain the nature of Chaucer's Englishness by isolating, identifying and describing as precisely as possible the uniquely English
quality of his poetry; to demonstrate that this quality is the
product of deliberate stylistic techniques for which Chaucer is
indebted to earlier English poetry; to establish, as a result,
not only that this uniquely English quality derives from the
native poetic tradition but marks Chaucer's poetry as belonging
firmly to that tradition; and so to provide a more accurate
assessment of Chaucer's place in the history of English literature.

While a complete investigation of Chaucer's relationship
to the native poetic tradition ideally would examine Chaucer's
poetry within the context of the whole corpus of English poetry
to his day, so enormous an undertaking seems to me beyond the
scope of any single investigation and less likely to yield meaningful results than would a more rigidly circumscribed approach.
Partly as a practical matter, therefore, I have chosen to limit
my investigation of the native tradition as it evolved after the
Conquest and its influence on Chaucer to the Middle English
lyrics, a limitation prompted by other considerations as well.
In the first place, Chaucer's indebtedness to earlier English
narrative poetry, particularly the romances, has already received
considerable attention, but there has been little serious

critical examination of his poetry in light of the lyric tradition. In the second place, my primary concern is with the sound
of Chaucer's poetry, and sound is the product of versification
techniques common to both narrative and lyric poetry. In this
respect generic distinctions become superfluous and because whatever conclusions about versification techniques can be reached
from a close analysis of the lyrics apply equally to narrative
poetry, exclusion of the latter results in no significant distortions of evidence. Finally, the Middle English lyrics are
representative of the native tradition in far more ways than
versification techniques alone. Spanning the entire period in
question, these lyrics treat every subject and every theme that
can be found elsewhere in the poetry of this period, and employ
virtually every stylistic and rhetorical device known to it.
There are religious lyrics and secular lyrics. There are lyrics
which are courtly and lyrics which are popular, popular at
least by destination if not by origin, to borrow Richard Greene's
terminology. And it is quite likely that in the popular lyrics
those elements of the tradition which have their roots in Old
English poetry are most clearly preserved. For it seems reasonable that at least some of these popular lyrics may have survived
as part of the oral tradition, passed on by word of mouth until
they came to be written down sometime after the twelfth century.
Thus, these lyrics would likely have been less affected by the
domination of French after the conquest than would the more
literary courtly poetry. But whether courtly or popular,
religious or secular, the Middle English lyrics were composed by
many different poets and were intended for a wide variety of
audiences, and we can assume, therefore, that they reflect the
characteristics common to the whole poetic corpus of the period,
at least those most popular with both poet and audience.

[1] Paull Baum, in his study of Chaucer's prosody, declares, "One thing may be said with security, that modern English versification starts with Chaucer. With him it was almost a de novo creation." Chaucer's Verse (Durham: Duke Univ. Press, 1961), 11. In much the same vein, Ian Robinson, in his concluding chapter, titled appropriately enough "Chaucer the Father," asserts, "So Chaucer is the father of English literature not by begetting it or influencing it but by creating its form." Chaucer and the English Tradition (London: Cambridge Univ. Press, 1972), 291. From a somewhat different perspective G.K. Chesterton devotes a chapter, "Chaucer as an Englishman," to the proposition that Chaucer represents the modern Englishman in the process of emerging. Chesterton suggests that traces of contemporary notions of the stereotypical "Englishman" can be found in Chaucer's life and are given their earliest literary manifestation in Chaucer's works. Chaucer (New York: Greenwood Press, 1956), 176-204.

[2] It is in fact precisely for this reason that W.J. Courthope claims that Chaucer is entitled to be called "the father of English poetry." A History of English Poetry (New York: Macmillan, 1895), I:6. So too H.S. Bennett, who writes, "It was for Chaucer, nourished in other literatures and stimulated by aristocratic demands, to make rapid advances on the road of English poetry." Chaucer and the Fifteenth century (Oxford: Oxford Univ. Press, 1947), 11.

[3] A Literary History of England (New York: Appleton-Century-Crofts, 1948), 263. Rossell Hope Robbins takes this point of view to its furthest extremes: "Chaucer, following the court fashion, was steeped in the new French poetry; he composed his early verses in French; through these French verses he acquired a court reputation as a poet; he later simply transliterated the French techniques and devices into English...If we accept these proposals, we are forced to believe that the traditional Father of English Poetry started his career by speaking French and writing French love poems." "The Vintner's Son: French Wine in English Bottles," in Eleanor of Aquitaine: Patron and Politician, ed. William W. Kibler (Austin: Univ. of Texas Press, 1976), 165. At the opposite extreme is S.R.T.O. D'Ardenne, who maintains, "Chaucer was English by birth and genius" and "remained English to the end." "Chaucer, the Englishman," in Chaucer und seine Zeit: Symposion fur Walter Schirmer, ed. Arno Esch (Tubingen: Max Niemeyer, 1968), 54.

[4] In A Critical History of English Poetry (New York: Oxford Univ. Press, 1946) Grierson and Smith comment, "The division of Chaucer's work into three periods, French, Italian, and English is not a happy one"(27). As early as 1915 G.L. Kittredge raised some pertinent objections. Chaucer and His Poetry (Cambridge, Mass: Harvard Univ. Press, 1915), 26-29.

[5]Medieval English Poetry: The Non-Chaucerian Tradition (London: Faber, 1957), 13. Similarly, Baugh remarks, "Chaucer is completely continental in his literary affiliations. He is remarkably indifferent to the English writings"(252).

[6]D.S. Fansler, Chaucer and the Roman de la Rose, Columbia Studies in English and Comparative Literature, 7 (New York, 1914); Hubertis M. Cummings, The Indebtedness of Chaucer's Works to the Italian Works of Boccaccio, University of Cincinnati Studies, 10.2 (Cincinnati, 1944); John Fyler, Chaucer and Ovid (New Haven: Yale Univ. Press, 1979); Bernard L. Jefferson, Chaucer and the Consolation of Philosophy of Boethius (Princeton: Princeton Univ. Press, 1917); Claes Schaar, The Golden Mirror (Denmark, 1967); Charles Muscatine, Chaucer and the French Tradition (Berkeley: Univ. of California Press, 1957); Grace W. Landrum, "Chaucer's Use of the Vulgate," PMLA 39(1924): 75-100.

[7]As R.A. Shoaf well observes, "Too much emphasis on the various traditions obscures the fact that Chaucer was an English poet." "Notes Toward Chaucer's Poetics of Translation," in Studies in the Age of Chaucer, 1(1979): 59-60.

[8]Ian Robinson declares, "Chaucer's composition of The Canterbury Tales is the creation of English Literature"(282).

[9]Ricardian Poetry (New Haven: Yale Univ. Press, 1971), 23.

[10] The Language of Chaucer's Poetry, Anglistica, 17 (Copenhagen: Rosenkilde and Bagger, 1972), 27.

[11] Old English and Middle English Poetry (London: Routledge & Kegan Paul, 1977), 199.

[12] In Troilus and Criseyde Chaucer refers to the state of confusion of English in his day. He is here addressing his book:

> And for ther is so gret diversite
> In Englissh and in writyng of oure tonge,
> So prey I God that non myswrite the,
> Ne the mysmetre for defaute of tonge. (V, 1793-1796)

And this passage from The Legend of Good Women may be taken as a reference to Chaucer's own sense of inadequacy or, as is more likely, another reference to the limitations of the language:

> Allas, that I ne had Englyssh, ryme or prose,
> Suffisant this flour to preyse aryght! (Prol. F, 66-67).

The Black Knight in The Book of the Duchess encounters a similar problem when he tries to describe Blanche:

> But which a visage had she thertoo!
> Allas! myn herte ys wonder woo
> That I ne kan discryven hyt!
> Me lakketh both Englyssh and wit
> For to undo hyt at the fulle....(895-899)

So too the Squire in describing Canacee:

> But for to telle yow al hir beautee,
> It lyth nat in my tonge, ny'n my konnyng;
> I dar nat undertake so heigh a thyng.
> Myn Englissh eek is insufficient.(34-37)

13
    Paul Strohm, on the basis of what scanty records there are of book ownership during Chaucer's day, concludes that the tastes of the great lords and ladies who might have been among Chaucer's audience were primarily for French works, particularly French romances. "Chaucer's Audience," Literature and History 5 (1977): 31. This leads Strohm to agree with Alfred David ("The Man of Law vs. Chaucer: A Case in Poetics," PMLA 82 (1967): 217-225) that the established literary tastes of the upper nobility might have prevented them from "appreciating the most innovative qualities of his [Chaucer's] poetry..."(31).

14
    "Geoffroi Chaucier, Poète Français, Father of English Poetry," Chaucer Review 13(1978):94. Diametrically opposed to Robbins' view is that of H.S. Bennett, who maintains that in the thirteenth century there was already a well-established tradition of secular lyric poetry in English and that Chaucer's "many a song and many a lecherous lay" had been written "in an effort to follow in this tradition"(10). John H. Fisher agrees with Robbins about Chaucer's early immersion in French, but presents a more moderate view of its impact on Chaucer's early work, one that does not exclude the probability of native influence. "Chaucer and the French Influence," in New Perspectives in Chaucer Criticism, ed. Donald M. Rose (Norman: Pilgrim, 1981), 177-191. Pursuing some of the implications of Fisher's essay, E. Talbot Donaldson points out several features of Chaucer's language that are unusual in English, and suggests that these derive from French idioms and colloquial expressions. "Gallic Flies in Chaucer's English Word Web," in New Perspectives in Chaucer Criticism, 193-202.

15
    Oliver Emerson Farrar argues convincingly, based largely on evidence provided by the "Roman manuscript" of Froissart's history, that not only did Edward III know and use English but that his great nobles did as well. "English or French in the Time of Edward III," in Chaucer: Essays and Studies (1929; rpt. Freeport: Books for Libraries Press, 1970), 271-297. And R.A. Shoaf remarks, "Chaucer's choice of English when French or Latin was still a possible alternative, especially in a court circle, is sufficient witness in itself that the pre-eminence of those languages was on the wane..."(59-60).

16

Chaucer and the Making of English Poetry (London: Routledge & Kegan Paul, 1972), vol. 1, *Love Vision and Debate*, 1. Larry Benson expresses much the same view: "That Chaucer might also have made artistic use of the English literary tradition was seldom considered by earlier critics. That he knew the tradition well is clear not only from 'Sir Thopas'...but from his occasional use of alliterative lines...and what E.T. Donaldson calls...'The Idiom of Popular Poetry in the Miller's Tales.'" "A Reader's Guide to Writings on Chaucer," in *Writers and Their Backgrounds: Geoffrey Chaucer*, ed. Derek Brewer (Athens: Ohio Univ. Press, 1975), 337.

17

Wolfgang Clemen, *Chaucer's Early Poetry*, tr. C.A.M. Sym (London: Methuen, 1963), 7. Similarly, R.H. Robbins writes, "Chaucer's fortune was to be in the right situation at the right moment in history to render the French styles into English"(115).

18

Fansler, whose primary concern is Chaucer's indebtedness to the *Roman de la Rose*, issues a similar caution: "But one must not forget the English poet's acquaintance with medieval romances, medieval Latin writers, and, not least of all, Middle English literature in general; for it is inconceivable that such a varied, idiomatic, correct use of our language as the author of the *Canterbury Tales* displays could have resulted merely from following foreign models"(73).

19

Medieval English Lyrics (London: Nelson, 1963), 35. Davies, when referring to the native tradition, has in mind primarily the Middle English secular lyrics. But while identifying both these lyrics and Chaucer's poetry as belonging to the same tradition, he denies any significant influence of the lyrics on Chaucer's poetry: "Though the poetry of Chaucer is written in the same tradition as that in which many of the early secular lyrics were written, there is no reason to think Chaucer was aware of continuing in it..."(35).

20

"The Relationship of Chaucer to the English and European Traditions," in *Chaucer and Chaucerians*, ed. D.S. Brewer (London: Nelson, 1966), 1.

21

Chaucer's Prosody (London: Cambridge Univ. Press, 1971), 239.

22

Wolfgang Clemen, for example, observes, "Yet despite this close familiarity with French and Italian thought and expression, how very English Chaucer in essence remains! So English, indeed, that many passages from his work can still be quoted for their typically English quality"(7-8).

23
In this regard I concur completely with George Economou's judgment that The Canterbury Tales is no more or less "English" than the Book of the Duchess or the House of Fame, that "it is more a question of the difference between early and mature work than it is one of periods of influence." "Introduction: Chaucer the Innovator," in Geoffrey Chaucer: A Collection of Original Articles, ed. George D. Economou (New York: McGraw Hill, 1975), 4.

24
"Chaucer's Good Ear," RES 23(1947): 201-208.

25
"Chaucer's Colloquial English: Its Structural Traits," PMLA 67(1952): 1116. Since Schlauch's pioneering essay, the colloquial and idiomatic qualities of Chaucer's language have received increasing attention. Among the more recent studies are Norman E. Eliason, The Language of Chaucer's Poetry, 1972; Ralph W.V. Eliott, Chaucer's English (London: Deutsch, 1974); Norman Davis, "Chaucer and the Fourteenth-Century English," in Writers and Their Backgrounds: Geoffrey Chaucer, ed. Derek Brewer et. al. (Athens: Ohio Univ. Press, 1975), 58-84; Vivian Salmon, "The Representation of Colloquial Speech in The Canterbury Tales," in Style and Text: Studies Presented to Nils Enkvist, ed. Hakan Ringbom et. al. (Stockholm: Sprakforlaget Skriptor AB, 1975), 263-277; Morton Donner, "Derived Words in Chaucer's Language," Chaucer Review 13(1978): 1-15.

26
"A Survey of Medieval Verse," in The Age of Chaucer, vol. 1 of A Guide to English Literature, ed. Boris Ford (Baltimore: Penguin, 1954), 21.

27
Baum is primarily concerned with Chaucer's long line, which he believes to be essentially metrical, "a series of five iambs," and for which be believes Chaucer had no native models; nevertheless, when Baum describes the rhythm of Chaucer's line, he falls back on the spoken language: "The rhythm of Chaucer's verse is a composite of the rhythm of contemporary spoken prose and the metrical forms which he adopted"(108).

28
"Chaucer and the European Literary Tradition," in Geoffrey Chaucer: A Collection of Original Articles, 43.

29
The Key of Remembrance (New Haven: Yale Univ. Press, 1963), 62.

30
Verses of Cadence (Oxford: Blackwell, 1954) and The Poetry of Chaucer and His Followers (Oxford: Blackwell, 1962).

31

In Southworth's opinion Chaucer's major achievement was to
bring this rhythmical tradition to its greatest pitch of perfection. Thus, he concludes,

> Chaucer's mature style is the perfect distilla-
> tion of the speech of his England--that of the
> urbane, sophisticated court of Richard II; that
> speech reflecting the strong influence of
> ecclesiastic writing and sermonizing; that of
> persons who have steeped themselves in popular
> romances; that of the court, the counting house,
> the village, and the field. His great achieve-
> ment lies in the artistry with which in his
> poetry he has eradicated the prolixity of daily
> speech without sacrificing its rhythms. (Prosody
> of Chaucer, 78).

32

But Robinson maintains that, although Chaucer's lines are
built on these "pieces of speech," they are also metrical, and
in this fusion of the alliterative and metrical traditions Chaucer
has developed an essentially new and unique prosodic technique,
which Robinson calls "balanced pentameter." Thus, Robinson
asserts, "This compound of balanced pentameter is evidence of an
accomplished technique; but the intention triumphantly fulfilled
in the best of Chaucer is the concealment of technique--the
simulation of speech by a heightening of speech which can yet
seem fresh and natural..." (Prosody, 172). The phrase "balanced
pentameter," obviously refers to Chaucer's long line, but
Robinson sees the same principle at work in Chaucer's short line
as well.

33

According to Norman Eliason, it was from such English minstrels, who handed down a native oral tradition, that "Chaucer
took his cue" in developing the various guises he adopts as
narrator of his poems (71). And Derek Brewer remarks that
"Chaucer is the last of the English minstrels who walked wide
over the land, whose tone he had early caught, and whose modesty
and deference to his audience he adopts...." "Towards a Chaucerian
Poetic," Proceedings of the British Academcy 60(1974): 247.

34

"Sir Thopas and Sir Guy," MLN 23(1908): 73-77 and 102-106.

35

"Chaucer and the Auchinleck MS: 'Thopas' and 'Guy of War-
wick,'" in Essays and Studies in Honor of Carleton Brown (New
York, 1941), 111-128. In a subsequent article, "Chaucer and the
Breton Lays of the Auchinleck MS.," Speculum 38(1941): 14-33,
Loomis pointed out Chaucer's use of the Breton Lays in this
manuscript, especially with reference to The Franklin's Tale.

36
"Chaucer and the Custom of Oral Delivery," Speculum 13 (1938):
413-432. In her earlier essay, "Oral Delivery in the Middle
Ages," Speculum 11(1936): 88-110, which served to provide the
background for this study, Crosby pointed out that such devices
were characteristic of medieval narrative poetry in general and
resulted from the custom of oral delivery. However, she makes
two most significant points with regard to Chaucer. The first,
already mentioned, is that Chaucer's use of these devices closely
resembles that in the English romances. The second is that
Chaucer's immediate foreign sources frequently exhibit no evidence that they were intended for oral recitation and, consequently, do not always employ these devices. Hence, it is quite
likely that Chaucer is indebted to the English romances for such
stylistic features in his own poetry. Additional characteristics
of the Middle English rhyming romances that can be found in
Chaucer's poetry have been pointed out by Elizabeth D. Kirk:
"Brisk handling of action, exchanges in short dialogue, telling
and selecting concrete detail (but not in catalogs and formal
description), and a tone of humane realism interspersed through
a plot and an imaginary world unrealistic enough to be completely
flexible and in the best romances, richly symbolic." "Chaucer
and the European Literary Tradition," in Geoffrey Chaucer: A
Collection of Original Articles, 124.

37
It will be observed that Burrow reaches much the same conclusions, and it may be that Crosby's studies gave impetus to
his. But Burrow goes a step further by including the northern
alliterative poetry.

38
"The Idiom of Popular Poetry in the Miller's Tale, in English Institute Essays: 1950, ed. Adam S. Downes (New York, 1951),
116-140. Donaldson also believes that Chaucer's diction derives
to some extent from the Middle English lyrics as well, particularly the courtly lyrics. But his primary concern in this essay
is to show how Chaucer uses this diction in the Miller's Tale.
He concludes, "The idiom Chaucer borrows from popular poetry contributes to the directly humorous effect of the Miller's Tale,
and that is probably its chief function"(140).

39
See also Charles Muscatine's "The Canterbury Tales: Style
of the Man and Style of the Work," in Chaucer and Chaucerians,
88-113.

40
Both Kean and Brewer find Chaucer's indebtedness to these
romances to have been far more comprehensive still. Brewer, who
compares in detail the style of Guy of Warwick with Chaucer's
style, concludes his analysis of one particular passage (Guy I,
590-598) as follows: "This is the very true gallop of Chaucer's
earlier metre and style...There is no question of 'source-hunting'

here. Chaucer was not borrowing specific passages; he was using a traditional style" (6-7). Kean declares, "He [Chaucer] was a narrative poet, and there is every sign that the earlier English romances played an important part in the development of his narrative style and also influenced his approach to narrative structure" (Love Vision, 5).

41

A Preface to Chaucer (Princeton: Princeton Univ. Press, 1962), 281-284. A more general approach is taken by D'Ardenne, who sees as typically English characteristics Chaucer's humor, his love of nature, and his conception of fate, which, despite Chaucer's use of the word "fortune," D'Ardenne claims closely approximates the Anglo-Saxon conception expressed by the word "wyrd" (48).

42

"The Lecher, the Legal Eagle, and the Papelard Priest: Middle English Confessional Satires in MS. Harley 2253 and Else-where," in His Firm Estate: Essays Presented to Franklin James Eckenberry (Univ. of Tulsa Monograph Series, No. 2, 1967), 54-71.

43

Revard does not maintain that satirical, confessional poems are unique to English literature, but he distinguishes between the English poems of this type and those of the continental and classical traditions. He describes the English poems as follows: "All these works share the rhetorical device of presenting a speaker who, in his boasting or complaining (often simultaneous) of his lot, is unintentionally confessing himself to be in some part a knave and in large part a fool"(57).

44

Describing Chaucer's development as a poet, Norman Eliason writes, "From the never-never land of dreams which French poets had informed Chaucer of and the distant lands he had learned about in his old books, he turned to his own native England, to the land and its rivers, manors and farmyards, country-side, villages and cities, to its universities and grammar-schools, to its people, and to its language"(112).

I

THE MIDDLE ENGLISH LYRICS
AND
THE NATIVE POETIC TRADITION

On the Continuity of the
English Poetic Tradition

The literary history of medieval Europe is extremely complicated.
The countries of medieval Europe shared a cultural heritage,
rooted in ancient Greece and Rome, which evolved under and was
in many ways determined by the continually increasing domination
of the church.
     As part of this common cultural heritage, the literature
of medieval Europe was not constrained to any great degree by
national boundaries. Furthermore, medieval aesthetics did not
place great value on originality. Nor was there any concept of
copyrighting--all literature was, so to speak, in the public
domain. Writers like Chaucer borrowed freely whatever may have
appealed to them not only from the past, but also from the present; not only from their fellow countrymen, but also from those
foreign writers whom they admired. As a result it is rarely an
easy matter to determine with any assurance the precise source
or origin of a particular plot or style, much less of a particular convention, theme, motif, image, or figure of speech.
     The problem becomes even more acute when we consider Middle
English literature. For here we have to contend not only with
such conditions as described above, but also with a number of
other complicating factors largely attributable to the Norman
Conquest. Perhaps nowhere else, with the possible exception of
Moorish Spain, was there so complete a fusion of two so diverse
cultures as took place in England during the two centuries following the Conquest. That the Conquest had profound social and
political repercussions on English civilization need hardly be
mentioned. With respect to English literature the fusion of
Teutonic and Romance traditions resulted in the creation of an
essentially new poetic tradition.

The immediate effect of the Norman Conquest upon English poetry was twofold. First, the old poetic tradition, though never completely suppressed, was certainly pushed into the background. Second, the doors were opened wider than ever to continental influences. Hence, the complexion of English poetry was considerably altered, and it is not surprising that Middle English poetry in many ways resembles the poetry of continental Europe, so much so in some cases that much of it has been characterized as belonging to continental European traditions. As a result early English literature has been divided into two distinct periods--Old English and Middle English. For the most part literary historians and critics have treated these periods as separate entities and have disregarded or denied any significant connection between them. Instead, they view the Norman Conquest, which so dramatically altered the course of English history, as ushering in a new age of English poetry, an age dominated essentially by French influence.

Among the earliest examples of this "new tradition" are the Middle English lyrics. Viewed within the mainstream of the historical criticism of Middle English poetry in general, these lyrics have commonly been regarded as an outgrowth of continental traditions. In fact, the very existence of any lyric poetry in English before the Conquest has been questioned: "It is a commonplace of literary history that there is no lyric in the poetry of the Anglo-Saxons...Such dramatic pieces as the Seafarer, the Husband's Message, or the Wife's Lament, or such elegiac reflections as the Ruin, are lyrical rather than lyrics. Caedmon's Hymn, Eadwacer, and Deor, the last so fine in its simple unity and directness, come closest perhaps in expressing the personal emotion of the poet" (Baugh, 208).

Such an assessment of these Old English poems rests largely on the conception of lyric poetry as the intense expression of personal emotion. But attempts to distinguish lyric poetry on this basis, which is at best highly subjective and at worst totally meaningless, leads only to confusion and unnecessary complications. Who can say what is "intense" and what is not, or what degree of intensity is required in a poem to qualify it as a lyric poem? Does intensity in any way distinguish a lyric poem from an epic poem, Shelley's "Ode to the West Wind" from Milton's Paradise Lost, or for that matter, does it in any real sense distinguish lyric poetry from any other kind of poetry? Is not intensity in some degree intrinsic to the very nature of poetry itself? And who can say whether or not the emotions expressed in a particular poem are "personal"? Does not personal in this sense imply "private" and "sincere"; that is, the "real" or "true" emotions of the poet who is laying bare his soul? Are Shakespeare's sonnets or Marvell's "To His Coy Mistress" personal in this sense, and does it really matter? Are these any the less lyric poems than Milton's sonnet on his blindness?

Nevertheless, the intense expression of personal emotion remains for many the essential criterion of lyric poetry, and on the basis of so dubious a criterion rests the argument that there is no lyric extant in the poetry of the Anglo-Saxons, a precarious conclusion that results in a perplexing dilemma. If this is indeed the yardstick by which we are to measure lyric poetry, then surely poems like "The Ruin," "The Wanderer," "The Seafarer," "The Wife's Lament," "The Husband's Message," and "Deor" are, despite assertions to the contrary, lyric poems in the fullest sense of the term. For where in the whole corpus of English poetry can we find more clearly and distinctly the intense expression of personal emotion than in these poems? Certainly not among that body of poetry commonly referred to as the Middle English lyrics. And herein lies the real paradox. For those who maintain that there is no lyric in Old English do not hesitate to identify these Middle English poems as "lyrics." This despite the fact that these Middle English poems are conspicuous by the very lack of such expression of personal emotion.[1]

I do not mean, however, to suggest that these Middle English poems are not lyrics, nor that we must somehow consider them a special class of lyrics to some extent deficient in or lacking the characteristic expression of emotion. Nor does the very subtle and fine distinction between lyric poetry and poetry that is lyrical, a distinction that seems to be more a matter of semantics than one which identifies any significant qualitative differences in the poetry itself, help resolve the dilemma. Originally, a "lyric" was simply a short poem composed for singing to the accompaniment of a lyre, and the term subsequently came to be applied to any short poem whose basic qualities are those of a song. For the present purposes it will suffice to think of lyric poetry in this most general sense, and in this sense I am content to use the term to include both the Middle English and the Old English poems.

However, the crux of the problem here is not so much whether we can properly regard the extant Old English poems or these Middle English poems as lyrics, nor even whether there ever was any lyric poetry in Old English. The major difficulty arises when the assumption that there is no lyric poetry in Old English leads to the concomitant assumption that there is therefore no connection between the Middle English lyrics and the Old English poems.[2] As a result, attempts to trace the origins of the Middle English lyrics have, for the most part, ignored the older native poetry and have focused instead on foreign sources, primarily French and Latin.[3]

Among the best known of the early Middle English lyrics are those found in MS. Harley 2253. It has long been recognized that these poems, composed sometime during the latter part of the thirteenth century and the very early fourteenth century, bear certain striking similarities to Provençal lyric poetry, so striking in fact that some have argued these English poems were imitations of the Provençal poems or at least were strongly influenced by them.[4] Others have argued against the likelihood of direct influence by Provençal poetry upon the English lyrics and have suggested instead that Provençal influence may have reached England via the later northern French poetry of the trouveres.[5] Among these is Helen Sandison, who emphasizes the influence of the chanson d'aventure on Middle English poems of the same type. But Sandison concludes her study by stressing certain significant differences between the French and English poems belonging to this genre. She sums up her findings as follows: "The differences between the English and the French adventure-songs are so marked that one can safely conclude that English poets were not slavishly translating or imitating particular foreign models, but rather working in accord with familiar tradition. Doubtless the later English writers knew the tradition much better through its earlier English exponents than through the French."[6]

The last is a particularly important point. For much of the continental lyric tradition must have reached later English poets like Chaucer in a similar manner; that is, via the earlier Middle English lyrics. And the poets who composed these early lyrics, in adopting various aspects of the continental tradition and making it their own, also modified it in many respects, most importantly by incorporating elements from their own native tradition.

Investigations into the origins of the Middle English lyrics have also been influenced by the division of these poems into sacred and profane, categories often treated as being mutually exclusive.[7] Consequently, most of these investigations have focused on one or the other. And if French has generally been given the first place in influencing the development of the English secular lyrics, Latin has similarly been given the first place in influencing the development of the religious lyrics. And those who have sought to trace the origins of the religious lyrics have ransacked the Latin literature of the Middle Ages, suggesting as possible sources or influences everything from the liturgy to the patristic writings, from the sacred hymns to the Goliardic verses.[8]

Distinguishing between religious and secular lyrics does not seem to me necessary nor particularly useful when attempting to determine the sources of these Middle English poems or the influences that contributed to their development. Nor do I believe such a division especially helpful in considering the essential characteristics of these poems. In fact, it is not always so simple as it might seem to distinguish between the two. Is, for example, Thomas of Hale's "Love Ron" a religious lyric or a secular lyric in religious clothing? There are both religious and secular lyrics among the earliest extant poetry after the Conquest; both types continue to exist side by side throughout the following centuries; and these lyrics are remarkably

similar in many respects. Both frequently make use of the same
literary conventions. A knight riding out into the country may
be the introduction to a love lament or to a hymn in praise of
the Virgin; a pastoral garden may be the setting for a love
debate or for a confession of sins. Love of God and love of a
lady frequently lead to the same kinds of suffering. And just
as a mistress is commonly depicted as the only physician who can
cure a lover's malady, so Mary is commonly depicted as the only
physician who can cure a sinner's malady.

But what is perhaps even more significant are the similarities in diction, imagery and structure. We have only to look at
two well-known lyrics (perhaps lyric fragments would be a more
apt description), "Nou Goth Sonne Vnder Wod" (Brown, XIII, 1) and
"Foweles in Þe Frith" (Brown, XIII, 8), to illustrate the point.
The texts of both follow:

> Nou goth sonne vnder Wod,--
> me reweth, marie, þi faire Rode.
> Nou goþ sonne vnder tre,--
> me reweþ, marie, þi sone and þe.
>
> Foweles in þe Frith,
> Þe fisses in þe flod,
> And i mon waxe wod.
> Sulch[9] sorw I walke with
> for beste of bon and blod.

The first is clearly a religious lyric, the speaker reflecting on the crucifixion. The second is a secular lyric, though
a religious interpretation is not altogether unlikely. Because
the poem seems so clearly an expression of love longing, the
phrase "beste of bon and blod" most obviously refers to the poet's
beloved. But the "best of bone and blood" is also, of course,
Christ, and it is not unreasonable to interpret the poet's sorrow
as stemming from his recollection of Christ's suffering. Nor is
it altogether improbable that the poet intends just such an
ambiguity, for ambiguity is a technique commonly employed by the
poets who composed the Middle English lyrics. We find a similar
use of verbal ambiguity in the first poem. "Sonne" can mean
"sun" or "son"; "Rode" can mean "face" or "tree" or "cross."
Thus, the setting sun is also Christ dying on the cross, the
ultimate setting of the sun on this world. And is not Mary's face
a reflection of that cross? Does not the poet pity Mary's face
because he sees mirrored in it the agonies of the crucifixion?

More to the point, the diction of the two poems is similar
both in its extreme simplicity and, at the same time, its
effectiveness in conveying not only a wealth of meaning but also
a depth of emotion. The sense of sadness, for example, is con-
veyed primarily by a single word--"reweth" in the first poem,
"sorw" in the second. In both poems what imagery there is is also

simple, drawn from the world of nature, and visually concrete--
the sun going down, setting behind a forest or a tree; the fowls
in the woods; the fish in the water.

But perhaps most striking is the resemblance in the structures of the two poems. Here again both poems are remarkably
simple, and both depend more upon what is implicit rather than
what is explicit. Both begin with the simple image from the
world of nature. Both then abruptly shift their focus to the
speaker. In neither does the poet bother to make explicit the
relationship between image and speaker. He does not have to.
In both the connection, though implicit, is perfectly clear, as
is the essential meaning of the whole poem, though this meaning
is perhaps more perfectly felt than intellectually understood.

In the first poem the setting sun evokes a recollection of
the crucifixion, especially Mary's response to it. The speaker
pities Mary in her human aspect, as mother, and Christ as her
son; there is no reference to divinity. It is this pity for
Mary and her son that evokes the speaker's own sadness, which,
though never explicitly expressed, nevertheless controls the
whole poem. The sun sets "nou" as it did at Christ's death. It
sets now on the speaker's world as it did then on Mary's world.
And the setting sun is a continual reminder to the speaker of
the great sacrifice made long ago on his behalf by this mother
and her son.

In the second poem the fowls and the fish are in their
natural environment; for them, all is well. Not so for the
speaker, whose condition is, by implication, sharply contrasted
to theirs. For he is being driven mad by grief. However, we
know very little about the cause of this grief. All we know is
that it is on account of the "beste of bon and blod." But is
this a wife who has deserted him, a child who has died, a friend
who has betrayed him, or a mistress who has left him for another?
The point is that it really does not matter. What we have is a
poignant expression of the grief we experience at the loss of
someone near and dear to us. The world goes on; some things
never change. Fowls will still be found in their woods, fish in
the water, and we still walk the earth. But after such a loss
we ourselves are changed, and we walk our earth with sorrow.

Similarities and correspondences like the ones between
these two poems exist to a greater or lesser degree between
virtually all the Middle English religious and secular lyrics
and are evidence of the very significant interaction between
them. Attempting to determine which came first, or which
borrowed from or influenced the other is, in most cases, not
unlike attempting to resolve the well-known chicken-egg enigma.
Most probably such influence worked both ways--in some cases
the secular lyrics borrowing from the religious lyrics; in
others, just the opposite. While Latin literature may well
have exerted its strongest and most direct influence on the
religious lyrics, we can reasonably infer that its influence

on the secular lyrics, though perhaps more often indirect and
so less obvious, must have been considerable as well.

Rosemary Woolf makes much of the fact that secular courtly
lyrics do not appear in English until a relatively late date,
and suggests the reason was that English was a "depressed
vernacular," regarded as inferior to both Latin and French (2).
She goes on to point out that at the time the early religious
lyrics were being composed, religious theory was strongly influenced by the Bernardine emphasis on natural feeling, as a
result of which the composers of these lyrics were primarily
concerned with ordinary, everyday experience, and because this
depressed English vernacular was admirably suited to express
exactly what these writers required of it, the religious lyrics
were able to develop "untrammeled by the conventions and style
of a secular form" (2). Woolf's argument would seem to imply
that these early religious lyrics represent a new tradition in
English poetry, a tradition, according to Woolf, rooted in Latin
devotional verse and formed in large part by the exigencies of
the English language at that time, and she presents a strong
case in support of her view. But this is not the whole picture.
For even though English secular courtly poetry did not appear
until a relatively late date and even if English was a "depressed
vernacular," there was nevertheless, by the time of the earliest
extant religious lyrics, already a well-established native
literary tradition.

R.M. Wilson is, in fact, quite right in observing that when
English lyric poetry appears in writing it is already in many
respects highly developed (251). H.S. Bennett holds much the
same opinion, and he attributes the excellence of many of the
early lyrics to the force of tradition:

> The quality of the lyrics in the well-known
> manuscript in the British Museum, Harleian
> 2253, emboldens us to believe that the writ-
> ing of lyrics in English was much more common
> than their scanty survival would suggest. Work
> such as "Lenten ys come with loue to toune," or
> "Bytuene Mersh and Aueril" is not fashioned in
> a day, or without some tradition. (10)

Since tradition always implies a relationship to the past, this
tradition must then, at least to some extent, have depended upon
the general continuity of English literature.

Wilson has commented, "The ultimate effects of the Conquest
on English literature, either for the better or worse, were
exceptionally important, but today it is the essential continuity
between Old and Middle English literature, rather than any difference, which needs emphasis" (209). But while the continuity of
English prose from the time of Alfred to the time of More has
been ably demonstrated by R.W. Chambers,[10] with respect to poetry

such continuity is for the most part only vaguely hinted at or
alluded to in the most tenuous terms.

What discussions there have been of the continuity of
English poetry frequently make mention of tone and mood;[11] more
frequently, they gravitate toward the survival of alliteration.
But it is the Middle English alliterative poetry, culminating
in what has been termed the "Alliterative Revival," which exhibits the most obvious link between Old English and Middle English
poetry and so has not only been the focal point of most critical
discussions of poetic continuity,[12] but has also come to be
regarded by many as virtually the exclusive manifestation of the
survival of a native tradition, a tradition which is generally
set in contrast to the poetry of Chaucer.[13] Moreover, even where
some thread of continuity between Old English and Middle English
poetry is recognized, foreign influences on the development of
Middle English poetry after the Conquest have habitually received greater emphasis. And if little connection has been seen
between Old English and Middle English poetry in general, even
less has been seen between Old English poetry and Chaucer's
poetry in particular.[14] W.H. Schofield, for example, remarks,

> To regard the writers of the fourteenth
> century and later as the lineal descend-
> ents of Anglo-Saxon percursors is funda-
> mentally false. Chaucer did not exhibit
> the spirit of early times reawakened
> after a slumber of centuries, but was the
> product of conditions secured by Norman
> and Angevin rule. English literature did
> not go through a tunnel on a long under-
> ground journey, as some conceive, to
> emerge at the end of it, the same in
> essentials of style.[15]

It is not my contention that Chaucer is a lineal descendent
of Anglo-Saxon percursors. Nor is my primary purpose here to
argue at great length for the continuity between Old English and
Middle English poetry. Nevertheless, because my intention is in
part to show that Chaucer is not so far removed even from his
earliest English predecessors as has heretofore been thought, I
think it important and appropriate at this point to examine
whether the gulf between Middle English and Old English poetry
is indeed so vast as has commonly been supposed.

Old English Roots and Middle English Flowers:
The Middle English Lyrics and the Old English
Poetic Tradition

While there can be no doubt that Latin and French literature
exerted a considerable influence on the development of the
Middle English lyrics, this influence was of a secondary or
contributory nature. For these lyrics are fundamentally rooted
in the older native poetry, and it is the old poetic tradition
that is, at the most rudimentary level, the source of the Middle
English lyrics. George Saintsbury states the case well:

> From the Latin hymns and proses which our
> unknown song-writers were constantly hearing,
> from the French and Provençal romances and
> varied lyric forms of all kinds that they
> were in not a few cases reading, but most
> probably hearing still more, they drew rhyme
> and metre, stanza-form and trick of refrain,
> diction almost always and accent quantity
> sometimes. From their own ancestral tongue
> they took less in appearance--so much less
> indeed that careless or prejudiced inquirers
> have constantly undervalued and sometimes
> actually denied the importance of this factor
> in the problem. But those who had eyes to
> see have always seen the abiding influence
> of English phrase; the singular and probably
> unique effect produced by the intermixture of
> the two accentuations; and, above all, the
> characteristic--differencing from all French
> and from the majority of at least mediaeval
> Latin--of the great Old English principle so
> often ignored and to this very day mistaken
> or denied, the principle of Equivalence--
> of the allowance of two syllables as equal
> to one, not as a license, not as a mark of
> irregular or slovenly composition, not as an
> occasional device to produce a particular and
> exceptional effect, but as a main and principal
> feature of the language and as an ancestral
> beauty of the poetry.[16]

What is perhaps most significant here is the recognition
of the vital interaction between native and foreign elements,
a fact too often neglected or brushed aside. Not only did the
old poetic tradition contribute certain stylistic features to
the Middle English lyrics, but it also controlled to a large
extent the ways in which elements from foreign traditions manifested themselves in these lyrics. The Middle English lyricist

did not, by and large, simply transpose elements from foreign traditions into his own poetry. Rather, he adapted them in ways conducive to the exigencies of his own tradition. It was by grafting these new foreign elements unto the older native stalks that he was able to accommodate them within the framework of his tradition. The result of such hybridization was the creation of the Middle English lyric[17] and, in a larger sense, of the whole of Middle English poetry. For it is this kind of interaction which above all else is the force responsible for determining the shape of the English poetic tradition as it was to emerge after the Conquest, and the early Middle English lyrics played a vital role in this process.[18]

Merle Fifield has conclusively demonstrated that the Middle English lyrics were instrumental in preserving particular alliterative phrases from the older poetry, thereby keeping the alliterative tradition alive for later writers. However, it is not so much that she is able to show any specific or direct influence of the older poetry on the lyrics that seems to me of utmost importance. Rather, by establishing beyond question that the Middle English lyricist drew upon the older poetry for such phrases, she also establishes the fact that the older poetry was not only available and known to these Middle English poets, but also made use of by them.[19] And if these poets did draw upon the older poetry for such alliterative phrases, it seems reasonable that they might also have drawn upon it for other stylistic features as well.

What then are some of the marks of lyric continuity? Certainly, as has been mentioned, the common use of alliteration is one. Another mark of this continuity that has frequently been remarked upon is the melancholic tone or mood characteristic of these lyrics, which E.K. Chambers suggests may be a matter of "racial temperament." But in considering the role played by Old English poetry in shaping the Middle English lyrics, we have more to do with than a matter of "racial temperament" or the survival of alliteration, though these are important. We have to do with the whole force of the old poetic tradition as it influenced the development of these lyrics.

Old English poetry belongs to the utilitarian tradition of the early Middle Ages, a tradition that conceived of poetry as a social art and of poets as performing a particular social function, in Morton Bloomfield's words, that of "teachers or officials of a sort who were what we would call today priests, historians, archivists, or scientists."[20] The Middle English lyrics seem to me clearly to reflect a similar conception of poetry. For the fundamental impulse behind these lyrics is to provide in a pleasing form something practical and useful for the audience--"sentence and solass."[21] This does not, of course, necessarily mean that the Middle English lyricist derived his conception of poetry solely or directly from his Old English predecessors nor that his poetry belongs exclusively to the same tradition, for this utilitarian

tradition was common to the whole of medieval western Europe.
Nevertheless, it is significant that by the time the earliest
Middle English lyrics were being written down the change in the
conception of poetry from a social to an individual art,[22] which
began in the west with the Renaissance of the twelfth century,
was already well under way. That these lyrics do not reflect
such a change, despite England's having been brought into closer
contact than ever before with continental literature as a result
of the Norman Conquest, is strongly indicative of the abiding
influence of the old poetic tradition and suggests at least one
possibly crucial role played by the old tradition in shaping the
Middle English lyrics--that is as a kind of conservative buffer
against the incursion of the new continental fashions which were
making their impact upon English poetry during this period.

Far more important, however, with respect to its influence
on the Middle English lyrics is the manner in which this utilitarian tradition manifested itself in Old English poetry. Emphasizing the influence of Hebrew wisdom literature on Old English
poetry and defining the role of the poet in such literature as
that of prophet and teacher, whose voice is characterized by
"the existential quality of direct speech and admonition,"
Bloomfield describes the form in which this poetry is most
commonly cast:

> The speaker, or speakers in wisdom literature,
> is the poet speaking as prophet and teacher.
> He is mediating wisdom and is not speaking
> primarily of himself. His experiences are to
> be taken as representative experiences not
> personal experiences...But these speeches are
> not monologues but dialogues even when a
> second speaker does not appear...these are
> addressed to every man or to God (23).[23]

Bloomfield might equally well be writing here about the
Middle English lyrics. The pupil-teacher relationship, the
emphasis on direct speech and admonition, the re-creation of a
common, not uniquely individual, experience are altogether
characteristic of these lyrics. The poem "Worldes Blis Ne Last
No Throwe" (Brown, XIII, 46) is a perfect example:

> Worldes blis ne last no throwe,
>   it went and wit a-wey anon;
> þe langer þat ics it knowe
>   þe lasse ics finde pris þar-on,
> for al it is imeind mid care,
> with serwen and mid iuel fare,
> and atte laste poure and bare
>   it lat man, wan it ginth agon.
> al þe blis þis her and þare
>   bilocth at ende wep and mon.

Al þe blis of þese liue
　　þou salt, man, enden ine wep--
of hus and hom, of child and wiue.
　　sali man, nim þar-of kep!
þu salt al bileuen here
þeite war-of lord þu were;
wan þu list hup-on þe bere
　　and slapst þat suithe dreri slep,
ne salt tu haue with þe no fere
　　but þine werkes on a hep.

Al sal gon þat man hier houet,
　and al it schal bicome to naut;
he þat hier no gud ne sowet,
　　wan othre repen he wrth bikaut.
þinc, man, forþi wilstu auest mithe,
þat þu þi gulte hier arithe,
and werche gud bi dai and nithe,
　　har þan þu be of liue laut.
þu nost wan crist hure drithe
　　þe hosket þat þe hauet bitaut.

Man, wi sestu þout and herte
　　o werldes blis þat nout ne last?
Wi þolstu þat þe softe ismerte
　　for þing þat is unstedefast?
þu lickest huni of þorn iwis
þat seist þi loue o werldos blis

. . . .
　　ful sore þu mith ben of-gast,
þat hier despendest heite a-mis,
　　to ben þar-þurew in-to elle cast.

Þinc, man, war-to crist þe wroute
　　and do way prede and felthe and mud.
þinc wu dere he þe boute
　　o rode mid is swete blud;
im-self he gaf for þe ine pris,
to bein þe blis ȝif þu be wis.
bi-þinc þe þan, and up aris
　　of senne, and agin werchen gud
þar wils time to werchen is,
　　for siker helles þu art wud.

Schal no gud ben unforiolden,
    ne no qued ne wrth unbout;
wan þu list, man, under molden
    þu schalt auen as tu auest wrout.
biþinc wel forþi us ics rede,
and clanse of ecs misdede,
þat crist þe helpe at tine nede,
    þat so dere hauet þe bout,
an to euene blisse lede
    þat euere last and faillet nout.

The experience re-created in this poem is certainly commonplace enough--the imminence of death that confronts all men. The
theme is essentially that of the morality play, Everyman--all
worldly bliss becomes useless and irrelevant in the face of death,
for only good deeds can help man when his time comes. Thus, the
poet assumes the role of teacher-priest to advise man to prepare
himself for the common end all men must meet.
The poet sums up the wisdom he is mediating in the first
stanza:

Worldes blis ne last no throwe,
    it went and wit a-wey anon;
þe langer þat ics it knowe
    þe lasse ics finde pris þar-on....

He is passing on his wisdom, teaching what he has learned, in
the hope of benefiting man: "biþinc wel forþi us ichs rede...."
Consequently, the terms in which the poet refers to this world's
bliss are again not personal but quite commonplace:

Al þe blis of þese liue
    þu salt, man, enden ine wep--
of hus and hom, of child and wiue.
    sali man, nim þar-of kep!

Throughout the poem, the poet directly addresses man, questioning
him,

Man, wi sestu þout and herte
    o werldes blis þat nout ne last?
Wi þolstu þat þe softe ismerte
    for þing þat is unstedefast?

and admonishing him to think, to think about doing good deeds
while he still can,

þinc, man, forþi wilstu auest mithe,
þat þu þi gulte hier arithe,
and werche gud bi dai and nithe...

to think about why Christ made him and about Christ's suffering on his behalf,

> þinc, man, war-to crist þe wroute
>   and do way prede and felthe and mud.
> þinc wu dere he þe boute
>   o rode mid is swete blud...
> biþinc þe þan, and up aris
>   of senne, and agin werchen gud...

and especially to think about the glories of salvation that Christ alone can help him attain,

> biþinc wel forþi us ics rede,
> and clanse of ecs misdede,
> þat Crist þe helpe at tine nede,
>   þat so dere hauet þe bout,
> an to euene blisse lede
>   þat euere last and faillet nout.

This poem is also illustrative of both the prevailing mode and style of the Middle English lyrics, a mode which can best be described as expository, and a style admirably suited to such a mode. The essential qualities of this style are those of effective exposition--clarity, simplicity, sincerity, directness, concreteness. But the English lyricist was, after all, composing poetry, and in his attempt to convey his meaning as effectively as possible, he brought to bear all the technical and imaginative resources of poetry at his command--diction, meter, rhyme, imagery. What ornamentation there is, however, is largely unobtrusive and unostentatious. Devices of sound, like alliteration and assonance, devices of structure, particularly repetition, and figures of speech are characteristically functional rather than merely decorative. The English poet employs such devices not for their own sake, but only in so far as they contribute to his purpose; that is, in so far as they help to establish, elucidate, emphasize, and reinforce his meaning. Or, to put it another way, form is put at the service of content.

This emphasis on exposition is a characteristic feature of the Middle English lyrics, one which distinguishes them sharply from contemporary French lyrics, as Stuart Degginger and others have noted.[24] Degginger also points out another significant difference between the English lyrics and those of the troubadours when he compares the English "Lutel Wot Hit Any Mon" (Brown, XIII, 91) with similar Provençal lyrics:

> There is an evident difference between
> this English piece and the lyrics of the
> trobadors--a difference which is immediately
> felt by anyone who has read the Provençal
> poets. Nor is the difference merely one
> of language and age. What is missing in the
> English is that reflex character of Provençal
> song which is partly the result of reflective
> language but mostly the effect of psychologizing--
> the self-conscious analysis that is so constant
> among the trobadors (88-89).[25]

The Middle Enlgish lyric poet makes little if any attempt
to psychologize his case, to dissect and minutely analyze a
subjective experience. Instead, he is content to express his
condition and the reasons for it. But that he does not undertake
such subtle, self-conscious analysis does not necessarily mean
the English language was inadequate for such a purpose, as some
have suggested.[26] Nor does it mean that the English poet was
incapable of writing this kind of poetry. Certainly, the author
of "The Owl and the Nightingale" is not far removed from his
French contemporaries in this regard. What this absence of
psychological analysis from the Middle English love lyrics does
suggest is that this kind of analysis simply was not a major
concern of the English poet.

The tendency to eschew subtle argument and minute analysis
is just as characteristic of the religious lyrics in Middle
English as of the secular lyrics. The poet is not primarily
concerned with his own religious sensibilities or with difficult
theological subtleties. He knows what he knows, and what he
knows he writes about. Here, even more than in the secular
lyrics, the poet's foremost consideration is to make some significant point, to teach a lesson.[27]

The English poet is working in a different tradition from
that of the troubador and trouvere. But the intention to teach
a lesson does not manifest itself solely in simple platitudes or
direct moral admonitions, though this is not infrequently the
case. To achieve his purpose, the poet attempts to re-create an
objective experience as accurately as possible so as to make it
readily accessible to his audience, who might then share in that
experience. Lewis and Nancy Owen describe this particular aspect
of the Middle English lyrics especially well:

> The Middle English poet, who before the
> fifteenth century was usually anonymous,
> wrote in a lyric voice that might be intensely
> personal but rarely individual...Whether a
> poem is sacred or secular, the description of
> an event or the account of a psychological
> state of mind, it becomes an invitation for

the reader to participate in a response which
is assumed to be universal. We do not feel
that we are being introduced to a uniquely
personal perception of experience, but rather
being reminded of a commonly shared experience
whose nature and value are already established
and familiar.[28]

Even if his poem does not explicitly spell out a lesson, it
can nevertheless achieve the same effect by re-creating the
experience in such a manner that the audience itself can be made
to share in it and learn from it; thus, the poem itself becomes
the lesson. This is particularly true of the religious lyrics,
where the poet often attempts to re-create an experience in
which the audience can participate by portraying a scene so
vividly and concretely that the audience is invited to visualize
itself as part of that scene.[29] The result of such attempts is
one of the outstanding characteristics of these lyrics, their
visual concreteness.

This visual concreteness is perhaps most obvious in passages
on the crucifixion. For example, in the poem "Iesu for Þi Muchele
Miht" (Brown, XIII, 84) the poet does not simply allude to Christ's
wound but describes in detail the blood flowing from the wound:

> Whan y þenke on iesu blod,
> þat ran doun by ys syde,
> from is herte doun to is fot....(6-8)

When we turn from poems on the crucifixion to the large body of
moral-philosophical poems, such as the "Doomsday" poems, we find
the same characteristic concreteness. "Wenne Hi Þenche on Domes-
dai Ful Sore I Me Adrede" (Brown, XIII, 28a) affords a good
example:

> Þat fuir sal comen in þis world on one sonen-nist,
> Firbernen al þis middeherd so crist hit wole disten,
> Boþen watir & þed-lond, þe flurs þat beit briste--
> Hiheriet bo ure louerd, muchel is his miththe.(5-8)

Again the poet does not simply allude to or mention the destruction of the world. He makes graphically explicit that watery as
well as inhabited regions will be consumed, and his addition of
bright flowers to the list, almost as an afterthought, is an
exquisite touch. But most striking is his placing of the verb
"firbernen" at the beginning of the sixth line. Here, the
syntactic emphasis on the word is reinforced by the metrical
emphasis. Thus, the reader is forced, as it were, by the poetic
structure itself to stop and visualize this fiery destruction of
the world.

The emphasis on minute detail, on visual concreteness, is by no means limited to the religious lyrics. Sister Theresa Clare Hogan, in her study of the Harley lyrics, suggests that "particularization of detail" is yet another quality that sets these English lyrics apart from even those Provençal lyrics that might have influenced their composition.[30] She focuses on the well-known "Lenten Ys Come Wiþ Loue to Toune" (Brown, XIII, 81), which serves well to illustrate this "particularization of detail," as does virtually every English lyric in the Harley 2253 manuscript.[31] But we do not have to limit ourselves to the poems in Harley 2253 to find examples of this characteristic in the secular lyrics. "Sumer Is Icumen In" (Brown XIII, 6), for example, is constructed almost entirely of such details:

> Svmer is icumen in,
> Lhude sing cuccu!
> Groweþ sed and bloweþ med
> and springeþ þe wde nu.
> Sing cuccu!
>
> Awe bleteþ after lomb,
> lhouþ after calue cu,
> Bulluc sterteþ, bucke uerteþ.
> Murie sing cuccu!
> Cuccu, cuccu,
> Wel singes þu cuccu.
> ne swik þu nauer nu!

Although all the details are not visual, they are certainly concrete. Not only do we "see" the breeze blown meadow, where the ewe chases after the lamb and the calf after the cow, but we also "hear" the ewe's bleating, the calf's lowing, and, above all, the "cuccu" singing its song. We see, we hear, we feel-- we experience--the coming of spring in this most delightful poem.

Whatever the reasons, a high degree of visual concreteness is characteristic of the Middle English lyrics, and we may have here another link between the lyrics and the old poetic tradition. That visual concreteness is characteristic of Old English poetry need hardly be demonstrated. We need only recall the description of the wall in "The Ruin"; or the description of life at sea with which "The Seafarer" opens; or the gruesome description of Beowulf's triumph over Grendel or the description of Grendel's "mere" to assure ourselves sufficiently of this point. But perhaps most interesting in this respect is the glorious description of the rood, alternating with the horrific details of the crucifixion in "The Dream of the Rood":

```
            Geseah ic wuldres treow,
wædnum geweorðode,  wynnum scinan,
gegyred mid golde;  gimmas hæfdon
bewrigene weoðlice  wealdendes treow.
Hwæðre ic þurh þæt gold  ongytan meahte
earmra ærgewin,  þæt hit ærest ongan
swætan on þa swiþran healfe.  Eall ic
            wæs mid sorgum gedrefed,
forht ic wæs for þære fægran gesyhðe.
          Geseah ic þæt fuse beacen
wendan wædum ond bleom,  hwilum hi wæs
                    mid wætan bestemed,
beswyled mid swates gange,  hwilum mid
            since gegyrwed.(14-23)
```

The paradox reflected in the contrast between the glorious
vision of the rood, decorated with gold and gems, and the alternating horrific vision of the same rood, smeared with blood from
the crucifixion, brings to mind the fourteenth century lyric
"Steddefast Crosse, Inmong All Oþer" (Brown, XIV, 40). Here too
the poet plays upon the paradox inherent in the crucifixion:

```
Steddefast crosse, inmong alle oþer
þow art a tre mykel of prise,
in brawnche and flore swylk a-noþer
I ne wot non in wode no rys.
Swete be þe nalys,
and swete be þe tre,
and sweter be þe birdyn þat hangis vppon the!
```

Furthermore, the rood's account of the crucifixion itself,
especially the emphasis on the driving in the nails ("Þurhdrifan
hi me mid deorcan næglum. On me syndon þa dolg gesiene, opene
inwidhlemmas."), recalls many a Middle English lyric on the Passion, for the Middle English poet was rarely content to state
that Christ was on the cross. Rather, he paints the scene in all
its horrifying detail. "Ihesu, For þi Precious Blod" (Brown,
XIV, 123) is a somewhat extreme, but not untypical, example. I
quote only the third, fourth and fifth stanzas:

```
Ihesu, for þi blodi dropes,
þat þe scourge & þe ropus
  Made hem to renne a-doune,
Fede me wit mete & drink,
þat i neuere in synne sinke--
  Haue mercy on me, glotoun
```

Ihesu, for þi blodi heued,
þat wit thornes was beweued,
   longe, scharp, & kene,
Chast me þat am so wilde;
Make my herte mek & mylde,
   to be þi seruant clene.

Ihesu, for þi blodi strondes,
þat ran out of ȝoure handes--
   þe nayles þer-inne i-driue--
fro coutyse drawe me þouȝt,
more þan me nede ȝef me nouȝt,
   wiles þat i schal leue.

We might also note at this point the Old English poet's
tendency to place strongly stressed words at the beginning of
the line, words which regularly inaugurate the alliterative
series. It is particularly in those lines where the alliteration joins the verb to concrete nouns that are themselves emphasized by the alliteration that the visual quality of the poem
is most intensified. For example, "gegyred mid golde; gimmas
hæfdon," where the glorious beauty of the tree adorned with gold
and gems is made most visually concrete. Or again, "beswyled
mid swates gange hwilum mid since gegyrwed," where the miracu-
lous nature of the alternating vision is made most strikingly
visual. Most effective in this regard is the following:

   earmra ærgewin, þæt hit ærest ongan
   swætan, on þa swiþran healfe....

Here the meter and the syntax combine to rivet attention on
"swætan" and force us to focus on the bleeding.
   While there is nothing precisely of this kind in the
Middle English poem, there are what may be vestiges of the tendency to begin a line with a strongly stressed word. Lines 10
and 16 begin with the strongly stressed, concrete verbs "Fede"
and "Chast" respectively. Furthermore, in lines 8-9 we can
observe the meter and syntax combining to create a run-on effect,
though the verb "Made" does not have the same force and significance as "swætan" in the Old English poem:

   þat þe scourge & þe ropus
   Made hem to renne a-doun....

Finally, in line 17 we have an instance of an initial strongly
stressed word inaugurating an alliterative series: "Make my
herte mek & mylde...."
   To trace with any certainty a precise relationship between
the Middle English lyrics and Old English poetry with respect to

visual concreteness is extremely difficult at best, for visual
concreteness may be achieved by a variety of means, and neither
it, nor the techniques employed to achieve it, are in any way
unique to English poetry. Nonetheless, the Middle English lyrics
do, on the whole, exhibit a higher degree of visual concreteness
than do their continental counterparts, and an inference can be
drawn, albeit a negative one--since Old English poetry exhibits
a considerable degree of visual concreteness, there is nothing
to preclude the possibility that this feature of the Middle
English lyrics derives at least to some extent from the older
poetry. But the precise source for this characteristic of the
lyrics is not in itself as important as is the very fact that
English poetry, from Old English times to Chaucer's day, is
marked by a high degree of visual concreteness, and this visual
concreteness contributes to the English quality that is a mark
of the native tradition.

The emphasis in the Middle English lyrics on teaching a
lesson quite naturally results in poetry which is perhaps more
didactic than our modern sensibilities find comfortable. Indeed,
the charge most frequently levelled against these lyrics is their
didacticism, and the charge is not altogether unjust. But didacticism is not of itself antithetical to lyric poetry, nor is it
necessarily so negative a quality as current critical use of the
term would seem to imply. For when the imaginative resources of
poetry are put at the service of a didactic impulse, the result
can be poetry whose power and vitality, whose special beauty,
derives precisely from this conjunction of the didactic and lyric
impulse.

In the best of the Middle English poems the poet does not
simply preach nor deliver a sermon in verse, for the medium
through which he conveys his message is poetry in the finest sense
of the word. A brief glimpse at a few of these poems should suffice to illustrate the point.

The theme of "Man Mei Longe Him Liues Wene" (Brown, XIII, 10)
is a familiar one--the unexpected suddenness with which we may be
confronted by death. The text of the first two stanzas follows:

> Man mei longe him liues wene,
>   ac ofte him liyet þe wreinch;
> fair weder ofte him went to rene,
>   an ferliche maket is blench.
>   þar-vore, man, þu þe biþench,--
> al sel valui þe grene.
> wela-wey! nis King ne Quene
>   þat ne sel drinke of deth-is drench.
>   Man, er þu falle of þi bench,
>   þu sinne aquench.

```
Ne mai strong ne starch ne kene
  a-ȝyle deth-is wiþer-clench;
ȝung and old and brith an-siene,
al he riueth an his streng.
  vox and ferlich is þe wreinch,
ne mai no man þar to-ȝenes,
wei-la-wei!  ne iweping ne bene,
  mede, liste, ne leches dreinch.
Man, let sinne and lustes stench,
Wel do, wel þench!
```

The poet is primarily concerned with warning man to be always
ready, lest he be surprised in the midst of his sins by death.
The lesson of the poem is summed up in the last two lines,

```
Man, let sinne and lustes stench,
Wel do, wel þench!
```

But this lesson is brought home in a series of striking images.
Death is depicted as a hostile foe ("deth-is wiþer-clench") always
ready ("vox and ferlich") to lay some snare ("wreinch") for man.
Man, in the flower of his youth ("þe grene") has no thought of
death; he expects to live for a long time. But this is an illusion, and in the illusion itself lies the snare. For just as un-
predictable as the weather ("fair weder ofte him went to rene/an
ferliche maket is blench") is the course of man's life. All
("ȝung and old and brith an-siene"), no matter how strong, must
sooner or later succumb to death's power. Neither weeping, nor
riches, nor craft is of any use; nor is any physician's draught
more effective than a draught of ale.

The subject matter of the poem is certainly a serious one.
But there is a certain humor and playfulness that seem to reflect
the poet's bemused sense of life as a kind of game. In this game
death is the treacherous opponent, and man, the somewhat naive
victim who is unaware of the full consequences of losing. This
playfulness is particularly striking in the last lines of the
opening stanza. Here the poet makes his point in terms of an
amusing analogy to drunkenness. Death is depicted as proferring
to man a draught, similar in its effect to ale or wine. There is
no one, no king nor queen, "þat ne sel drinke of deth-is drench."
Thus, the poet sounds his warning,

```
Man, er þu falle of þi bench,
þu sinne aquench.32
```

Falling off the bench is both the result of excessive drinking and,
at the same time, a metaphor for dying, a metaphor particularly
appropriate within the context of the poem as a whole. For a

drunken stupor is the perfect metaphor for the life of the man
who plays the game unprepared for the consequences of losing.
The lesson is, of course, perfectly obvious. Man had better be
more concerned with "quenching" his sins than quenching his thirst.

The theme of "Wen Þe Turuf Is Þi Tuur" (Brown, XIII, 30) is
the transitory nature of worldly joy. In six short lines the poet.
forcefully drives home his lesson:

> Wen þe turuf is þi tuur,
> & þi put is þi bour,
> Þi wel & þi wite þrote
> ssulen wormes to note.
> Wat helpit þe þenne
> al þe worilde wnne?

The poem works by a series of ironically contrasted parallels--
"turuf" and "tuur," "put" and "bour." "Turf" and "pit" stand in
sharp contrast to "tower" and "bower," but at the same time they
serve a similar function. The irony is further developed in the
next two lines. For only the worms shall take note of the things
prized, "wel" and "wite þrote," by those who formerly inhabited
the "tower" and the "bower" but whose abode is now the "turf" and
the "pit."

The poem is obviously didactic; it is a powerful utterance
against vainglory. But nowhere does the poet preach at us.
Rather, his effective use of imagery forces us to recognize the
levelling power of death and the common end of all men. The
irony reinforces the theme and emphasizes the futility of pride
in worldly joys. Significantly, the poet does not conclude with
a direct admonishment but with a question:

> Wat helpit þe þenne
> al þe worilde wnne?

Of a different order is the poem, "Wose Seye on Rode" (Brown,
XIII, 34). In this poem, as in virtually all the lyrics on the
Passion, the poet's main purpose is to arouse in his audience the
great love for Christ that comes from the realization of the
suffering Christ willingly underwent on behalf of man:

> Wose seye on rode
> ihesus is lef-mon,
> (Sori stod him bi wepinde
> sent marie & sent Ion),
> Is hewid him al abutun
> wid þornis i-prikit,
> Is faire hondin & is waire wed
> wid naylis y-stickit,
> Ys rug wid yerdis suonken

ys syde wid sper y-vundit,
Al for sunne of mon,--
Sore he may wepin
& bittre teris letin,
mon þad of luue con.

The point of the poem is expressed in the two lines with which
it begins and the three lines with which it concludes--any man
who is capable of love, or who knows anything of love, will
surely weep bitter tears when he sees his beloved Jesus on the
cross. This is self-evident, and the poet does not belabor the
point. Rather, he concentrates his power on the image of the
crucified Christ, which he develops in vivid and minute detail--
His head pricked by thorns; His hands and feet pierced by nails;
His back scourged by rods; His side wounded by a spear. He
re-creates for his audience the scene on Calvary so powerfully
that they cannot help but "feel" Christ's suffering and, consequently, ponder its meaning. But "feeling" is the key. By
sharing the experience, by feeling the agonies of the crucifixion,
the audience comes to understand the meaning and power of love.
It was because of His love for man that Christ willingly underwent such torment. And it is only the power of love that can
sustain man in the face of such suffering. If, then, man can be
made to feel Christ's suffering, he can be made to feel Christ's
love for him. Once he feels the depth and power of Christ's love,
he cannot help but return that love--if, as the poet says, he is
at all capable of love. This, then, is the meaning of the poem--
to arouse in the audience love for Christ and to reinforce this
love by effectively re-creating the single most powerful manifestation of such love. This the poem admirably accomplishes.
     That the great majority of Middle English lyrics are didactic
can hardly be denied. That they are often, at the same time,
characterized by vigour and sincere feeling, that they are often
vital and beautiful, is the more to their credit. But it is not
so much the didactic element itself which distinguishes the Middle
English from the French and other continental lyrics; rather, it
is the particular form in which this didactic element manifests
itself in the English lyrics, what I have referred to as the
expository mode, that makes these lyrics unique.
     Love is also the subject of what is perhaps the best known
of all the Middle English lyrics, Thomas of Hales' "Love Ron"
(Brown, XIII, 43). The poem is set within a simple framework:

A Mayde cristes me bit yorne
   þat ich hire wurche a luue-ron,
For hwan heo myhte best ileorne
   to taken on-oþer soþ lefmon,
Þat treowest were of alle berne
   & best wyte cuþe a freo wymmon. (1-6)

The poet readily agrees--"Ich hire nule nowiht werne...." But
he does not intend simply to amuse her; rather, he intends to
instruct her--"Ich hire wule teche as ic con" --a purpose he
reaffirms in the penultimate stanza:

> Þis rym, mayde, ich þe sende
>   open and wiþ-vte sel;
> Bidde ic þat þu hit vntrende
>   & leorny bute bok vych del;
> Her-of þat þu beo swiþe hende....(193-197)

The lesson that the poem contains is not intended solely for
the maiden who requested its composition, but for all those who,
like her, desire to know about love:

> & tech hit oþer maydnenes wel.
> Hwo-so cuþe hit to þan ende,
>   hit wolde him stonde muchel stel.(198-200)

The theme of the poem proper is the transitory, unstable
nature of earthly love. As the poem begins, earthly love is set
within the larger context--the transitory and mutable nature of
all worldly things--and such love is "bute o res." The poet
depicts this transitory world in a series of simple but effective
images:

> Þeos þeines þat her weren bolde
>   beoþ aglyden so wyndes bles,
> Vnder molde hi liggeþ colde
>   & faleweþ so doþ medewe gres.(13-16)

In this world nothing is permanent; all things move toward their
appointed end. And here too the poet stresses the sudden unex-
pectedness with which we may be confronted by death:

> Pyne & deþ him wile of-dryue
>   hwenne he weneþ to libben best.(23-24)

There is no one, no matter how rich or noble, no matter how swift
or powerful, who can avoid this end. Nor can it be averted by
means of gold or silver or any other worldly riches. Hence, the
poet concludes,

> Þus is þes world, as þu mayht seo,
> Al so þe schadewe þat glyt away.(31-32)

All worldly things are transitory and unstable, subject to
constant change:

> Þis world fareþ hwilynde--
>   hwenne on cumeþ an-oþer goþ;
> Þat wes bi-fore nv is bihynde,
>   þat er was leof nv hit is loþ.(33-36)

And so it is with earthly love:

> Monnes luue nys buten o stunde:
>   nv he luueþ, nv he is sad,
> Nv he cumeþ, nv wile he funde,
>   nv he is wroþ, nv he is gled.
> His luue is her & ek a-lunde,
>   nv he luueþ sum þat he er bed;
> Nis ne neuer treowe i-funde--
>   þat him tristeþ he is amed.(49-56)[33]

Just as death brings an end to joy in worldly riches, so it brings an end to earthly love--" Al deþ hit wile from him take" (64).

The poet reinforces the point in the well-known, exquisite ubi sunt passage:

> Hwer is paris & heleyne
>   þat weren so bryht & feyre on bleo,
> Amadas & dideyne,
>   tristram, yseude and alle þeo,
> Ector, wiþ his scharpe meyne,
>   & cesar, riche of wordes feo.
> Heo beoþ i-glyden vt of þe reyne
>   so þe schef is of þe cleo.(65-72)

While the ubi sunt motif is commonplace in the literature of the Middle Ages and such passages abound, we might note here the similarity between this passage and the ubi sunt passage in the Old English poem, "The Wanderer," which it so closely resembles in function and structure. Particularly striking is the similarity in phrasing of the concluding lines, where the Middle English, "Hit is of heom also hit nere," literally translates the Old English, "swa heo no wære." Also of interest is the fact that these passages occur in poems having a clearly defined narrative framework, which, as Dronke has pointed out, is an important element in the English lyric tradition.

The ubi sunt passage in the "Love Ron" is the culmination of the poet's demonstration that earthly love is transitory. Having established that such love is devoid of any permanent value, the poet now takes up his real purpose:

> Mayde, if þu wilnest after leofmon
>   ich teche þe enne treowe king.(87-88)

The poet proceeds then to tell the maiden about this "treowe king." First, his appearance and character:

> he is feyr & bryht on heowe,
>   of glede chere, of mode mylde,
> of lufsum lost, of truste treowe,
>   freo of heorte, of wisdom wilde....(91-94)

Next, his riches:

> He is ricchest mon of londe
>   so wide so mon spekeþ wiþ muþ,
> Alle heo beoþ to his honde,
>   est & west, norþ and suþ.(97-100)

If she gives her love to him, he will dress her in the finest garments:

> He brouhte þe to suche wede
>   þat naueþ king ne kayser non.(111-112)

And she will live in the most splendid dwelling:

> Hwat spekestu of eny bolde
>   þat wrouhte þe wise salomon
> of iaspe, of saphir, of merede golde,
>   & of mony on-oþer ston?
> Hit is feyrure of feole volde
>   more þan ich eu telle con;
> Þis bold, mayde, þe is bihote
>   if þat þu bist his leouemon.(113-120)

This "treowe king" is clearly the paragon of all lovers, and the poet is obviously referring to Christ. But the terms in which the poet describes Him, though always superlatives, are those equally appropriate to worldly lovers. In fact, it is not until the seventeenth and eighteenth stanzas that the "king" is explicitly identified, and even here it is somewhat indirectly. The poet is continuing his description of the magnificent dwelling:

> Þer ne may no freond fleon oþer,
>   ne non fur-leosen his iryhte;
> Þer nys hate ne wreþþe nouþer,
>   of prude ne of onde, of none wihte.
> Alle heo schule wyþ engles pleye,
>   some & sauhte in heouene lyhte.
> Ne beoþ heo, mayde, in gode waye
>   þat wel luueþ vre dryhte?(129-136)

But even here the poet does not completely abandon the metaphor
of earthly love:

> Nere he, mayde, ful seoly
> þat myhte wunye myd such a knyhte?(143-144)

The poet goes on to describe a great treasure that this
"king" has committed to her care, a treasure "betere þan gold
oþer pel." This treasure has remarkable powers--"He heleþ alle
luue wunde." The treasure is called "Mayden-hod," and it is the
most precious of all jewels:

> Hwat spekstu of eny stóne
> þat beoþ in vertu oþer in grace --
> Of amatiste, of calcydóne,
> of lectorie and tupace,
> Of iaspe, of saphir, of sardone,
> smaragde, Beril and crisopace?
> A-mong alle oþre ymstone,
> þes beoþ deorre in vyche place.(169-176)

Throughout the poem, then, the poet teaches heavenly love
and spiritual values, but he does so almost exclusively in
worldly terms. He does not engage in abstract theology. He is
not vague or mystical; he does not speak of joys or rewards beyond
all human comprehension. Nor is he argumentative. True, he
promises much. But his frame of reference is always the concrete
reality of worldly experience, though certainly a romanticized and
idealized version of this reality. The paradox is functional as
well as effective. For he translates a spiritual experience into
existential reality and in so doing makes it comprehensible and,
consequently, meaningful in human terms. The result is perhaps
the most perfect example among the Middle English lyrics of what
can be achieved in the expository mode, particularly of the vitality and beauty that can be generated by the conjunction of the
didactic and lyric impulse when skillfully structured in this mode.
While the early English lyricist seemed to have directed his
efforts toward re-creating an objective experience in which the
audience could share, the Provençal poet consciously and characteristically directed his efforts toward analyzing his own personal
situation or psychologizing his condition. And this seems to be,
generally speaking, the raison d'etre for the great majority of
troubadour lyrics.
By the twelfth century continental lyric poetry, particularly
that of the troubadours, already clearly reflects a conception of
poetry as an individual art. The troubadour poets were fully and
self-consciously aware of the fact that they were engaged in an
artistic endeavor. William IX, for example, the first of the
troubadour poets about whom we know anything at all, begins his
poems time and again with the phrase, "Farai un vers." William's

conception of his role as a poet is that of a performing artist,
an entertainer, not a "teacher" in any significant sense of the
word. It is a role that he seldom seems to take very seriously,
and his attitude is reflected quite clearly in the half-humorous,
half-ironic manner that he approaches his art. Thus, he begins
one poem, "Farai un vers, pos mi somelh," and another, "Companho,
faray un vers...convinen...." William is primarily concerned
with entertaining, with amusing, his audience, not with imparting
a lesson. Even "nothing" is suitable subject matter for him, and
he begins another poem, "Farai un vers de dreyt nien...."
     Even when William does, on occasion, become somewhat more
serious in his poetry, he, like other troubadour poets, is still
not primarily concerned with teaching a lesson or with any other
practical considerations; rather, he is primarily concerned with
analyzing his own subjective experiences. Such introspective
analysis was, in fact, the overriding concern of the troubadour
poets. We can observe this tendency quite well in William's
lovely poem, "Ab La Dolchor Del Temps Novel." Unlike Thomas of
Hale, whose poem is directed at the maid who requested its composition and whose purpose is to instruct her as best he can,
William is concerned, as he tells us in the second stanza, with
his own condition:

> ni no m'aus traire adenan,
> tro que eu sacha ben de fi
> s'el' es aissi com eu deman.(10-13)

(I do not dare make a move until I know for certain the outcome
will be that which I ask for.)

Moreover, William's concern with his own condition leads him to
an analysis of the love affair itself, an analysis manifested in
the exquisite, elaborate, and complex simile of the third stanza:

> La nostr' amor vai enaissi
> com la branca de l'albespi
> qu'esta sobre l'arbre tremblan,
> la nuoit, a la ploia ez al gel,
> tro l'endeman, que·l sols s'espan
> per la fueilla vert e·l ramel.(13-18)

(Our love is like the branch of a sturdy hawthorne tree, trembling
all night in the rain and frost, until the next day when the sun-
shine envelops both green leaf and branch.)

Here, William employs images from the natural world. But the
images do not stand by themselves, as they so often do in the
English lyrics. They are not simply alluded to as examples of the
poet's lesson or as emblems of his condition, or the condition of

mankind in general. Rather, they are woven into an intricate pattern, a pattern which itself comments upon the nature of love as the poet himself experiences it. Of particular note is the poet's use of descriptive phrases and adjectives to depict the experience. He does not simply tell us that his love, like the hawthorn branch, is renewed each day. He analyzes the process of renewal itself in minute detail. The branch "trembles" in the "rain" and "frost" of the night. But with the coming of day the sun's rays envelop both green leaf and branch, warm them, give them new life. So love is threatened by the uncertainty of darkness, of separation, and is subject to the whims of elements beyond the lover's control. But with the coming of each new day, this love is not only resumed, it starts afresh, invigorated by the brightness of the sun, which supersedes the gloom, the uncertainty of the night. Clearly, the use of imagery here is of a different order from that in such English lyrics as "Nou Goth Sonne Vnder Wod" or "Foweles in þe Frith."

On the whole, the Middle English lyricist was primarily concerned with what he had to say; the troubadour poet, with how splendidly he said it--that is, the argument itself was secondary to the manner in which that argument was presented. Hence, form and technique became the major preoccupations of the troubadour poets.

Where the prevailing mode of the Middle English lryics was expository, the prevailing mode of Provençal lyric poetry can perhaps best be described as analytical. The poems of Bernart De Ventadorn are as typical as any of this analytical mode. In the poem, "Can Vei La Lauzeta Mover," Bernart assumes the role of the bewildered lover struggling to understand the perplexities of love:

> Ai, las! tan cuidava saber
> d'amor, e tan petit en sai....(9-10)

(Alas! how much I thought I knew about love, and how little I know.)

The paradox and complexity of the situation is reflected by the structure of the lines. How much the speaker thought he knew is contrasted with how little he in fact knows. The reason he knows so little is that the subject is love, and it is love, "amor," that structurally occupies the position precisely between the two clauses. In effect, "love" causes the transition from "how much" to "how little" and accounts for the speaker's bewilderment.

But the key word is "know," and this is emphasized not only by the repetition of the verb at the conclusion of both lines, but also by the rhyme. For it is precisely what he knows, or rather doesn't know, in his pursuit of love that is the poet's foremost concern here. Bernart's dilemma in this poem arises from what is the most commonplace situation of the courtly love

tradition, the dilemma that the troubadour poets, as well as
their successors in the tradition, most frequently find themselves in and attempt to analyze--he cannot help loving his lady,
despite the fact that she doesn't return his love:

> car eu d'amar no·m posc tener
> celeis don ja pro non aurai.
> Tout m'a mo cor, e tout m'a me,
> e se mezeis e tot lo mon;
> e can se·m tolc, no·m laisset re
> mas dezirer e cor volon.(11-16)

(For I cannot help loving one who will grant nothing in return.
She possesses my whole heart and my whole being, her own self
and the whole world. And when she left me, she left me nothing
but desire and a longing heart.)

   The expression of Bernart's dilemma in this second stanza
is an expansion of the indirect question he raises at the conclusion of the first stanza:

> meravilhas ai, car desse
> lo cor de dezirer no·m fon.(7-8)

(I wonder why my heart does not melt with desire.)

In this first stanza Bernart employs an elaborate image to describe his condition:

> Can vei la lauzeta mover
> de joi sas alas contral rai,
> que s'oblid' e·s laissa chazer
> per la doussor c'al cor li vai....(1-4)

(When I see the lark joyfully move his wings toward the light,
forgetting himself and letting himself fall because of the
sweetness that enters his heart....)

The flight of the lark represents for Bernart exuberant joy, not
his own, but the joy of those who, unlike him, are happy in their
situation:

> ai! tan grans enveya m'en ve
> de cui qu'eu veya jauzion(5-6)

(Oh, how great an envy toward all whom I see joyful seizes me.)

The joy of those he envies, like the joy of the lark, stands in
sharp contrast to Bernart's own misery, a misery implied in his

envy of those who are happy, a misery which results from unrequited love. But he cannot seem to understand why his "heart,"
that is, his emotional being, does not simply "resolve itself
into a dew" as a result of his unfulfilled desire. And so he
proceeds to identify the precise nature and cause of his suffering in the second stanza.

In the third stanza Bernart describes the effect the lady
has had on him since the moment he first saw her:

> Anc non agui de me poder
> ni no fui meus de l'or' en sai
> que·m laisset en sos olhs vezer
> en un miralh que mout me plai.
> Miralhs, pus me mirei en te,
> m'an mort li sospir de preon,
> c'aissi·m perdei com perdet se
> lo bels Narcisus en la fon.(17-24)

(I have had no control over myself nor been myself from the
moment I was permitted to look into her eyes, into a mirror that
pleases me greatly. Mirror, since I saw myself reflected in you,
the sighs from deep within me have been the death of me, and I
was lost just like fair Narcissus was lost in the fountain.)

Particularly effective is the poet's use of the mirror image,
which leads to the metaphoric death and culminates in the allusion to Narcissus. Not only was the pool Narcissus' mirror, but
Narcissus was also left powerless as a result of gazing into it
and ultimately pined away, sighing over the unobtainable reflection.

It is a subtle and intricate progression from the poet's
state in the first line of the stanza to Narcissus' fate in the
last, and Bernart handles it most carefully and logically. But
the process of going from the one to the other and then of linking the two together is an intellectual one or, in slightly
different terms, an analytical one.

Striking also is the cleverness of the poet's technique in
developing the metaphoric death as a theme in the poem. In the
fourth stanza the lady is responsible for destroying him ("vas
leis que·m destrui e·m cofon"); in the sixth, she lets him die
("laisse morrir, que no l·aon"); and finally in the seventh
staza, where she has succeeded in bringing about his death
("mort m'a"). Thus, it is as a dead man that he is now speaking:
"e per mort li respon...."

This last line is illustrative also of the sophisticated wit
which underlies the whole poem. We can observe this most clearly
in the fifth stanza where the poet paradoxically blames his lady
for behaving like a woman instead of like a man:

> D'aisso's fa be femna parer
> ma domna, per qu'e·lh o retrai,
> car no vol so c'om voler,
> e so c'om li deveda, fai.(33-36)

(In this way my lady behaves like a woman, for which I blame her;
for she does not want what one should want, and that which one
forbids her, she does.)

This kind of sophisticated wit, quite different from the occasional
playfulness and simple humor found in some of the Middle English
lyrics, is an important characteristic of the analytical mode and
in general marks the poetry of the troubadours.

The northern French poets, influenced by the poetry of the
troubadours, inherited not only many of the conventions of
Provençal poetry but also this analytical mode, together with its
emphasis on form and technique.[34] Conon De Béthune, for example,
in the poem, "Si Voirement Com Chele Dont Je Cant," finds himself
in much the same dilemma as Bernart--his love too is unrequited,
though not because his lady spurns him, but rather because he is
unable even to bring himself to tell her of it, an equally commonplace situation in the courtly love tradition. Thus, he bewails
his condition:

> Hé, las! dolens je ne sai tant canter
> ke me dame perchoive mes tormens,
> n'encor n'est pas si grans mes hardemens
> ke je li os dire les maus ke trai,
> ne devant li n'en os parler ne sai....(25-29)

(Alas! suffering, I do not know how to sing so that my lady might
perceive my torments, nor is my courage so great that I can speak
to her of the pains that I endure; no, I do not even know how to
speak directly to her....)

In this poem too the key word is "sai," a word which occurs,
in one form or another, five times. Here too Conon develops the
paradox of how much he thought he knew about love in theory and
how little he knows in practice:

> Ains ke fusse sorpris de cheste amour,
> savoie jou autre gent conseillier,
> et or sai bien d'autrui jeu enseignier
> et si ne sai mie le mien juer....(17-20)

(Before I was surprised by this love, I knew how to counsel others.
And even now I well know how to teach another the game, but know
not how to play mine.)

The paradox is further developed in two extended similes. In
the first, Conon compares himself to a chess player who has great
skill in teaching the game to others, but fails miserably when
actually playing himself:

> si sui com chil ke as escas voit cler
> et ki tres bien ensaigne autres gens,
> et cant il jue, si pert si sen sens
> k'il ne se set escoure de mater. (21-24)

(I am like one who clearly understands the game of chess and who
can teach others very well, but when he plays so loses his senses
that he cannot avoid checkmate.)

In the second, he compares himself to a champion who has long
studied the arts of war, but who forgets all he has learned when
it comes to putting what he has learned into practice on the
field:

> si vait de moi com fait dou campïon
> ke de lonc tens aprent a escremir,
> e cant il vient ou camp as cous ferir,
> si ne set rien d'escu ne de baston. (37-40)

(What happens to me is like what happens to the champion who
practices for a long time at weaponry but, when it comes to
striking blows on the field, knows nothing of shield nor spear.)

The two similes are effective. They are carefully chosen to
reflect the conception of love which underlies the whole poem--
love as a kind of game difficult to master and love as a kind of
battle in which the participants are frequently helpless--and both
are just as carefully developed to emphasize the inexplicability
of it all. Moreover, the essential quality of both similes is
intellectual; that is, they do not depend upon a sensuous or
emotional response on the part of the reader. There is no immediately obvious connection between the lover and the chess player
or between the lover and the champion. The reader is forced to
work out the connection, though he is, of course, guided by the
particular way in which the simile is developed by the poet.
Conon is most concerned in this poem with analyzing his in-
ability to act, to ease his suffering by addressing the lady and
attempting to win her love. This analysis is carried out primarily in the two similes. Like the skilled chess player and the
well-trained champion, Conon knows what to do, but he cannot do
it. Such introspective analysis is an attempt to deal with the
mysteries of love itself. But the particular form it takes here
results from the tradition of fin amour and its associated conventions, a tradition introduced and developed by the troubadours
and subsequently refined by the northern French poets.

Among the most important conventions of this tradition was
secrecy, not only the secrecy that was required of the lover when
the affair was progressing well, but also the secrecy that was
required when the affair was not progressing well or not progressing at all. The dilemma of the poet arises not infrequently
from this necessity for secrecy. The lady who is the object of
the poet's love is conventionally, for one reason or another,
inaccessible so that the poet cannot reveal his feelings to her.
Nor can he reveal them to anyone else for fear of exposing both
his lady and himself to ridicule and shame. Because keeping
such emotions pent up leads to unbearable frustration and even
madness, the poet, to relieve the frustration and to avoid madness,
must somehow give voice to his emotions, and he does so by the
only means available to him--through his poetry. His poetry
serves, then, as an outlet for his emotions. But more than this,
it serves also to replace the ordinary human discourse that is so
vital to the well-being of one who suffers from love's malady;
that is, it serves to replace the friend with whom he could share
his secret and discuss his problems. In a sense the poem becomes
the vehicle through which the poet is able to share the secret,
if only with himself, and so is able to discuss and examine his
condition.

As a result, the psychological analysis in these poems
commonly takes the form of the poet's conversation with himself.
The poet typically begins by relating his wretchedness and the
cause of it. He then proceeds to examine the nature of his misery,
the courses of action he may take to alleviate it and the possible
consequences of such actions, or else the consequences for him of
not taking any action at all. An extremely important part of the
poet's technique in such poems is the use of questions, for the
most part rhetorical, to give impetus to the discussion and to
help move it along. Gace Brulé's "De Bone Amour" affords a good
example of the method in general and this technique in particular:

> De bone amour et de leaul amie
> me vient sovant pitiez et remembrance,
> si que ja mais a nul jor de ma vie
> n'oblierai son vis ne sa semblance;
> pouroec, s'Amors ne s'en vuet plus sosfrir
> qu'ele de touz ne face a son plaisir
> et de toutes, mais ne puet avenir
> que de la moie aie bone esperance.
>
> Coment porroie avoir bone esperance
> a bone amor ne a leal amie,
> ne a vairs yeuz, n'a la douce semblance
> que ne verrai ja més jor de ma vie?
> Amer m'estuet, ne m'en puis plus sosfrir,
> celi cui ja ne vanra a plaisir;
> et si ne sai coment puist avenir
> qu'aie de li ne secours ne ahie.

Coment avari ne secors ne ahie
vers fine Amour, la ou nus n'a puissance?
Amer me fait ce qui ne m'ainme mie,
dont ja n'avrai fors ennui et pesance;
ne ne li os mon corage gehir
celi qui tant m'a fait de max sentir,
que de tel mort sui jugiez a morir
dont ja ne quier veoir ma delivrance.

Je ne vois pas querant tel delivrance
par quoi amors soit de moi departie;
ne ja nul jor n'en quier avoir poissance,
ainz amerai ce qui ne m'ainme mie,
n'il n'est pas droiz que li doie gehir
por nul destroit que me face sentir;
n'avrai confort, n'i voi que dou morir,
puis que je sai que ne m'ameroit mie.

Ne m'ameroit? Ice ne sai je mie;
que fins amis doit par bone atendance
et par soffrir conquerre haute amie.
Més je n'i puis avoir nulle fiance,
que cele est tex, por cui plaing et sopir,
que ma dolor ne doigneroit oïr;
si me vaut mieuz garder mon bon taisir,
que dire riens qui li tort a grevance.

Ne vos doit pas trop torner a grevance
se je vos aing, dame, plus que ma vie,
car c'est la riens ou j'ai greignor fiance
quant par moi seul vos os nonmer amie,
et por ce fais maint dolorous sopir
que ne vos puis ne veoir ne oïr,
et quant vos voi, n'i a que dou taisir,
que si sui pris que ne sai que je die.

Mes biaus conforz ne l'en porra garir;
de vos amer ne me porrai partir,
n'a vos parler, ne ne m'en puis taisir
que mon maltrait en chantant ne vos die.

Par Deu, Hüet, ne m'en puis plus soffrir,
qu'en Bertree est et ma morz et ma vie.[35]

Not only does Brulé reflect upon his condition, but he does
so in a manner which successfully captures the strain he is under
because he cannot reveal his suffering to anyone, least of all to
her who is responsible for it. As the frustration of the poet
increases, the tension of the poem mounts until it explodes in the

emotional outburst of the last few lines, where the poet is no
longer able to restrain himself. He can no longer keep silent;
he must give voice to his love and his grief--but it is only in
his "song" that he finally does so.

Brulé achieves this effect of frustration accumulating to
the breaking point in two ways: first, through the use of the
rhetorical questions that introduce stanzas two, three, and
five, questions which serve not only to keep the discourse going,
but at the same time also create the impression of a person de-
bating with himself; second, through his use of repetition, both
verbal and structural.

Echoing the silent fears haunting the poet are phrases that
time and again come back almost as if to taunt him; for example,
"ce qui ne m'ainme mie" (She who does not love me), which occurs
in stanza three and twice in stanza four. Such verbal repetition
reflects not only the doubts tormenting the poet, but also the
very state of his mind itself, a mind in turmoil and confusion.
Also contributing to this effect, as well as creating the sense
of one thing piling on top of another, is the most important
structural device Brulé employs in the poem--entrelacement.
Moreover, this kind of repetition of a key word or phrase from
the last line of one stanza in the first line of the subsequent
stanza accurately represents the form that introspective debates
commonly take. Not only does this going back and forth reflect
the tumultuous state of the poet's mind as he engages in such a
debate, it also attests to the strain he is under. It is almost
as though the poet is engaged in a continuing struggle to express
what is in his heart, a struggle made all the more difficult by
the constant welling of his emotions. It is a struggle that is
renewed with each successive stanza. For just as the poet seems
to have his emotions under control and so is able to complete one
stanza, they once again come rushing to the fore, and the struggle
begins all over again. Thus, the poet continually grasps for some
key word at each successive stage of the debate in order to keep
clear in his mind what he is trying to say, and he clings to that
word until he can once again compose himself and order his thoughts.
It is only in this manner, in the continual process of stopping and
going back, of repeating a key word or phrase to help crystallize
his thoughts, that the poet is able to proceed at all.

Brulé is primarily concerned in this poem with his emotional
condition. Yet, despite even the emotional outburst of the last
few lines, he is always completely in perfect control of his
medium, as attested to by his careful use of entrelacement, his
perfectly regular decasyllabic lines, and even more by his intricately worked-out rhyme scheme, as well as the rhyme words themselves.

The poem is built upon three rhymes, the a and b rhyme being
reversed in alternating stanzas. The pattern is ababcccb/babaccca,
and this pattern is repeated three times. The only variation
occurs in the final stanza, which consists of six lines rhyming

cccaca. Thus, the poem consists of three paired stanzas and one
concluding stanza. These paired stanzas, linked initially by
entrelacement, are bound even more firmly together by the recurrence of the c rhymes in identical positions structurally, in
lines five, six, and seven. Moreover, the rhyme words in these
positions are the same in each pair of stanzas--"sosfrir,"
"Plaisir," "avenir" in stanzas one and two; "gehir," "sentir,"
"morir" in stanzas three and four; "sopir," "oïr," "taisir" in
stanzas five and six. In fact, the same words are used again
and again in the rhyme positions so that only twenty-six different
words occupy the fifty-four possible rhyme positions. These are,
of course, the most crucial words in the poem--"amie," "remembrance," "vie," "semblance," "sosfrir," "plaisir," "avenir,"
"esperance," "ahie," "puissance," "mie," "pesance," "gehir,"
"sentir," "morir," "delivrance," "departie," "atendance," "fiance,"
"sopir," "oïr," "taisir," "grevance," "die," "garir," "partir"--
and they are emphasized not only by their recurrence throughout
the poem, particularly at the end of the lines, but by the rhyme
scheme itself. It is precisely such words that make up the
conventional poetic language of the tradition of fin amour and
so help reflect the conventional attitudes of this tradition.

In sum, the very structure of the poem, though carefully
controlled and meticulously organized, contributes to the effect
of mounting frustration and helps to emphasize the poet's dis-
traught condition. The poet is suffering; he is bewildered and
confused. And the poem represents his attempt to define and so
to come to grips with his situation. But it is a most difficult
process; confusion and uncertainty constantly interfere with his
efforts; and he must continually go backwards, repeating words
and patterns, before he can get anywhere at all.

Only in the last stanza, where the poet decides that he must
give voice to his feelings, if only in his song, is the pattern
broken, or, to be more accurate, modified. The shorter stanza,
as well as the modified rhyme scheme, appropriately corresponds
to his emotional outburst. For the change here in the structure
of the poem reflects a change in the condition of the poet. He
has finally arrived at a decision, though admittedly it is one he
could not help making. He will no longer keep silent. Just as
he has found release from the repetitious thought pattern in
which he had to this point been trapped, the poem has been released
from the repetitious structural pattern in which it had previously
been trapped. The change in structural pattern as the poem comes
to an end thus reflects the change in the condition of the poet,
reinforcing the sense of relief he experiences in giving voice
to his emotions; that is, the sense of relief he finds in the
very act of writing poetry. For it is only in his poetry that he
can so express himself.

The emphasis of this French lyric differs completely from
that of the Middle English lyrics. The English poems are

externally oriented, intended for an audience to whom the poet
is teaching a lesson and therefore addresses directly. Even in
such lyrics as "Blow, Northerne Wynd," where the poet does seem
concerned with the expression of personal feelings, the form
such expression takes differs from the French. The experience
is externalized and made objective. In Spitzer's words, "Just
as the portrait of the lady offered by our poet was an objective
summary of all virtues conceivable in a lady, so the lover's
feeling is objectified" (15). Spitzer goes on to argue that in
the poem the "lawsuit" against the lady represents the inner
struggle in the heart of the poet made explicit, and Spitzer
suggests French models for this kind of externalization of an
inner debate (17). However, on those few occasions in the English
lyrics where such debates occur, they are invariably externalized;
never is there the kind of internal dialogue, the poet's conversation with himself, that we find in Brulé's poem.36

The medieval French love poem is internally oriented, the
poet addressing himself. The tradition that the troubadour and
trouvere love poet works in and its conventions, demanding secrecy
on account of the delicate subject matter, together with the concomitant pose assumed by the poet, precludes any direct address
to an external audience. Moreover, the poet working in this
tradition has no lesson to teach. He himself does not have the
answers to the questions he raises, and his poetry is occasioned
precisely by the fact he does not have these answers. These
questions are, in a general way, the fundamental questions of the
tradition in which the poet is working. But in any given poem,
they are acutely and particularly those of the individual poet
himself, and all he can really do is to set forth the problem as
it pertains to him and somehow attempt to work it out for himself.

This same conception of poetry as an individual art, which
underlies the French secular lyrics and to such an extent controls
their form and style, underlies the French religious lyrics as
well, though it manifests itself somewhat differently. In the
religious lyrics the poet is not primarily concerned with describing his emotions nor with analyzing his experience. He is above
all concerned with expressing his devotion as best he knows how--
by glorifying Christ or Mary or both in his poetry. His poetry
serves as the poet's own particular and very personal offering
to them, and he concentrates all his efforts on making this offering as worthy and as nearly perfect as possible. Consequently,
the foremost consideration of the French poet in the religious
lyrics, as in the secular lyrics, is with the aesthetic, and while
he does not adopt directly the analytical mode for his religious
lyrics, he does adopt many of the techniques of the secular poetry
as well as many of the conventions characterizing the tradition
of fin amour.

The dependence of the French religious lyrics upon the secular poetic tradition is most graphically illustrated by those poems celebrating the Virgin, poems written in imitation of secular love poems and borrowing from them diction, imagery, meters, and other essentials of style. These French Marian lyrics differ considerably from the English ones, in part because there was no well-established body of secular courtly love lyrics in English to influence the development of the English Marian lyrics and in part because these English lyrics were the product of a different poetic tradition. As a result, the differences between the English and French Marian lyrics reflect, in a broader sense, the fundamental differences between the English and French lyric traditions.

Concerning the English Marian lyrics Rosemary Woolf remarks, "In these lyrics there is a strong attempt...to describe a personal and private relationship rather than to make a beautiful object" (157-158). Woolf is certainly right. For the Middle English lyricist the creation of a "beautiful object" is not a major concern. Rather, his foremost concern is, as we have already seen, to teach a lesson. To that end, the "personal" and "private" relationship he describes is externalized and transformed into that of "Everyman," and his poem is as equally well suited for public as for private use; the language he uses to relate his experience is the everyday language of the common people; his use of concrete details and simple images drawn from the world of nature helps re-create the experience in a manner readily accessible to the audience. In short, his emphasis on teaching a lesson results in a style that effectively serves to diminish the distance between his audience and his poem, for it is a style designed to invite the audience to share the experience so that they may feel it, ponder it, and learn from it.

The French religious lyric, on the other hand, is the product of an artist consciously engaged in the endeavor to create just such a "beautiful object." It is like an exquisite painting, exquisitely framed by its highly elaborate and meticulously wrought structure. In his effort to create this beautiful object, the French poet adopts a style which has just the opposite effect from that of the English poet. It is not only a style designed in every way to enhance the beauty of the poem, but one which effectively serves to maintain a certain distance between the audience and the poem, a distance necessary if the poem is to be fully appreciated. Anyone, for example, who has had the experience of viewing a painting will realize that it must be viewed from a proper perspective. If it is viewed too close-up, the picture becomes blurred, and if one focuses on any single feature of the whole, the total impression is lost. And it is, after all, the total product, the entire picture in its frame, to which the viewer must respond if he is to derive the maximum satisfaction and pleasure from his experience. Thus, where the form and style of the English religious lyric invite the reader to share and even participate in the experience itself, the form and style of the

French religious lyric invite the reader to stand back and admire
the beautiful object. For like a painting on display the French
religious lyric can be fully appreciated only if viewed from the
proper perspective, and so the poet is most careful to keep the
reader at a distance, to force him, as it were, to remain behind
the restraining cord.

The following song to the Virgin by Guillaume Le Vinier
illustrates quite well the particular qualities and the typical
style of the French religious lyrics:

> Glorieuse Vierge pucele,
> Qui Dieu fustes mere et ancele
> Et encore vous est pere at fieus,
> Qui vous sert de cuer sans favele
> Amender en doit sa querele.
> Secourez moi, dame gentieus!
> Priez vo fil, beaus dous cuer pieus,
> Qui rien que veuilliez ne rapele,
> Qu'en la sainte clarté des cieus
> Soit fais et devisés mes lieus
> Et chascun qui de cuer l'apele.
>
> Precieuse dame tres bele,
> Talent ai que vos biens espele
> Selon ce que pourrai au mieus.
> Va douceur est la fontenele
> Qui sourt sous la plaisant gravele,
> Qui rent talent as maladieus.
> Les mors cuers pereceus et vieus
> Esprendez d'ardant estincele
> D'estre en l'amour Dieu talentieus.
> Vo douceur dont tant croit li rieus
> Le monde arose et renovele.
>
> De tout est dame et damoisele
> Cele dont issi la flourcele
> Et la source des fontenieus
> Dont li cours n'estanche n'engele;
> Terre gaste arose, et praiele;
> La où court est tempres avrieus;
> Les durs cuers negligens targieus
> Font et molie et esquartele
> Com fait contre soleil gresieus;
> Repentance, rosee et mieus,
> L'amour Dieu i ferme et seële.

De dous trenchant est l'alemele
Qui le cuer desous la mamele
Fent sans angoisse et sans perieus;
Si souef le roisne et quarele
Que sons de harpe ne viele
N'est plus dous ne plus melodieus;
Clarté remet en orbes yeus
Et parole en langue muele;
Les mors membres fait poestieus
Et fers et sentables quant Dieus
Les surrexist de grace isnele.

Bien peut mestraire la merele
Cil qui si sa char n'afincele
Et estraint qu'il ne soit decieus.
Sire en qui tous biens amoncele,
Gardez mon cors qu'il ne chancele.
Trop est cist siecles malaisieus,
Tant i a article doutieus
Dont la char soronde et revele.
Se vo secours ne m'est hastieus,
Tost puis estre atains et consieus
Au tournoi sans frein et sans sele.

Seigneur, la gaitans mors soutieus
Tient la queue de la paiele.
Ainsi à s'eslite et son kieus
Aussi tost prent jeunes et vieus.
Pour ce a bien fait la martele.

Chantez, arcangles sains Mikieus,
Devant Dieu ma chançon nouvele
Tant qu'il vous commant que recieus
Soit de vous mes espris doutieus
Quant mors li toudra sa cotele.[37]

This poem is indeed beautifully framed. It is built upon
only two rhymes, but the repetition of rhyme words is minimal.
Only three words are repeated in the sixty-five rhyme positions--
"doutieus," "mieus," and "vieus." The poem is organized into
seven stanzas; the first five consisting of eleven lines each
with the rhyme pattern aabaabbabba, and the last two consisting
of five lines each with the rhyme pattern babba, the same pattern
as the last five lines in the longer stanzas. The lines themselves are, with few exceptions, regularly octosyllabic. The
only significant variation is the six syllable line with which
the first two stanzas begin. In both these instances the poet
is directly addressing the Virgin. Both lines consist only of
the noun by which he addresses her--"Vierge" in the first, "dame"

in the second--and appropriately laudatory adjectives. There
are no subordinate or extraneous elements whatsoever. Semantically, contextually, syntactically, and metrically each of
these lines is a self-contained unit standing apart from the
remainder of the stanza. It is as though the poet is giving
the Virgin a place all her own, placing her on a pedestal so to
speak, at the head of each of these stanzas.

That the poet lavishes such care on the structure of the
poem is an indication of his conscious effort to create a
beautiful object, an effort stemming from the attitude with
which he approaches his art. This attitude is made manifestly
clear in the last stanza where he invokes the archangel
Michael to sing this song in the presence of God. The poet is
concerned that his soul be received in heaven when he dies.
Thus, like the tumbler in the well-known story who was anxious
to show his devotion in the only way he knew how, by performing
his little ritual before the statue of the Virgin in the hope
of pleasing her, the poet is anxious to show his devotion in
the best way he knows how, by composing a song he hopes God
will find pleasing. Just as the tumbler's performance is a
testament to his devotion and his own very personal offering to
Mary, so too is the poet's performance, his song, a testament
to his devotion and his own personal offering to God. Like the
tumbler, the poet makes the offering in the hope that it will
help him to attain salvation. And like the tumbler's offering,
the poet's offering is the most beautiful and perfect one he
is capable of making.

This last stanza is illustrative also of the predominant
style of the whole poem. It is a highly elaborate style that
stands in sharp contrast to the stark plainness and simplicity
characterizing the style of the English religious lyrics. The
poet seems to go out of his way to avoid saying anything simply
or directly. Instead, everything is couched in complex metaphors.
Thus, he does not simply say that he hopes his soul will be
received in heaven but rather that God might command Michael to
receive his spirit, one full of misgivings ("espris doutieus"),
when death takes its shell ("Quant mors li toudra sa cotele").

Even when he sets out to ennumerate the virtues of the
Virgin in the second and third stanzas, he uses these complex
and elaborate metaphors. Though he says that he is going to
describe all her goodness as best he can, he devotes almost the
entire second stanza to her "sweetness." Her sweetness is the
"fountain that gushes forth from under the pleasant sand and
gives hope to the sick." It "inflames dead hearts and rekindles
in these vile and wretched hearts the desire for the love of
God." It is "an ever growing stream that cleanses and revitalizes
the world":

> Vo douceur dont tant croit li rieus
> Le monde arose et renovele.

This metaphor of the stream that revitalizes the world is picked up and further elaborated in the third stanza. She is "the source of the springs" whose "course neither dries up nor freezes." Her sweetness waters both the desert ("Terre gaste") and the meadow ("praiele"), and where it flows, it brings a mild spring, metaphorically represented by the month of April. Her sweetness "melts and softens hard hearts," as the sun melts the hail, and it "secures and seals" in these now softened hearts the love of God.

This is a highly intellectual style and of a completely different order from the style of the English lyrics. For example, where the French poet elaborates upon the qualities of the Virgin in a complex metaphoric manner, the English poet is, for the most part, content simply to list her virtues.[38] Over and over again we find in the English Marian lyrics such lines as, "þu ard god & suete & brit" (Brown, XIII, 27: 5) and such passages as:

> Edi beo þu, heuene quene,
> folkes froure & engles blis,
> moder unþemmed & maiden clene--
> spich in þorld non oþer nis.
> On þé hit is þel eþ sene
> of alle þimmen þu hauest þet pris....(Brown, XIII, 60:
> 1-6)

The absence from the English lyrics of this intellectual quality so typical of the French in itself represents a fundamental difference between the two, and this difference manifests itself in yet another significant way. The absence of this intellectual quality prevents in the English lyrics an equal emphasis on the dual nature of both Christ and Mary, their divine and human aspects, and as a result leads to, in Rosemary Woolf's words, "the exclusion of paradox arousing wonderment." "Nou Goth Sonne Vnder Wod," for example, derives its effect precisely from the singular emphasis on the humanity of Christ and the Virgin. Even when the English poets refer to the immaculate conception or the Virgin birth, they do so simply and matter-of-factly. For example,

> Seinte marie, leuedi brist,
> moder þov art of muchel mist,
> quene in heuene of feire ble.
> gabriel to þe he liste
> þe he brovste al wid riste
> þen holi gost to listen in þe.   (Brown, XIII, 18:   1-6)

Or, the following description of Christ's birth:

> Of a meide he was iborin,
> Y-comin of heiye cunne....(Brown, XIII, 24:   11-12)

Or, this description of Mary's unique role as the mother of
Christ:

> Mayden heo was uid childe & Maiden hcr biforen,
> & maiden ar sot-hent hire chid was iboren;
> Maiden and moder nas neuer non wimon boten he--
> wel mitte he berigge of godes sune be. (Brown,
> XIII, 31: 17-20)

Certainly, especially in the last example, the poet is aware
that he is in the presence of a miracle, and like all miracles
it is a mystery. But he does not dwell upon the mystery. He
simply accepts it and is content to relate it, emphasizing only
its uniqueness. Never before has there been a woman who was a
maiden both before and after giving birth. Mary is unique as a
woman; she is unique with reference to her human condition. But
there is no sense of paradox here.[39]

Guillaume, on the other hand, not only alludes to the
paradox ("Qui Dieu fustes mere et ancele"), but it is precisely
this paradox that he emphasizes ("Et encore vous est pere et
fieus"). It is not the mystery or the miracle that is his concern,
nor is it the uniqueness of Mary's situation. Rather, it is the
paradox of Mary's relationship to God, the paradox of one who is
the daughter of her son, that he attempts to convey. And he does
so by expressing the relationship in a manner resembling a riddle,
a riddle which the reader must work out for himself.

The style of the French lyrics differs considerably from
that of the Middle English lyrics. For the essential features of
this style--the meticulously taut structure, the carefully balanced
phrases, the intricate rhyme schemes, the perfectly regular syllabic versification, the highly specialized and elaborately
stylized diction; in short, a style designed to appeal to the
intellect rather than to the emotions by way of the physical
senses--are those conducive to an analytical, or intellectual,
mode. The French poet did indeed pay very close attention to
form and technique. But his close attention to technical detail
emphasized, and his perfect control of form reinforced, the subtle,
minute, intricate analysis that was so often the subject of his
poetry. If the Middle English lyrics are, on the whole, free
from the introspection which is so much a feature of the French
analytical mode, the French lyrics are, on the whole, equally free
from the overt didacticism that is so much a feature of the English expository mode. And while the vitality and beauty of the
best of the English lyrics often results from a conjunction of a
didactic impulse with the lyric impulse, the vitality and beauty
of many of the best French lyrics results from a similar conjunction of an analytical impulse with the lyric impulse. Just as
the English lyric, in form and style, is an effective vehicle for
its content and admirably suited to its purpose, so the French
lyric is just as effective a vehicle for its content and just as
admirably suited to its purpose.

There is one other significant factor we must consider with
regard to the style of the Middle English lyrics, and that is
the long and continuing tradition in England of oral recitation.
Middle English poetry seems even as late as the fourteenth
century to have been largely intended for oral delivery. That
this is so even in Chaucer's day, when English poetry had finally
taken its rightful place in the court, is attested to by the well-
known drawing of Chaucer himself reading to an obviously aristocratic audience. That the Middle English lyricist intended his
poetry for oral recitation is clearly evident from his conscious
concern with meeting the demands of aural comprehension. Nor can
we emphasize enough the importance of this factor in shaping the
style of the Middle English lyrics. For it is precisely this
concern that determines the characteristic style the lyricist
adopts, a style carefully designed for and eminently conducive to
poetry meant to be read aloud and listened to.

Many of the stylistic features we have previously noted--
the absence of ornate rhetorical flourishes, of abstractions in
favor of direct statement, of complex metaphors in favor of concrete images drawn from the world of nature, and especially the
simplicity of the diction and clarity of expression--are largely
the direct result of the fact that the lyrics were intended for
oral recitation. Even the structure of these lyrics, both internally and externally, reflects the poet's concern with making his
meaning as clear as possible to a listening audience. Sentence
structure, for example, is predominantly simple and straight-
forward, the poet preferring to build up and link his sentences
through coordinating constructions rather than to develop his
ideas through subordinate relationships. Moreover, clear and
simple transitions are commonly provided. The rhyme schemes too
are rarely intricate or elaborate, the poet being content with
simple and regular patterns, most commonly the couplet or alternate rhyme, though occasionally the pattern is extended to include
three line units of the type "aab ccb" or some variation thereof.
But the single most important structural principle in the lyrics
arising from the need to meet the demands of aural comprehension
is repetition. Not only are the lyrics characterized by verbal
repetition, by repetition of alliterative and other stock phrases,
but also by repetition of grammatical and metrical structures.[40]

We have already seen that certain characteristic features
of the Middle English lyrics--the emphasis on teaching a lesson,
and thus the expository mode, the dialogue form, the visual concreteness, the use of alliteration--quite possibly have their
roots in the older English poetry. Old English poetry, composed
primarily in an oral tradition, also provides models for many of
the stylistic features of the Middle English lyrics reflecting
the concern with aural comprehension. Especially important is
repetition, not only of stock, formulaic phrases, but also of
syntactic structures.

One of the dominant characteristics of Old English poetry is the technique of parallel variation--the reiteration of key terms or crucial concepts through subsequent substitution, frequently in parallel structures or structures but slightly modified, of equivalent or nearly equivalent expressions. We can observe this technique, used simply but effectively, in Caedmon's "Hymn":

> Nu sculon herigean heofonrices weard,
> meotodes meahte ond his modegeþanc
> weorc wuldorfæder, swa he wundra gehwæs,
> ece drihten, or onstealde.
> He ærest sceop eorðan bearnum
> heofon to hrofe halig scyppend;
> þa middangeard monncynnes weard,
> ece drihten, æfter teode
> firum foldan, frea ælmihtig.

The poem is a paean to God in His aspect as creator. The poet refers to God in a series of parallel variations, each one of which identifies a particular aspect of His Being. He is the "heofonrices weard," the "meotode," the "wuldorfæder," the "ece drihten," the "halig scyppend," the "monncynnes weard," and the "frea ælmihtig." But the poet does not use these different epithets simply for the sake of variety. Each epithet occurs in a separate line and in a slightly different context. In each case the particular connotation of the epithet used is apropos to the context in which it appears. In the first line God is identified in His omniscient and omnipresent aspect, Whose presence not only exists in the heavens above, but Who is Himself the "guardian" or ruler of those heavens. In the second line it is His might and purpose as "creator" that is the subject of the praise. In the third line it is the work of the "glorious father," that is, the father Who is the originator of, Who gives life to, each of these marvels. And in the line which concludes this first passage, God is most appropriately the "eternal lord" Who is time-less, Who is, through the act of creation, the source of the beginning of mankind.

The second passage deals with the three stages of creation. Thus, God is the "holy shaper" Who first gave form to the universe by creating the heavens as a roof for the children to Whom He was subsequently to give life. Next it is God as the "guardian of mankind" Who creates the earth as a place for these children to reside. And then it is once again the "eternal lord" Who creates mankind and Who is, consequently, Himself the beginning of human history. The prayer concludes most fittingly with the reference to God in His omnipotent aspect, the "lord almighty" Who has performed all these wonders and Whose power is indeed unlimited.

Repetition in the form of parallel variation is also used
by the Old English poets to intensify a scene. The description
of Bryhtnoth's reply to the invading Vikings in "The Battle of
Maldon" is a good example of this technique:

> Byrhtnoð maþelode, bord hafenode,
> wand wacne æsch, wordum mælde,
> yrre and anræd, ageaf him andsware.... (42-44)

"Wordum mælde" and "ageaf him andsware" are variations of the
initial formula, "Byrhtnoð maþelode." And the poet's use of
repetition here seems an attempt to convey the intensity of
Bryhtnoth's anger and resolve. It is as though Bryhtnoth has to
start over several times, raising his shield and brandishing his
spear each time, before he can finally give vent to his strong
emotions. Bryhtnoth's speech, when he finally does deliver it,
affords another example of the poet's effective use of parallel
variation:

> Gehyrst þu, sælida, hwæt þis folc sęgeð?
> Hi willað eow to gafole garas syllan,
> ættrynne ord and ealde swurd,
> þa hęregeatu þe eow æt hilde ne deah. (45-48)

"Garas," "ættrynne ord," "ealde swurd," "hęregeatu"--all are
metaphoric parallel variations of the tribute ("gafole") the
Englishmen are prepared to pay the Vikings, tribute that will
not be to their liking, for it consists of the implements of war
the Englishmen are prepared to use against them. Here, the poet's
use of parallel variation, by underscoring the ironic implication
of Bryhtnoth's words, seems again clearly intended to heighten the
dramatic intensity of the scene.

There are numerous other ways in which the Old English poets
used repetition, and we must mention at least one more of these--
the refrain. For it is generally held that the Middle English
lyric poets borrowed this device from continental poetry. Perhaps
they did. But the splendid use of this device by the poet who
composed "Deor," the haunting repetition of the well-known line,
"þæs ofereode; þisses swa mæg" at the conclusion of each stanza,
attests to the fact that the device was known in English poetry
long before the Conquest. And the poet's flawless handling of
the refrain in this poem suggests that its use may have been more
common than this one existing example of it might indicate.

Models exist in Old English poetry for many of the most
common forms of repetition found in the Middle English lyrics.
Moreover, the ways in which the poets who composed these lyrics
used repetition frequently bear a close resemblance to the ways
in which repetition is used in the older poetry. We find, for
example, in the lyrics, the continual use of variant epithets:

Leudi sainte marie, moder and meide...(Brown, XIII, 2: 1)

Seinte marie, luedi brist,
moder þov art of muchel mist,
quene in heuene of feire ble. (Brown, XIII, 18: 1-3)

Iesu, lefman suete...(Brown, XIII, 63: 41 and 51)

Swete ihesu, king of blisse....(Brown, XIII, 51: 1)

In this last poem, "Swete Ihesu, King of Blisse," we find another common device--the use of structurally parallel variant descriptive phrases. Each stanza begins with a line which addresses Christ and describes the speaker's relationship to Him:

Swete ihesu, king of blisse,
Min herte loue, min herte lisse...

Swete ihesu, min herte liȝt...

Swete ihesu, mi soule bote...

Such parallel constructions are commonplace in the Middle English lyrics and serve primarily to reinforce the poet's meaning, to make it as clear and precise as possible. "Leude Sainte Marie, Moder and Meide," (Brown, XIII, 2) affords another good example of this technique:

Ifurn ich habbe isunehed mid þorke & mid þorde,
hþile in mine bedde & hþile atte borde,
ofte þin idrunke & selde of þe forde;
muchel ich habbe ispened, to lite ich habbe an horde.

The poet tells us not only that he has sinned, but that he has sinned "mid þorke & mid þorde." He has sinned continually, both while asleep "in mine bedde" and while awake "atte borde." He has drunk wine "ofte," but "selde" from the right vessel. Finally, he has spent much, but saved little. The poet does not merely tell us that he has sinned; he conveys to us his own sense of the very great extent to which he has sinned and makes us feel, as he feels, the weight of those sins. For he describes his sinful state in terms that are very particular, but have, at the same time, very wide and general application. The situation in which he describes himself becomes one in which we can easily identify ourselves. By making his condition so clear to us, the poet forces us to recognize our own similar sinful condition.
But perhaps the most common form of repetition in the lyrics is the stringing together of synonymous or nearly synonymous words in a coordinate series. Here the poet's purpose is almost always to intensify meaning. Such series may consist of nouns,

Vroure & hele, folkes fader, heóuenliche drichte...
(Brown, XIII, 59: 5);

adjectives,

Nov þov art in huene quene
mit tine sone brist and scene...(Brown, XIII, 18: 52-53)

Nou is mon hol & soint...(Brown, XIII, 20: 1);

or verbs,

Ne helpit hit no þinc þenne to wepen ne to remen...
(Brown, XIII, 28a: 11)

And ich þid þel michel wrong
soregh and murne and <fast>....(Brown, XIII, 7: 5-6)

Certainly such verbal and structural repetition is not
unique to English poetry. Nor is there an exact congruence in
the kinds of repetition, either verbal or structural, that occur
in the Middle English lyrics and Old English poetry. But the
principle is essentially the same, as is the purpose the repetition serves--to clarify, emphasize, and intensify meaning. And
there are enough resemblances between the use of repetition in
the lyrics and in the older poetry to at least suggest that the
Middle English lyricist may have inherited some of these techniques from his Old English predecessors.
     The Middle English lyricist dealt generally with the same
themes as his continental counterpart--love and death, morality
and religion. But though the subject matter was much the same,
the treatment, i.e., style, was, as we have seen, very different.
The qualities most often pointed to as characteristic of the
Middle English lyrics--their simplicity, their sincerity, their
directness, their concreteness--are precisely those by which the
English lyrics are most commonly contrasted to the sophisticated,
ornate, and artificial French lyrics. In part this difference
may be due to the fact that while the English language and English
poetry in the thirteenth century were just beginning to reassert
themselves, French lyric poetry had been flourishing unmolested
for centuries. By the thirteenth century French lyric poetry had
already had a long history of association with the court. Not
only were the French lyrics composed essentially for the highly
sophisticated and cultured aristocratic circles, but in many
cases the poets themselves belonged to this same aristocracy.
The aristocracy in England during this same period was primarily
Norman, and the court was dominated by French fashions. What
courtly poetry there was, was composed for the most part in
Anglo-Norman. The poetry composed in English was intended for a

broader and a more simple audience than either the French or
the Anglo-Norman poetry; it was, one might say, poetry intended
for "everyman." Consequently, as Rosemary Woolf suggests,
"There can, perhaps, never have been a poetry which was more
exclusively written in the language of the common people..."(8).[41]
Even in the fourteenth century, when poets like Chaucer sought
to give English poetry "the entrée to the court," the native
tradition upon which they built was strongly marked by a didactic purpose, and the poetic language of this tradition upon
which they drew was still very much "the language of the common
people."

1

Raymond Oliver stresses the "impersonal, generalized, public quality of the Middle English poems...." He further notes, "The poets show practically no interest in subtle, unique experiences and feelings, neither their own nor anyone else's." Poems Without Names: The English Lyric, 1200-1500 (Berkeley: Univ. of California Press, 1970), 124. Similarly, Rosemary Woolf observes, "Their [the Middle English poets] personal moods and emotions are...not revealed in their poetry, for they are not concerned with the question of how they feel individually...." The English Religious Lyric in the Middle Ages (Oxford: Oxford Univ. Press, 1968), 6. Interestingly enough, F.N. Robinson makes much the same point in his introductory remarks to Chaucer's short poems: "In so far as lyrical poetry is an intensely individual expression of thought or feeling, it would seem not to have been natural to Chaucer's temperament" (The Works of Geoffrey Chaucer, 519). And Patricia Kean, commenting on Robinson's remark, writes, "The same, however, might be said of all Chaucer's contemporaries and predecessors. Apart from odd snatches of song, generally surviving as refrains, there is no medieval English lyric in this sense. To expect Chaucer's short poems to fill the gap is to miss their point. They exist as a witness to a poetic activity which was, above all, social" (Love Vision and Debate, 44-45).

2

Among those taking such a position is R.M. Wilson, who writes, "There is no direct evidence for the existence of lyric poetry in England before the twelfth century, and even then only odd fragments of it have been preserved before the following century... There is little in the Middle English lyric which we can claim as an unmistakable development from Old English, but since we know nothing of Old English lyric poetry--not even whether it existed or not--the fact that we can trace no connexion is of little value as evidence." Early Middle English Literature (London: Methuen, 1939), 251.

3

Though it is generally recognized that Latin and French exerted the strongest foreign influence on the development of the Middle English lyrics, investigations into the origins of the lyrics have not been limited to these two literatures. As early as 1916 Margaret Medary and Carleton Brown in a joint study, "Stanza-Linking in Middle English Verse," Romanic Review 7(1916): 243-283, suggested the possibility of Celtic influence on the lyrics. More recently, A.T.E. Matonis has argued for an even greater influence of Celtic poetry on the Middle English lyrics, particularly the Harley lyrics, in "An Investigation of Celtic Influence on MS. Harley 2253," Modern Philology 70(1972): 91-108.

4

See in particular J. Audiau, <u>Les Troubadours et l'Angleterre</u> (Paris: Vrin, 1927); also, Elinor Rees, who suggests not only an identity of conventions and rhyme-schemes between the English and Provençal poems, but an identity of themes and subject matter. "Provençal Elements in the English Vernacular Lyrics of Manuscript Harley 2253," in <u>Stanford Studies in Language and Literature</u>, ed. Hardin Craig (Stanford, 1941). The "English poet" to whom Rees attributes the Harley lyrics is hypothetical. The lyrics found in Ms. 2253 were most likely composed by a number of different poets, residing in various locales throughout England, despite the fact that the manuscript has come down to us in the handwriting of a single scribe. For a full discussion of the subject, see G.L. Brook, "The Original Dialects of the Harley Lyrics," in <u>Leeds Studies in English and Kindred Languages</u> 2(1933): 38-61. On the subject of French influence, Peter Dronke expresses a dissenting opinion, emphasizing the differences between the Harley lyrics and French lyric poetry. He writes, "There are no songs of such a kind in Provençe; in France the short dance-songs and refrains tend to be permutations of traditional phrases--they do not create an individual situation in a few lines, they do not have this stark plainness of language." <u>Problems and Interpretations</u>, Vol. 1 of <u>Medieval Latin and the Rise of the European Love-Lyric</u> (Oxford: Oxford Univ. Press, 1969), 113. Dronke goes on to suggest German lyric poetry as a possible source for these English lyrics. Pointing out that both have a common ancestry in alliterative rhythms, Dronke concludes, "It is with medieval German love-lyrics, not with Romance, that the English have the truest affinities" (113).

5

Perhaps the leading proponent of this position is H.J. Chaytor, <u>The Troubadours and England</u> (London: Cambridge Univ. Press, 1923). But for a strong objection see the introduction by Rossell Hope Robbins, ed., <u>Secular Lyrics of the XIVth and XVth Centuries</u> (Oxford: Clarendon, 1952), Li ff. Robbins points out that Chaytor's arguments are based almost entirely on Ms. Harley 2253 and that the emphasis on these poems creates a distorted picture. Robbins maintains that when the whole corpus of Middle English lyrics is taken into consideration, French influence is substantially less significant than suggested by Chaytor.

6

<u>The "Chanson D'Aventure" in Middle English</u>, <u>Bryn Mawr College Monographs</u>, Series XII (Bryn Mawr, 1913), 44.

7

Baugh, for example, offers the following capsule summary of the possible origins of these lyrics:

> In considering the origins of the Middle
> English lyric we must of course distinguish
> between religious and secular types. The
> religious lyric belongs to an ecclesiastical
> and literary tradition which knows no
> national boundaries. It is as wide as the
> Christian faith itself. The secular lyric,
> on the other hand, could conceivably have
> roots in the native soil, or in Continental
> poetry--French or Provençal--or in the secular
> Latin lyric which is conveniently, if somewhat
> loosely, characterized by the term Goliardic.
> (209)

8
　　Frank Allen Patterson suggests that the liturgy and the
patristic writings were the most significant Latin influences
on the Middle English religious lyrics. The Middle English
Penitential Lyric (New York: Columbia Univ. Press, 1911).
Natalie White, in her doctoral dissertation (The English
Liturgical Refrain Lyric Before 1450 with Special Reference to
the Fourteenth Century), maintains the liturgy to have been
the main formative element in the creation of the majority of
these lyrics. Sarah Weber has emphasized the indebtedness of
these lyrics, particularly with respect to purpose, form,
structure and texture, to the liturgy as sacred history.
Theology and Poetry in the Middle English Lyric (Columbus:
Ohio State Univ. Press, 1969). Rosemary Woolf, on the other
hand, has argued most convincingly that the English religious
lyrics grew directly from a Latin devotional movement and so
have their sources in Latin works that are overtly and unmis-
takably meditations (The English Religious Lyric in the Middle
Ages).

9
　　Carter Revard's argument that the confusion between the
"beaver-tailed" capital "S" and "M" has resulted in a misread-
ing of the fourth line of this lyric seems to me convincing.
"Sulch Sorw I Walke With," Notes & Queries, NS 25(1978): 200.
Hence, I have adopted his reading of the first word in line four
as "Sulch" rather than "Mulch."

10
　　On the Continuity of English Prose from Alfred to More and
His School (London: Oxford Univ. Press, 1932). But Chambers,
who himself argues so eloquently for the continuity of English
prose, sees no significant continuity in English poetry. He
writes, "Old English poetry had its home in the Anglo-Saxon hall,
and had to go into the highways when the hall passed into Norman
hands. But unlike English poetry, English prose was not suddenly
overthrown..."(Lxxxi).

11

See C.W. Wyld, "Diction and Imagery in Anglo-Saxon Poetry," Essays and Studies 11(1925) and, for a more detailed discussion of this subject, Elinor Rees, "A Portrayal of Moods and Emotions in Early English Vernacular Poetry," Stanford University Bulletin, Abstracts of Dissertations XI(1935-1936): 57-63.

12

Ronald Waldron, for example, sees the survival of allitera-tive meter as evidence of "an unbroken tradition of alliterative verse from the Anglo-Saxon period." "Oral-Formulaic Technique and Middle English Alliterative Poetry," Speculum 32(1957): 793. J.P. Oakden regards the poetry of the "Alliterative Revival" as the strongest evidence for the continuity of an English poetic tradition. "Alliterative Poetry in Middle English (Manchester: Manchester Univ. Press, 1935), II, 42.

13

J.A. Burrow, who is primarily concerned with demonstrating the similarity between all the major English poetry of the second half of the fourteenth century, writes in this regard, "Unlike Chaucer and Gower, the poets of the Alliterative Revival were heirs to a tradition which had in English a long and distinguished history, going right back to the bards or 'scops' of Anglo-Saxon times"(23).

14

W.J. Courthope, in his usual direct and succinct manner, com-ments, "Between the poetry produced in England before the Norman Conquest and the poetry of Chaucer there is absolutely no link of connection"(4). Even C.L. Wrenn, who argues for the continuity of English poetry in subject matter, thought pattern, tone and mood, nevertheless denies any significant relationship between Chaucer's poetry and Old English poetry. "On the Continuity of English Poetry," Anglia 76(1958): 41-59. Among the few who have maintained that there is a strand of continuity from Old English to Chaucer are L.C. Gruber, "The Wanderer and Arcite: Isolation and the Continuity of the English Elegiac Mode," Four Papers for Michio Masui (Denver: The Society for New Language Study, 1972), 1-10; Raymond P. Tripp, "On the Continuity of English Poetry between Beowulf and Chaucer," Poetica (1976): 1-21; and "The Dialectics of Debate and the Continuity of English Poetry," Massachusetts Studies in English 7 (1978): 41-51.

15

English Literature from the Norman Conquest to Chaucer (New York: Macmillan, 1906), 453.

16

The Historical Character of English Lyric. Warton Lecture on English Poetry (London, 1912), 3. Saintsbury is, of course, rid-ing his own hobby-horse here with his emphasis on what he refers to as "the principle of Equivalence," a position he was to make famous in his later, more important work, A History of English Prosody (London: Macmillan, 1923). But he is basically correct in pointing out a relationship between the Middle English lyrics and the older native poetry.

17

    Leo Spitzer's analysis of "Blow, Northerne Wynd" (Brown, XIII, 83) implies that this lyric is the result precisely of such hybridization. Spitzer sees the poem as falling into two distinct parts--the body, what Spitzer calls "the 'courtly' love-poem" and which he describes as "lengthy, courtly, elaborate, intellectualized, calm, static, didactic, and rhetorical"; and the refrain or burden, which he describes as "short, popular, simple, emotional, violent, dynamic, natural, musical...." Spitzer further notes that while the courtly love-poem is marked by the use of Gallicisms, there are no Gallicisms or Latinisms in the refrain. Spitzer maintains that the courtly love-poem is very similar to French lyrics and suggests French models for some of its features. "Explication de Texte Applied to Three Great Middle English Poems," Archivum Linguisticum 3(1951): 1-22. However, even this "courtly love-poem" itself reflects the process of hybridization, for many of the stylistic features noted by Spitzer as characteristic of it--repetition (including synonymous doublets), alliteration, anaphora--are characteristic of the Middle English lyrics in general and derive largely, as we shall see, from the older native poetic tradition.

18

    As Merle Fifield perceptively notes, "By preserving old forms and utilizing more modern ones, the thirteenth-century lyric plays a role in the continuity of the alliterative tradition and in the evolution of a new tradition." "Alliteration in the Middle English Lyrics," Diss. Univ. of Illinois 1960, 46-47. Raymond Oliver also emphasizes the relationship between the Middle English lyrics and the older poetry, particularly the Old English elegies and gnomic verses. Oliver's sense of the very basic yet comprehensive nature of the continuity of the English lyric tradition seems to me precisely right: "The most striking and important marks of lyric continuity, from Anglo-Saxon England through the sixteenth century, are neither mainly stylistic/ structural nor mainly thematic but both at once, because form and content imply each other" (132).

19

    Fifield does not contend that this alliterative tradition survived intact and unchanged into the Middle English period. Rather, she suggests that the thirteenth century saw the beginning of a new alliterative tradition, but one that drew much from the old, and that it was the Middle English lyrics which were primarily responsible for preserving the old tradition and making it accessible to the poets of the new tradition. In her own words from a subsequently published article, "The thirteenth-century lyrics were written in a century which saw the end of the vigorous old tradition and the beginning of a new alliterative language, which was to include some of the ancient phrases... Thirteenth-century lyrics can be proved neither the direct antecedents of later alliteration nor direct descendents of the

old tradition, but they have been proved preservers of Old
English alliterative phrases and contributors to the continuing
expansion of alliteration." "Thirteenth-Century Lyrics and the
Alliterative Tradition," JEGP 62(1963): 118.

20
    "Understanding Old English Poetry," Annuale Mediaevale
9(1968): 6. While Bloomfield is not concerned here primarily
with the question of continuity, he does suggest that the function performed by the Middle English poet was similar to that
performed by the Old English poet. Specifically, he sees the
Old English scops as ancestors of the late medieval court poets
and heralds, and the "popular singers" as ancestors of the late
medieval wandering minstrels (9). See also Stephen G. Nichols,
Jr., "The Medieval Lyric and Its Public," Medievalia et
Humanistica, NS 3(1972): 133-153.

21
    Such also is the view of Oliver and underlies much of his
study of these lyrics. As he puts it, "The anonymous lyrics in
Middle English make up a single tradition, public in status and
shaped by practical considerations" (135). According to Oliver
the three main intentions of these lyrics are to celebrate, to
persuade, and to define. Oliver's sense of the utilitarian function of these lyrics is somewhat more rigid and also perhaps,
more pragmatic than my own. I would prefer to say simply that
the main intention of the Middle English lyric is to inform.
Obviously, Oliver's is a more specific statement of essentially
the same point. But whereas the great majority of the lyrics
fit easily the more general mold, fitting certain of the lyrics
into the more specific mold might be somewhat like fitting them
to a procrustean bed. But more important, Oliver points out
that these lyrics have "a high degree of stylistic coherence"
and further suggests that this stylistic coherence derives from
"the anonymous, practical, and public nature of the poems" (3).
Here, I am in complete agreement, and I will take up the
relationship between purpose and style in subsequent pages.

22
    Another way of thinking of this change is the transition
from "folk" or "popular" lyric to "literary" or "art" lyric.
In Arthur K. Moore's terms it is the transition from the
"embryonic" stage of the lyric to the "perfected" stage. In
the histories of English literature, it is Geoffrey Chaucer who
is commonly credited with being the first major poet to make
this transition. But even Chaucer's poetry, not only in its
purpose, but also in its form and style, is, as I hope to show,
still strongly marked by this utilitarian tradition.

23
    Bloomfield also acknowledges the important influence of
Graeco-Roman wisdom literature on Old English poetry. His main
point, however, is that the Hebrew wisdom literature may have
exerted a stronger influence on the form of Old English than did
the Graeco-Roman. The most important model for Bloomfield's
argument is Ecclesiastes, and he points to similarities between

it and Old English poems like "The Seafarer" and "The Wanderer,"
both of which, according to Bloomfield, are organized around the
same themes and exhibit the same general structure as the Hebrew
poem. In fact, Bloomfield suggests that what have been commonly
referred to as the Old English "Elegies" are not really, in the
strict sense of the word, elegies at all, but rather that these
are types of wisdom literature.

24
    "The Earliest Middle English Lyrics 1150-1325; An Investiga-
tion of the Influence of Latin, Provençal and French," Diss.
Columbia Univ. 1953, 23. Degginger argues that the emphasis on
exposition in these lyrics is strongly suggestive of Old English
homiletic influence, and he sees this influence as being trans-
mitted primarily by way of the West Midland prose sermons.
Degginger is, I believe, right as far as he goes. But, as I
shall attempt to show, the roots of these lyrics reach even more
deeply into the old poetic tradition.

25
    Others too have noted this difference, most often with re-
spect to the secular love lyrics. Thus, R.M. Wilson remarks,
"Whilst some of the ideals of courtly love may occasionally be
reflected in the Middle English lyric, the technical vocabulary
of love is largely absent and there is not the same delight in
sentimental analysis" (252). Albert C. Baugh emphasizes much
the same difference when he compares the English with the French
love lyrics: "The [French] poet analyzes his emotions, theorizes
about the cause and effect of love, and finds enjoyment even in
the suffering which he endures. The monotony with which the
chansons courtoises repeat their conventional attitude is the
fault with which they are most often charged, and to pass to the
English love-lyric is like stepping from make-believe into the
real world. Here we have not Frauendienst of the knightly class,
but feelings natural to two young people between whom there is no
social gulf. The English lyric is frank and outspoken" (211).

26
    See, for example, H.J. Chaytor, The Troubadours and England,
118; and Arthur K. Moore, The Secular Lyric in Middle English, 45.
Degginger, in fact, effectively refutes this notion by examining
a number of early English lyrics in close detail. He concludes
his analysis as follows: "Actually the language is quite sophisticated and quite capable of conveying the subtle nuances of the
courtly tradition...If to this secular vocabulary we were to add
the affective terms occurring in the religious lyrics additionally, there could be no question of a deficiency in early English
with regard to its ability to express fin amour" (75).

27
    Rossell Hope Robbins stresses this function of the religious
lyrics. "The Authors of the Middle English Lyrics," JEGP 39
(1940): 230-238. Robbins argues persuasively that the English
religious lyrics before 1350 were composed in most cases by
Franciscan friars. He points out that religious minstrelsy was

characteristic of the Franciscans and that they were an order
devoted to teaching. Hence, Robbins contends this emphasis on
teaching a lesson in these lyrics supports his argument for
Franciscan authorship.

28
   Middle English Poetry (New York: Bobbs-Merrill, 1971), 5.
29
   Rosemary Woolf calls attention to this quality of the
religious lyrics in accounting for their content: "The main
subjects of the medieval religious lyrics are those central to
medieval meditation, the Passion, and the Last Things, especially
death, with the emotions proper to them, love and fear. In order
that the reader of the poems may feel these emotions personally
and keenly, he is persuaded by the lyric to imagine himself in
a scene which will provoke them, and which is described often in
minute visual detail" (19). Douglas Gray puts the matter somewhat differently but equally effectively. He suggests that the
purpose of the lyrics was "to provide a sensible object of piety
for the eye of some devout beholder to rest on in the work of
meditation, and to excite the inward feelings so that he might
say with Margery Kempe that Christ's death and passion was as
fresh to him as if He had died that same day." "The Five Wounds
of Our Lord," NQ 208(1963): 169. We might also note here Thomas
Ross' discovery of five fifteenth century "emblem" poems in Brit.
Mus. Addit. Ms. 37049. These five poems are accompanied by
graphic illustrations that are directly related to the verse, and,
according to Ross, the subject matter of both the graphic and
poetic treatment is the same. Ross, in seeking for the sources
of the emblem verses that became so popular with seventeenth
century English poets, suggests "a native tradition which may be
added to the history of 'emblems.'" "Five Fifteenth Century
'Emblem' Verses from Brit. Mus. Addit. Ms. 37049," Speculum 32
(1957): 274.

30
   "A Critical Study of the Middle English Lyrics of British
Museum MS. Harley 2253," Diss. Notre Dame Univ. 1962.

31
   Spitzer, for example, emphasizes the detailed, ordered
description of the lady's beauty in "Blow, Northerne Wynd": "The
procedure of description is to break down the 'totality' of the
figure of the Beloved into minute details" (1). Her physical
features are described, as Spitzer points out, from head to toe
in accordance with medieval rhetorical precepts. Of greater
significance is the purpose Spitzer maintains the description
serves in this lyric--to aid the audience in "visualization of
the perfect--visualization of the principle of perfection" (8).

32

It seems to me we can hear echoes of such lines in Chaucer's poetry, for example, at the conclusion of The Physician's Tale, where the narrator, like the poet here, addresses the reader directly with the lesson to be derived:

> Therefore I rede yow this conseil take:
> Forsaketh synne, er synne yow forsake. (285-286)

33

I am indebted to Charles Muscatine for bringing to my attention the similarity between these lines and the following passage from Chaucer's The Knight's Tale, where the subject is also the contrary effects of erotic love:

> Now in the crope, now doun in the breres,
> Now up, now doun, as boket in a welle.
> Right as the Friday, soothly for to telle,
> Now it shyneth, now it reyneth faste,
> Right so kan geery Venus overcaste
> The hertes of hir folk....(1532-1537)

34

In his Introduction to the Study of Old French Literature, tr. Francis M. Du Mont, 3rd. ed. (Halle: Max Nieymeyer, 1931), Carl Voretzsch observes, "The French took over from the troubadours, in a fully developed condition, the conventional character of their lyric poetry..." and, he continues, "Poetry became less the expression of personal experiences and feelings than a somewhat ingenious handling of conventional thoughts in more or less new forms" (334). That the northern French poets, like the troubadours, were primarily concerned with form is also implied by Voretzsch as he traces the development of their poetry through the fourteenth century: "Definite metrical forms were prescribed for several lyric types, in opposition to the lyric poetry of the golden age, when each poet was obliged to invent constantly new metres and new rhythms. The concept of the lyric type is now [fourteenth century] determined less by its content and its peculiar sensibility than by its metrical form" (334).

35

(So often do feelings of pity and the memory of a good love and a faithful lover come to me that never in all my life will I forget her face or her appearance; therefore, if Love is not willing to cease doing as he pleases with all, it cannot be that I may have good hope.

How can I have good hope of a good love or a faithful lover, or of gray eyes or the sweet appearance that I will never again see in all my life? Love drives me; I cannot stop myself, even though she is one whom I can never please. And I know not how it might happen that I should obtain from her either succor or help.

How can I hope for succor or help against true Love, where none has any power? Love makes me love her who loves me not; therefore, I will have nothing but sorrow and grief. Nor dare I reveal my heart to her who makes me feel so many pains; thus, I am doomed to die a kind of death from which I do not search for my deliverance.

I do not search for such deliverance as would free me from love, nor do I seek to ever have this power; rather, I will ever love her who loves me not. Nor is it proper to reveal it to her, no matter the anguish it causes me. I will never have any comfort, and so see no way out but to die, since I know she would never love me.

Would never love me? I really do not know that for sure. For a true lover should, through careful diligence and through suffering, win a noble love. But I can put no faith in that, for this one is such, the one for whom I weep and sigh, that she would not deign to hear about my grief. And so it seems better to keep my good silence than to say anything that might upset her.

It should not so very greatly upset you if I love you, lady, more than my life, for the only thing that sustains me is to call you my love when I am all alone. And because I cannot see nor hear you, I utter many a mournful sigh; and when I see you, I am capable only of silence, for I am so taken that I do not even know what I am saying.

No sweet comfort can ever heal me; I cannot cease loving you; I can no longer keep silent, about my misery.

By God, Huet, I can stand the suffering no longer, for upon Bertree depends both my death and my life.)

36

Spitzer concludes his analysis of this lyric by suggesting that the poet sought to couple two approaches to love--"one the lyrical (popular), the other the didactic (courtly)--and that his predecessors in such attempts to integrate these two voices were the thirteenth century French lyric poets. While Spitzer may well be right in this particular regard, in my view his analysis here, as elsewhere, despite his emphasis on the elaborateness and courtliness of the poem, points not so much to the English poet's attempt to emulate these French models as to his striving to incorporate the foreign elements he draws upon in a manner compatible with the native tradition he is working in.

37

(Glorious Virgin maid, God's mother and servant, and He both Father and Son to you, whoever serves you with a pure heart, in doing so makes his peace. Succor me, gentle lady! Beautiful, sweet, pious heart, pray to your Son, Who denies you nothing you wish, so that in the pure holiness of the heavens a place may be made and prepared for me and for everyone who calls to Him from the heart.

Precious lady, so very beautiful, my desire is to set forth
all your goodness as best I can. Your sweetness is the fountain
that rises from beneath pleasant sands and restores desire to
the sick. Dead hearts, impotent and decrepit, you rekindle with
a blazing spark to yearn for the love of God. Your sweetness is
an overflowing stream that cleanses and renews the world.

Lady and mistress of all is she from whom issued forth the
flower and the source of springs whose course neither dries up
nor freezes, but waters both barren land and meadow, and where it
flows brings mild April, thawing, softening and appeasing hard
hearts, negligent and remote, like hail in the sun. And Repent-
ence, the dew and honey, fixes and seals the love of God in them.

Sweetly piercing is the knife that without anguish and without peril lays open the heart within the breast. It pierces and
searches so gently that the sound of neither harp nor viol is not
more sweet nor more melodious. It brings light to the eyes' orbs
and words to mute speech. It makes dead limbs powerful and hard
and feeling when God resurrects them with His quick grace.

One who is not able to master well and control his flesh so
that he is not deceived is in a bad way. Sire, in Whom all goodness abounds, keep watch over my body so that it does not falter.
Great is the evil of these times. There are so many dubious
things which lead the flesh to indulge and to rebel. If Your
help does not come quickly to me, I may be entered in the tournament and attacked without bit and without saddle.

Gentlemen, death, cunning and unremitting, disburses the
final wage. He takes at his whim the young as readily as the old.
He has for that purpose a well-made hammer.

Sing, archangel, holy Michael, my new song in the presence
of God so that he may command that my soul, full of misgivings,
be received by you when death has taken its shell.)

38

So too in the secular lyrics, as Spitzer notes with regard to
"Blow, Northerne Wynd." He characterizes the detailed description
of the lady's virtues in this poem as "a loose-jointed enumeration
of qualities..."(6).

39

Spitzer makes much the same point with regard to the well-
known fifteenth century lyric, "I Sing of a Maiden." He points
out that the language is eminently simple, and the image used in
the similes to re-create the miracle, the dew, is drawn from the
natural world and is perfectly familiar: "The miracle is immediately
described in terms of a regular phenomenon in nature which works
quietly, with unassuming consistency" (155).

40

Stylistic features such as repetition, particularly of stock
phrases, and the use of clear and simple transitions are, as
Ruth Crosby has shown, equally characteristic of Chaucer's poetry
("Chaucer and the Custom of Oral Delivery"). Crosby attributes

Chaucer's use of these techniques to the practice of oral delivery and suggests that he may have learned them from the Middle English romances. The most important issue here is not whether Chaucer learned these techniques from the romances, the lyrics, or some other specific source, but that such stylistic features are common to the whole of Middle English poetry from the earliest lyrics to the work of Chaucer himself. Rooted in the older native poetry, they are, in fact, characteristic features of the native tradition as it developed following the Conquest. And it is from this native tradition as a whole rather than from any one particular manifestation of it that Chaucer most likely derived not only these but other elements of style as well.

41
   Woolf is here referring to the religious lyrics in particular, but her comment is equally applicable to the secular lyrics. Sister Hogan, for example, remarks, "Those who wrote the poems in Harley 2253...were Englishmen...They were men of clerical education...but they had a feeling of kinship with the people rather than the court" (211).

II

BRIDGING THE GULF: FROM <u>BEOWULF</u> TO CHAUCER

In a lecture delivered in 1920 on the place of the West Midland
alliterative poets in the history of English literature, Sir
Israel Gollancz remarks,

> Even when these poets chose their matter from
> France, or from Latin sources, the spirit of
> the handling is characteristic and altogether
> differentiated from the Chaucerian method.
> All the West Midland poets may not have the
> technical skill and finish attained by the
> poet of <u>Cleanness</u> and <u>Patience</u>, but where
> the treatment shows a weaker hand, <u>the pur-</u>
> <u>pose is none the less marked, namely, that</u>
> <u>the lesson is the first consideration, trans-</u>
> <u>cending all effort in search of the artistic</u>
> <u>and aesthetic.</u>[1]

Gollancz implies that this difference between Chaucer and the
alliterative poets may be due to a more direct link between the
alliterative poets and the old poetic tradition. Nonetheless,
there is considerable evidence that in this very regard Chaucer
shares many of the same concerns with both his alliterative contemporaries and English predecessors; that his poetry has much in
common with theirs; that, in fact, his poetry, like theirs, still
exhibits signs of the influence of the Old English poetic tradition and so attests further to the general continuity of English
poetry.

    We have already noted that the Middle English lyrics reflect
a conception of poetry as a social art and that the poets who
composed these lyrics seemed less concerned with the intense expression of personal emotion or with creating a beautiful object
than with conveying their lesson; for them too the lesson was the
first consideration. And if we are to believe Chaucer's own words,
either as spoken by the dreamer-narrator in so early a work as
the <u>House of Fame</u> ("And listeneth of my drem to lere," 511), or
by himself in his "Retraction," the lesson, the "sentence," was an

equally important consideration for him as well throughout his
entire career: "For oure book seith, 'Al that is writen is
writen for oure doctrine,' and that is myn entente." Thus,
Chaucer goes on to revoke those "translacions and enditynges of
worldly vanitees" and those Canterbury tales that "sowen into
synne," but not the "bookes of legendes of seintes, and omelies,
and moralites, and devocioun." Didacticism is, in fact, so pervasive an element of Chaucer's works that it cannot be denied.
Far too often, however, it has been shunted aside or has merely
been tolerated as an annoying inconvenience which, at best, dis-
tracts us from Chaucer's more important qualities--his narrative
skill, his realism, his good humor and geniality, his bawdiness,
his eye for detail and ear for speech rhythms, his poetic virtu-
osity. But if such qualities constitute the flesh and bone and
sinew of his art, didacticism is the life blood coursing through
its veins.[2]

On more than one occasion Chaucer emphasizes the qualities
of morality and virtue in connection with a particular tale. The
Parson, for example, who cannot "geeste 'rum,' 'ram,' 'ruf' by
lettre," and who considers "rym...but litel bettre," says his
tale will be one of "moralitee and vertuous mateere." And so it
is. Similarly, the narrator uses almost the identical phrase
with reference to The Tale of Melibee: "It is a moral tale
vertuous...." Even the Pilgrims as a whole, on the one occasion
when they express a preference for a particular kind of tale,
call for "som moral thyng, that we may leere...."

This outburst by the Pilgrims seems to me a significant
comment upon their expectations as an audience. It occurs when
the Pardoner is called upon to tell his tale:

> Nay, lat hym telle us of no ribaudye!
> Telle us some moral thyng, that we may leere
> Som wit, and thanne wol we gladly heere. (VI, 324-326)

Why should the Pilgrims object to ribaldry and request a "moral
thyng" at this particular point, more than half way through the
journey, with the first cycle of tales more than half completed?
They have already heard a number of bawdy tales, none of which
they seem to have found offensive. In fact, Chaucer makes it a
point to emphasize at the conclusion of The Miller's Tale that no
one, save the Reeve, was offended:

> Ne at this tale I saugh no man hym greve
> But it were oonly Osewold the Reve. (I, 3859-3860)

We know that Oswald has his own personal reasons for being
agrieved. Nor does the Pilgrim's response at this juncture seem
to signal a change in their attitude as they approach nearer to
Canterbury. The remainder of the tales do not differ substantially
from the preceding ones; in fact, the tale which immediately

follows the Pardoner's in many of the best manuscripts, including Ellesmere, is another fabliau, The Shipman's Tale; yet, no
one objects to it. Quite the contrary. The Host is most pleased
by the tale--"Wel seyd," he cries out and then goes on to summar-
ize the lesson that is to be derived from it: "A ha! felawes!
beth ware of swich a jape...Draweth no monkes moore unto youre
in." What the Pilgrims are objecting to, then, it seems to me,
is not so much a tale whose content may be bawdy, but rather to
ribaldry for the sake of ribaldry. They are perfectly willing
to listen to a bawdy tale so long as it has some substance, some
lesson about life to teach them. What they do not want to hear
is just a dirty joke.

In the "Retraction" Chaucer is speaking not simply as a
raconteur of romances, not as a teller of amusing, if sometime
bawdy tales, but in propria persona. Nor can we dismiss the
"Retraction," as has too often been done, simply as an anomaly
or as a conventional "deathbed" apology.[3] For the attitude
expressed here is altogether significant of and consistent with
Chaucer's attitude toward his art throughout his literary career
and had, as we shall see, a significant impact on the style of
his poetry.

This attitude manifests itself in part in Chaucer's concern
with what constitutes the proper subject matter for poetry, a
problem which he intricately weaves into the very structure of
The Canterbury Tales. At the conclusion of the "General Prologue" the Host, Harry Bailly, suggests that each of the Pilgrims
tell a number of tales to help pass the time on their journey to
Canterbury. He further suggests that whoever tells the best tale
be honored with a supper at the expense of the rest of the company when they return from their pilgrimage, and he offers to go
along himself to act as judge, an offer readily accepted by the
assembled Pilgrims. Hence, Harry Bailly's conception of what
constitutes a good tale is crucial not only to the Pilgrims, but
to the narrative framework as a whole. Moreover, his views are
equally significant for us. For we discover, as we accompany
the Pilgrims on their journey and listen to their tales and to
Harry Bailly's comments upon these tales, that he is a sensible,
perceptive, and sometimes even an astute critic.

In Harry Bailly's own words the best tales are, "Tales of
best sentence and most solaas...." Nor is it merely coincidental
that this view is shared by the Pilgrim-Narrator.[4]

Before proceeding to relate the Miller's tale, the Narrator
warns his audience that it is a churlish tale, and he suggests
that anyone who might find such a tale offensive can go on and
choose another:

> For he shal fynde ynowe, grete and smale,
> Of storial thyng that toucheth gentillesse,
> And eek moralitee and hoolynesse. (I, 3178-3180)

Clearly, that the Narrator feels he must apologize for the
Miller's tale while recommending tales that touch on "gentil-
lesse," and "moralitee," and "hoolynesse" indicates that he considers the latter, if not superior, at least more suitable. But
if there is "ynowe" of the latter kind of tale, why then does he
see fit to include the former kind? The Narrator himself answers
the question quite explicitly:

> And therefore every gentil wight I preye,
> For Goddes love, demeth nat that I seye
> Of yvel entente, but for I moot reherce
> Hir tales alle, be they bettre or werse,
> Or elles falsen som of my mateere. (I, 3171-3175)

That Chaucer is most sensitive to the problem involved in
relating a tale whose subject matter is questionable is attested
to by the fact that the Narrator is here reiterating a point he
has already made in the "General Prologue," where he is also
addressing his audience:

> But first I pray yow, of youre curteisye,
> That ye n'arette it nat my vileyneye,
> Thogh that I pleynly speke in this mateere,
> To telle yow hir wordes and hir cheere,
> Ne thogh I speke hir wordes properly.
> For this ye knowen al so wel as I,
> Whoso shal telle a tale after a man,
> He moot reherce as ny as evere he kan
> Everich a word, if it be in his charge,
> Al speke he never so rudeliche and large,
> Or ellis he moot telle his tale untrewe,
> Or feyne thyng, or fynde wordes newe.
> He may nat spare, althogh he were his brother;
> He moot as wel seye o word as another. (I, 725-738)

Chaucer's emphasis on relating a tale accurately, regardless of its content, so as not to falsify his subject matter is
indicative of his attitude toward his art. For Chaucer poetry
must be, above all, truthful. It should be an honest representation of life and so ideally should reflect its infinite variety.
Hence, Chaucer finds all aspects of life, the bad as well as the
good, the base as well as the noble, the ugly as well as the
beautiful, to be suitable subject matter for his poetry. Nor is
this necessarily inconsistent with his acceptance of the view
that all that is written is written for our doctrine. For what
is doctrine if not truth? And the primary responsibility of the
poet, if his poetry is indeed written for our doctrine, must be
to reveal the truth as best he can.

The truth for Chaucer is not just some abstract concept.
Rather, it is an active principle, the recognition of which can
be beneficial to us and guide us to a better life. In Chaucer's
own words from the "Balade de Bon Conseyl," "And trouthe thee
shal delivere, it is no drede." Chaucer's conception of himself as a poet writing for our doctrine is essentially that of
the prophet-teacher whose primary function is to reveal the
truth to us so that we may learn how better to conduct our
lives.[5] We have as much to learn from Alison as from Custance,
from the Pardoner as from the Parson, for the poet teaches us
not only what to emulate, but also what to avoid. And in this
respect there may be as much of "doctrine" in The Miller's Tale
or The Merchant's Tale as in The Man of Law's Tale or The Physician's Tale or even the Parson's sermon.

That the first consideration for Chaucer was the lesson is
further attested to by his attitude toward the aesthetic element
in his poetry. For Chaucer, as for the majority of early Eng-
ish lyricists, the emphasis is on "sentence," and, consequently,
he shares with the lyricists a greater concern for conveying
his "sentence" than for displaying craftsmanship.

In fact, scholars have, in the past, occasionally dismissed
what they consider irregularities in Chaucer's poetry, particularly with regard to metrics, for this very reason. In the
Preface to his 1737 edition of The Canterbury Tales, Thomas
Morell writes, "I conclude that an exact Numerosity... was not
Chaucer's main Care; but that he had sometimes a greater Regard
for the Sense than the Metre." Similarly, W. J. Courthope ex-
cuses what he terms "the defective line" in Chaucer's poetry as
follows: "The blot, when it is found in Chaucer, doubtless proceeds from sense being attended to before sound..." (331).[6]

Chaucer would, I think, be the first to agree that he was
most of all concerned with being clearly understood, that he was
more concerned with "sense" than with sound, meter, or any other
aspect of craftsmanship. At least this is the common position
taken by each of Chaucer's personae who is ever made to comment
on the matter. For example, the Dreamer-Narrator of The House
of Fame, as Book III opens, invokes Apollo to guide him, "The
Hous of Fame for to descryve":

       O God of science and of lyght,
       Appollo, thurgh thy grete myght,
       This lytel laste bok thou gye!
       Nat that I wilne, for maistrye,
       Here art poetical be shewed;
       But for the rym ys lyght and lewed,
       Yit make hyt sumwhat agreable,
       Though som vers fayle in a sillable;
       And that I do no diligence
       To shewe craft, but o sentence. (1091-1100)

Apollo is invoked here not as the god of poetry, but rather as
the god of science and light, the god who reveals truth. For
the Dreamer-Narrator expresses no desire that "art poetical" be
shown here; he has no concern for "craft" but only for "sentence."
So too the Dreamer-Narrator of The Legend of Good Women declares,

> For myn entente is, or I fro yow fare,
> The naked text in English to declare.... (Prol. G, 85-86)[7]

Certainly Chaucer lavishes as much "craft" on these two
poems as on any others, more than the passages just quoted would
seem to indicate. Nor am I suggesting that Chaucer was not concerned with craftsmanship. The point is simply that here, as
always, Chaucer's professed attitude is that "sentence" comes
first and that "craft" is only important in so far as it contributes to conveying the "sentence" in a manner "sumwhat agreable."[8]
What is perhaps the clearest and most explicit statement of this
attitude is made by Harry Bailly. In calling upon the Clerk to
tell a tale, Harry Bailly imposes upon him the following injunc-
tion:

> Telle us som murie thyng of aventures
> Youre termes, youre colours, and youre figures,
> Keepe hem in stoor til so be that ye endite
> Heigh style, as whan that men to kynges write.
> Speketh so pleyn at this tyme, we yow preye,
> That we may understonde what ye seye. (IV, 15-20)

The Clerk readily assents. He says that he learned the tale he
is about to tell from Petrarch, the laureate poet "whos rethorike
sweet/ Enlumyned al Ytaille of poetrie...." Furthermore, the
Clerk continues, although Petrarch began the tale with a prologue,
written in the high style, describing the Italian countryside, he
himself will pass over this prologue. The Clerk's reason for
doing so is again most significant:

> And trewely, as to my juggement,
> Me thynketh it a thyng impertinent,
> Save that he wole conveyen his mateere.... (IV, 53-55)

D. W. Robertson has remarked, "When the parson says that he
will mingle no chaff with his wheat, he means that he will, as an
expositor should, explain his text clearly and straightforwardly"
(335). Chaucer was a poet, not an expositor. But Robertson's
comment here can be taken as an emblem for Chaucer's attitude
toward poetry, an attitude we find echoed in the words of the
Parson:

> Why sholde I sowen draf out of my fest
> Whan I may sowen whete, if that me lest? (X, 35-36)

Chaucer revokes certain of his works in the "Retraction" not because of their subject matter, but rather because he fears his intention to teach some moral thing may be misunderstood and so that these works may have the opposite effect upon his audience from the one intended. It is because he fears he may, in fact, have "sowen draf" rather than "whete" that he retracts those works.[9]

To whatever extent Chaucer may have shared with his English predecessors a conception of poetry as a social art, the most essential function of which was to teach some lesson, he was also very much aware that in his own poetic milieu this conception was changing. Patricia Kean goes so far as to imply that it was primarily Chaucer who gave impetus to the change in England, and attributes his doing so in part to a change in the nature of the audience for whom his poetry was intended:

> While Chaucer and some of his contemporaries seem to aim at an audience which would be interested in the actual techniques of poetry and would be capable of reacting as connoisseurs to details of workmanship, the aim of earlier writers seems to have been an appeal to the audience based almost entirely on subject-matter; and the art with which they get this across is largely concealed. (Love Vision and Debate, 4)

No doubt Chaucer's audience differed as much from the one for whom the early lyrics were intended as that audience differed from the audience of the Old English poet. And surely Chaucer knew perfectly well that if he was to succeed with his poetry he had to satisfy the expectations of his audience.

The Canterbury Tales is a pageant of English life as Chaucer knew it. But that there are no "common people" to speak of among the Pilgrims, no representatives from the mass of farmers and laborers who constituted the bulk of English society in Chaucer's day,[10] is significant of the fact that the assembled company does not so much represent a cross-section of English society, but rather that part of society in which Chaucer himself moved or with which he had the closest contact. It would seem, then, that the make-up of this company can be taken to represent more or less accurately the general make-up of the actual audience for whom Chaucer most likely intended his poetry.[11] Consequently, while the audience for whom the early lyrics were intended was, to a significant extent, composed of the "common people," Chaucer's audience was not only considerably more sophisticated, or at least more literate, but also had more leisure time for such things as poetry. For Chaucer's audience poetry was, in large measure, a form of recreation, a pleasurable pastime. But it was an audience capable also of responding to and appreciating

the aesthetic aspects of poetry, not just the subject matter,
and so demanded more than moral preachments or simple stories.
It was an audience which demanded entertainment, an audience
as desirous of being amused, if not more so, as of being in-
structed.

Chaucer's role as a poet must be viewed from this twofold
perspective. If, on the one hand, Chaucer, like the early
lyricists, regarded the role of the poet as primarily that of
prophet-teacher, he also recognized, on the other hand, that in
his own day his audience demanded, to a greater extent than ever
before, that the poet be an entertainer as well. Nor did Chaucer
find this dual role irreconcilable or even inconsistent, for he
fully realized that if one is to teach effectively he must hold
the interest of his audience, in a very real sense, entertain
his audience. Chaucer emphatically and most dramatically makes
just this point in the Host's response to the Monk's tale:

> For sikerly, nere clynkyng of youre belles,
> That on youre bridel hange on every syde,
> By hevene kyng, that for us alle dyde,
> I sholde er this han fallen doun for sleep,
> Althogh the slough had never been so deep;
> Thanne hadde your tale al be toold in veyn.
> For certeinly, as that thise clerkes seyn,
> Whereas a man may have noon audience,
> Noght helpeth it to tellen his sentence. (VII, 2794-2802)

Wolfgang Clemen suggests that one of Chaucer's most important accomplishments was to achieve a new way of uniting entertainment with instruction, pointing out that Chaucer characteristically toned down and made more subtle the didactic element
in his poetry (9). Throughout his analysis of Chaucer's early
works, Clemen emphasizes the fact that Chaucer does not overtly
make moral judgments, that he does not preach at his audience.
Rather, Chaucer creates a poetic experience and allows his audience to draw their own conclusions by witnessing that experience
filtered through the eyes and ears of the narrator-persona. But
in this respect also, it seems to me, Chaucer can be regarded as
continuing in the tradition of the early English lyricists. For,
as we have seen, in the best of the lyrics the poet does not
simply preach at his audience; he too avoids direct moral admonitions. Rather, he teaches by implication, by re-creating an experience from which the audience can learn. To this end he too
employs all the resources of poetry at his command. He too seeks
to find new ways of uniting entertainment with instruction.

Certainly there are fundamental differences between
Chaucer's poetry and these lyrics, but this does not negate the
fact that the didactic impulse is as much at the heart of
Chaucer's poetry as of the lyrics. If Chaucer's poetry is less
overtly didactic, it is, in part, because Chaucer was writing

for a different kind of audience, an audience with different
expectations regarding poetry; in part, because Chaucer was
primarily a narrative poet and so worked in an essentially
different poetic mode; but most of all, because of Chaucer's
own individual genius. Chaucer clearly recognized, as did the
lyricists, the importance of the aesthetic element even in
poetry designed, above all, to teach some lesson. Not only did
Chaucer recognize, as did the lyricists, that art could be made
to serve doctrine, but what is more, for Chaucer, as for the
lyricists, this was the chief end of art.

Chaucer's poetry clearly reflects his concern with aesthetic matters, a concern no doubt stimulated at least in part
by the expectations of a new kind of English audience. But at
the same time, Chaucer himself, by continually pointing to that
which is moral and virtuous in his subject matter, by continually emphasizing that "sentence" and "doctrine" take precedence
over all other considerations in his poetry, still clearly indicates that for him the first consideration remains the didactic
one. Thus, Chaucer acknowledges a kinship to his English predecessors, whose poetry, like his, belongs in this respect to the
same, older utilitarian tradition. He shares with these poets
not only a more or less similar attitude toward poetry, but
also certain similar artistic concerns deriving in some measure
from the old poetic tradition. But what is even more important,
Chaucer's poetry itself, in form and style, like that of these
other English poets, also still shows signs of its Old English
ancestry.

That Chaucer was to some extent familiar with the alliterative tradition is attested to not only by the frequent occurrence of alliteration and alliterative phrases in his poetry,
but also by such well-known passages as the description of the
tournament in The Knight's Tale and the sea-battle in the
"Legend of Cleopatra," both of which closely approximate the
manner and style of traditional alliterative verse, not to mention the Parson's overt reference to "rum, ram, ruf."[12] But
these vestiges of the alliterative tradition are only one aspect
of the continuity from Old English poetry to Chaucer's poetry.

In many respects Beowulf and Chaucer's The Knight's Tale
are, both figuratively and literally speaking, worlds apart.
They are separated not only by the intervening centuries, but
even more so by the enormous changes poetic technique and the
language itself had undergone during those centuries. They
differ in conception and in execution. Yet the gulf between
these two poems is not so vast as may appear on the surface.
For both poems are in certain significant respects shaped by
similar concerns. And the similar manner in which the respective poets develop these concerns, the similar methods and
techniques they both employ, must, it seems to me, be attributed
to something more than coincidence.

I do not mean to suggest that <u>Beowulf</u> was in any sense a direct source for Chaucer's poem any more than "The Wanderer" was a direct source for the "Love Ron." The main point here is that models existed in the older poetry for many of the features characteristic of Middle English poetry; hence, it is not always necessary to go outside of the English tradition itself to account for these features. Nor is it necessary to argue that Middle English poets like Chaucer had direct contact with Old English poetry or could even read or understand it. For despite how different in retrospect Old English seems, and indeed is, from Middle English, we must never lose sight of the fact that the transition from the former to the latter was a very gradual one, occurring over a period of several centuries. In this gradual process of change certain features of the older poetry must have survived, deeply embedded in the language itself and also, not only in whatever poetry may have been preserved from the older period, but in whatever poetry may have been composed during the centuries of transition themselves.

On the most fundamental level, the particular form, as described by Bloomfield, that the utilitarian tradition takes in Old English poetry is almost as clearly reflected in <u>The Knight's Tale</u> as in <u>Beowulf</u>. But in neither poem does the poet himself directly assume the role of teacher. Instead, both poets create a character who serves precisely this function--Hrothgar in <u>Beowulf</u> and Theseus in <u>The Knight's Tale</u>. Nowhere in <u>Beowulf</u> is this function of Hrothgar better illustrated than in his well-known speech to <u>Beowulf</u> after the hero has presented the aged king with the head of Grendel's dam. Similarly, we can observe Theseus performing precisely the same function in the equally well-known "Firste Moevere" speech.[13]

Hrothgar's speech has commonly been referred to as a sermon, and indeed both his speech and Theseus' exhibit the qualities and structure of a sermon. Fittingly enough Theseus' speech occurs at the conclusion of <u>The Knight's Tale</u> and so occupies a position in relationship to the whole poem that structurally parallels the position of the Parson's sermon in relationship to <u>The Canterbury Tales</u> as a whole. The speech comes at a time when the violence and bloodshed that preceded have come to an end, but still cast a dark shadow over Athens. In this speech, occasioned by the unfortunate events, Theseus attempts to derive some meaning from them, some lesson which he can impart to the assembly he is addressing. That Theseus is himself conscious of his role as teacher is attested to by his own words, "But that me list declaren my sentence."

That Hrothgar is equally conscious of such a role is like-wise attested to by his words:

```
                        Ðu þe lær be þon,
        gumcyste ongit!    Ic þis gid be þe
        awræc wintrum frod.    (1722-1724)
```

Hrothgar's speech, however, does not come at the conclusion of
the whole poem; nevertheless, it occupies, in relationship to the
episode which it does conclude, a position structurally parallel
to that of Theseus' speech. Here too the speech comes at a
moment when violence and bloodshed come to an end--Beowulf has
finally put an end to the ravagings of Grendel and his dam. But
the memory of recent horrors, dramatically symbolized by the
monster's head, still hangs heavily over Heorot. Here too the old
king attempts to derive some meaning from the events, some lesson
which he can impart to the hero. But though Hrothgar's speech is
directed to Beowulf, the lesson is intended just as much for the
entire assembly gathered in the hall and for the poem's audience
as well.
        Theseus is presiding over what is in essence a funeral ser-
vice and is delivering a funeral oration. The purpose most
commonly underlying such an oration is consolation, and this is
precisely the point of Theseus' speech:

```
        I rede that we make of sorwes two
        O parfit joye, lastynge evermo.  (I, 3071-3072)
```

Hrothgar, on the other hand, is presiding over a celebration--
the great evil that had so long plagued the Danes has finally
been overcome. It is for Beowulf his greatest triumph, his
moment of glory. And the gathered assembly are revelling in the
hero's triumph as well as in their own good fortune. It is at
just such moments that men may all too easily fall prey to the
most grievous of sins--Pride. Hrothgar's "sermon," in large part
a lecture on conduct and duty, therefore quite fittingly takes
the form of an admonition against this deadliest of the seven
deadly sins:

```
        Bebeorh þe ðone bealonið, Beowulf leofa,
        secg betsta,  ond þe þæt selre geceos,
        ece rædas; oferhyda ne gym,
        mære cempa!  (1758-1761)
```

        The most important function of a sermon is to teach a lesson.
The lesson that Hrothgar's sermon teaches is expressed in the
lines just cited--Beware of this great evil...choose that which
is better, eternal rewards; be not intent upon pride. Theseus'
"sermon" is intended to teach a somewhat different lesson. But
here too the lesson is explicitly stated:

```
        Thanne is it wysdom, as it thynketh me,
        To maken vertu of necessitee,
        And take it weel that we may nat eschue,
        And namely that to us alle is due.  (I, 3041-3044)
```

Because the primary function of a sermon is to teach a lesson, the sermon is organized in a manner designed to make its point most effectively, to drive home the lesson clearly and forcefully. In general a sermon begins with a statement of the Text that is to be its subject--some biblical quotation, some proverbial expression, some maxim, epigram, or aphorism; in short, some familiar or easily remembered capsular form of the lesson. Then this text is interpreted and explained, most commonly through the use of examples. The sermon is concluded with a direct statement of the lesson and its application to the immediate situation. Of course there may be variations within any given sermon--the whole pattern, or parts of it, may be repeated, and, in some cases, even rearranged.[14] But the pattern here described is essentially the model for the structure of most formal medieval sermons. In every case, however, these elements--text, example, and application--are the vital constituent parts.

The structure of both Hrothgar's and Theseus' speeches clearly reflects such a pattern, though there are, to be sure, certain variations. Neither speech, for example, begins with the direct quotation of a specific text. Yet it would be a quite simple matter to provide such a text for each--perhaps, Proverbs, XVI, 18, "Pride goeth before destruction, and an haughty spirit before a fall," for the former; and Ecclesiastes, III, 1, "To every thing there is a season, and a time to every purpose under the heavens," for the latter.

Be this as it may, the text of a sermon serves essentially as an introduction. It is a statement of the subject to be dealt with, one usually of some concern at the particular moment, and calls forth the examples and application which follow. Both Hrothgar and Theseus begin with a somewhat abstract and rather general observation that introduces the subject of their respective discourses and has significant implications for the situation at hand. Hence, these opening lines serve in each case the same function as a text.

Hrothgar wishes to praise Beowulf for the great deeds the hero has performed. But the old king is well aware of the difference between praise that is one's just and proper due and flattery that inflames pride. He is further aware that the source from whom such praise comes and the terms in which it is expressed can to a great extent influence the sense in which it is received and the manner in which it is borne, and so Hrothgar prefaces the accolades he is about to bestow with a carefully phrased comment upon those from whom such praise may rightly come. This, then, is the very first concern of his speech and the "text" of his sermon:

> Þæt, la, mæg secgan se þe soð ond riht
> fremeð on folce, feor eal gemon,
> eald eþelweard, þæt ðes eorl wære
> geboren betera! (1700-1703)

Obviously, Hrothgar is here referring to himself, thereby placing in proper perspective the praise for Beowulf that follows.
It is as though Hrothgar is saying to Beowulf, "I who am old
and wise may rightly honor you and be secure in the knowledge
that you will not misconstrue my intentions, but will bear
these honors in the proper and fitting manner."

In order to reinforce the message and, at the same time, to
make certain that there will be no misunderstanding whatsoever,
Hrothgar relates the story of Heremod--a blatant example of the
manifestation of misdirected pride. Hrothgar concludes this
example with a direct statement of its application:

Đu þe lær be þon,
gumcyste ongit! (1722-1723)

Hrothgar next launches into a lengthy discourse on how
pride can creep into the soul of a man who is not constantly
on guard, especially when such a man is at the height of his
powers and all things seem to be going particularly well for
him:

                    ac him eal worold
weneð on willan; he þæt wyrse ne con--,
oð þæt him on innan oferhygda dæl
weaxeð ond wridað; þonne se weard swefeð,
sawele hyrde; bið se slæp to fæst,
bisgum gebunden.... (1738-1743)

The implied allusion to Beowulf's own situation is perfectly
clear, yet here again Hrothgar makes the direct application:

    Bebeorh þe ðone bealonið, Beowulf leofa,
secg betsta, ond þe þæt selre geceos,
ece rædas; oferhyda ne gym,
mære cempa! (1758-1761)

Pride is the result of too great a concern for worldly
joys. However, as Hrothgar well knows, all the material things
of this world, as well as man himself, share the same inevitable
end, and so Hrothgar, in the next portion of his speech goes on
to emphasize the transitory nature of such joys.

Hrothgar concludes his speech with a final example, one
that is particularly striking and effective, for he himself is
its subject. Hrothgar, like Beowulf, has known such moments of
glory and has been accorded similar honors:

    Swa ic Hring-Dena hund missera
weold under wolcnum ond hig wigge beleac
manigum mægþa geond þysne middangeard,
æscum ond ecgum, þæt ic me ænigne
under swegles begong gesacan ne tealde. (1769-1773)

But what is of the utmost importance is the subtle hint
implied in the last clause. For it suggests that Hrothgar, in
circumstances that parallel those now surrounding Beowulf, was
himself guilty of pride. The ensuing consequences were, of
course, inevitable:

> Hwæt me þæs on eþel   edwenden cwom,
> gyrn æfter gomene,   seoþðan Grendel wearð,
> ealdgewinna   ingenga min;
> ic þære socne   singales wæg
> modceare micle. (1774-1778)

It is as though the ravages of Grendel and his dam were intended
to punish Hrothgar for his pride and to teach him the lesson he
now passes on to Beowulf.

The technique Hrothgar employs here is quite common to
sermons. In such sermons the speaker confesses to some wrong-
doing of which he has himself been guilty and uses his own
experiences as an example of the consequences of such actions.
But equally important, the speaker has, as a result of some
event or other, seen the error of his ways. Having learned
from his own experience, he is now in a position to instruct
his audience.

This is precisely the situation in Hrothgar's case and what
makes the final example doubly effective. Hrothgar's own history
is not intended simply as another example of the dangers of
pride--the account of Heremod has already illustrated this point
more than adequately. Rather, Hrothgar's history is meant to be
contrasted with that of Heremod. For where Hrothgar has learned
from his experience, Heremod did not. Moreover, having learned
from these experiences, Hrothgar has come himself to embody the
standard of conduct he teaches. He teaches this lesson then not
only through words, but by his very presence. He is himself not
only an example of what to avoid, but even more, he is the best
example of what to imitate. He is himself a living model of the
lesson taught in his sermon.[15]

It is now that we can perhaps better understand the full
significance of the first few lines of Hrothgar's speech.
Hrothgar remembers all that is past, and he has learned much from
this past. He has experienced similar good fortune to that which
now attends Beowulf, but he has also experienced the reverse,
which Beowulf has not. Hence, he knows what Beowulf cannot yet
know. He knows the fickleness of glory; he knows the transitory
nature of worldly joys; he knows the danger of pride. It is
precisely because he has learned these things from his own experience that a person such as Hrothgar can honor a person such
as Beowulf and, at the same time, instruct him in how to properly
bear his glory. It is in these first few lines that Hrothgar lays
the foundation for the structure of the whole sermon. The example

of Heremod and the discourse on the transitory nature of earthly
joys are the pillars that support the structure. But these are
only the skeleton, like the bones of the body or the frame of a
building. What finally and perfectly completes this structure,
what holds it together, what gives it real substance, is the
concluding example of Hrothgar himself. And the labor expended
on it is justified by the result, by the effectiveness with
which the poet has achieved his purpose. In the concluding passage Hrothgar seems to say, "Consider not only my words, but
also me. When you recall my words to you, recall also me. For
I am living proof of the lesson I have taught you." Thus, the
audience, like Beowulf and his companions and the Danish war-
riors assembled in Heorot, is left not simply with the lesson
itself, but with a vivid and concrete manifestation of the
application of that lesson--the example of Hrothgar himself who
embodies the very lesson he teaches. We may forget the exact
words of Hrothgar's speech, but we cannot erase the image of
the aged king that has been implanted in our minds. It is this
image of Hrothgar that, more than his words alone could ever do,
drives home the lesson.

The major concern of Theseus' speech, as we have noted, is
to derive some consolation from Arcite's apparently random and
meaningless death. To this end, Theseus places Arcite's death
within the larger context of the orderly and meaningful progression of all things in the universe:

> The Firste Moevere of the cause above,
> Whan he first made the faire cheyne of love,
> Greet was th'effect, and heigh was his entente.
>   (I, 2987-2989)

This is essentially the text of his sermon. For the remainder
of the speech is a demonstration that all things, including
Arcite's death, serve the lofty purpose, the "heigh entente,"
of the First Mover, i.e. Jupiter, God, the Creator.

All things, save the Creator himself, are mutable, and
Theseus goes on to explain that this is itself according to the
divine will:

> That same Prince and that Moevere,...
> Hath stablished in this wrecched world adoun
> Certeyne dayes and duracioun
> To al that is engendred in this place,
> Over the whiche day they may nat pace....(I, 2994-2998)

In his wisdom the Creator has allowed for a kind of permanence
which works through and transcends this mutability itself and
so gives it meaning within the divine scheme:

> And therfore, of his wise purveiaunce,
> He hath so wel biset his ordinaunce,
> That speces of thynges and progressiouns
> Shullen enduren by successiouns,
> And nat eterne.... (I, 3011-3015)

Next follow a series of examples to illustrate the point--
the oak that lives so long, yet at the last is wasted; the hard
stone that turns to pebbles and dust; the river that dries up;
the great towns that disappear; and, finally, men and women
themselves, of every degree and station, who meet with the same
common end. This brings Theseus to the lesson that his sermon
is intended to teach:

> Thanne is it wysdom, as it thynketh me,
> To maken vertu of necessitee,
> And take it weel that we may nat eschue,
> And namely that to us alle is due. (I, 3041-3044)

What follows is the application of the lesson to the situation
at hand:

> And certeinly a man hath moost honour
> To dyen in his excellence and flour,
> Whan he is siker of his goode name;
> Thanne hath he doon his freend, ne hym, no shame,
> And gladder oghte his freend been of his deeth,
> Whan with honour up yolden is his breeth,
> Than whan his name apalled is for age,
> For al forgeten is his vassellage.
> Thanne is it best, as for a worthy fame,
> To dyen whan that he is best of name. (I, 3047-3056)

Herein, then, lies the meaning and the consolation that can
be derived from Arcite's death. To be sure, Arcite has been
denied the kind of permanence that Theseus alludes to earlier in
his speech, the kind of permanence that results from the process
of change itself, the continual cycle of death and birth, the
kind of permanence symbolized by the marriage of Palamon and
Emily. For Arcite has died wifeless and childless; he has left
no offspring through whom some part of his being can continue to
exist. Yet there is another kind of permanence, one which manifests itself in the memories of men and endures so long as the
human race itself endures. It is the permanence achieved not
only by Socrates and Homer, by Alexander the Great and Julius
Caesar, but also by Hercules and by Lancelot, by Achilles and
Aeneas. Arcite has taken his place next to these and many, many
more like them. This, then, is the immortality Arcite has
achieved. In this lies the meaning of his life and, even more
importantly, the real meaning of his death and the consolation
we are to derive from it.

The first part of Theseus' speech does not occur in
Boccaccio's Teseida, Chaucer's immediate source for The Knight's
Tale, though Teseo does iterate the notion that our days on this
earth are determined by the Creator.[16] Instead, it depends to a
great extent upon Boethius.[17] But the vast differences in purpose, form, and style between the Chaucerian and Boethian passages are self-evident and need no elaboration here.[18]

The second part of the speech is a fairly close translation
of Teseo's speech. But though the two speeches are similar in
content, they differ significantly in emphasis, structure, and
style. For not only do these speeches serve essentially different purposes in the respective works, they also reflect in a
general way the different traditions to which these works respectively belong.

We have already seen that Theseus' speech resembles, in
style and structure, a sermon, and, consequently, its primary
function is to teach a lesson, this lesson taking the form of
the consolation to be derived from Arcite's death. The emphasis
of the speech is on the meaning of Arcite's death within the context of the orderly and meaningful progression of all things
according to the divine will. Thus, the speech occurs at the
very end of the whole work, where it brings to a fitting conclusion the events that have transpired.

Teseo's speech, on the other hand, occurs at the beginning
of Book XII and serves to introduce a series of discourses on
one of Boccaccio's major concerns in the work as a whole--the
justification of the marriage between Palamon and Emily.

In both works this marriage is suggested by the dying
Arcite, but only in Boccaccio's does the propriety of the
marriage become an issue. When Theseus proposes the marriage
at the conclusion of his sermon, he makes no reference to Arcite,
nor any attempt to justify the proposed union:

> I rede that we make of sorwes two
> O parfit joye, lastynge evermo.
> And looketh now, wher moost sorwe is herinne,
> Ther wol we first amenden and bigynne. (I, 3071-3074)

In Chaucer's version the marriage simply follows in the natural
and orderly progression of things, the theme developed in the
first part of Theseus' speech; the marriage itself, together
with Palamon's and Emily's future happiness, is only very
briefly alluded to as the poem comes to a close. It is almost
as though the marriage of Palamon and Emily and their future
happiness serve as a final example to support the lesson.

Teseo, on the other hand, introduces the question of the
marriage not only by a direct reference to Arcite's dying wish,
but also with a reference to Foroneo, the law-giver, that
supports the validity of such a request:

> E oltre a ciò, quel ch'esso ultimamente
> pregò, si pensi mettere ad effetto;
> però che Foroneo, che primamente
> ne donò leggi, disse che il detto
> estremo di ciascun solennememte
> doveva con ragione esser perfetto;
> e el pregò ch'Emilia fosse data
> a Palemon, che l'avea tanto amata. (XII, 18)

(And furthermore, we ought to consider doing what he asked in
his last extremity, for Foroneo, who first gave us laws, said
that the last wish of each person ought to be solemnly and
reasonably carried out. And he asked that Emily be given to
Palamon, who loved her so dearly.)

This reference to Foroneo seems to reinforce the notion
that what we really have to do with here is a questione d'amore
posed before a court of love. Consequently, what follows is
essentially a debate centering on the question of the propriety
of a marriage between Palamon and Emily. When Teseo has fin-
ished, Palamon speaks, accepting the proposed marriage and
justifying it in terms of his love for and loyalty to Arcite.
Then Emily, still hesitant and wavering, expresses some doubts,
but her doubts are soon allayed by Teseo, and she is finally
persuaded. The poem culminates in the lengthy and elaborate
description of the magnificent wedding, which overshadows, if
it does not completely obscure, Arcite's recent death. In this
way Boccaccio achieves his purpose; the marriage is justified
not only in the eyes of men, but also in the eyes of the gods.
For surely the splendor of the spectacle we witness is the final
and most powerful testimony in favor of the union.
This difference in purpose helps explain the difference in
emphasis. Chaucer is very much concerned with the meaning of
Arcite's death in the larger scheme of things. Boccaccio is
more concerned with life, with the marriage of Palamon and Emily.
But in order to get to this marriage, he must first overcome the
grief that has been occasioned by Arcite's death. This is the
primary function of Teseo's speech. Unlike Chaucer, then,
Boccaccio does not attempt to derive any consolation from
Arcite's death; rather, he attempts to demonstrate that it was,
in fact, not only a glorious death but even a desirable one, one
which need, therefore, occasion no tears. Thus, Teseo's speech
is perfectly structured as a logical argument demonstrating this
point.
Teseo begins with the premise that death is the natural
consequence of living:

> Così come alcun che mai non visse
> non mori mai, così si pò vedere
> ch'alcun non visse mai che non morisse....
>   (XII, 6, 1-3)

(Just as anyone who has never lived cannot have died, so it can
be seen that anyone who ever lived did not escape death.)

He then proceeds to support this premise with examples from
nature: the long lived oak that eventually dies; the hard stones
that are worn away; the old rivers that dry up (XII, 7). The
conclusion that follows is inevitable--men are subject to the
same end (XII, 8).
     This leads to the next step in his argument. Since death
eventually comes to all, it is better to die in one's prime than
in the miseries of old age:

> E certo io credo ch'allora migliore
> la morte sia quando di viver giova....(XII, 9, 1-2)

(And indeed I believe that death is best while one enjoys living.)

He supports this conclusion by referring to the fame that attends
one who is at the height of his glory and perpetuates his memory
long after his death: "fama li serba suo debito onore." Therefore, he maintains, there is no cause for excessive grief when
one dies under such circumstances, for such grief can lead only
to madness, but can never bring the person back (XII, 13).
     Teseo now comes to the crucial point to which his argument
has been leading--the death of Arcite. Since Arcite was as gal-
lant a figure as ever lived in Greece and has been magnificently
honored at his funeral, since Arcite's fame is thus assured,
there is no further purpose to continue in mourning:

> E certo s' el fu giammai lagrimato
> in Grecia nessun uom valoroso,
> si è debitamente Arcita stato
> da molti re e popol copioso;
> e con onor magnifico onorato
> è stato ancora al suo rogo pomposo,
> e ben solvuto gli è ogni dovere
> che morto corpo dee potere avere.
>
> E è ancor, sí come noi veggiamo,
> durato il pianto più giorni in Attene;
> e ciascheduno ancora abito gramo
> portato n'ha quale a ciò si convene,
> e noi massimamente che qui siamo,
> da cui agli altri prender s'apartiene
> essemplo in ciascuno atto e seguitare
> massimamente nel bene operare.

> Dunque da poi parimente ci more
> ciò che ci masce, e sia pur che si voglia,
> e è fatto per noi il debito onore
> a colui per lo quale ora avem doglia,
> estimo con ragion che sia il migliore
> se questo abito oscur da noi si spoglia,
> e lascisi il doler, ch'è feminile
> atto più tosto che non è virile. (XII, 14-16)[19]

From here Teseo turns to the proposed marriage between Palamon and Emily.

In translating Teseo's speech, Chaucer adheres fairly closely to Boccaccio's version, but there is a distinct difference in purpose and form. Boccaccio is primarily concerned with presenting a subtle, intricate but logical argument, and he constructs the speech in a manner closely approximating the analytical mode that is so much a feature of the continental tradition, as exemplified by the French lyrics we have previously examined. Chaucer, on the other hand, like the Beowulf poet, is primarily concerned with teaching a moral and virtuous lesson, and so, like the Beowulf poet, he casts the speech in a form more conducive to achieving this end, that of a sermon, and adopts a manner more nearly approximating the expository mode characteristic of the Middle English lyrics.

As a result, there is also a distinct difference in tone between the two speeches. Teseo's speech has emphasized the honor, glory and fame achieved by Arcite, and, while dignified throughout, his tone is one of hopeful optimism as he urges the people to leave off weeping and wailing and to be cheerful: "Però da mo' in avanti ciascum festeggi, e 'l piangere e l' omei si lasci star..." (XII, 17, 5-7). Teseo concludes his speech on a celebratory note, ordering the cessation of mourning and the preparation for the festive occasion to follow--the marriage of Emily to Palamon:

> Però diposte queste nere veste
> e il pianto lasciato e il dolore,
> cominceren le liete e chiare feste;
> e prima che si parta alcun signore,
> de' due già detti nozze manifeste
> celebrerem con debito splendore.
> (XII, 19, 1-6)

(When these dark garments have been removed and the weeping and grief ceased, let us begin the joyful and brilliant festivities. And before any of these lords depart, let us celebrate with the splendor due the already promised wedding of these two.)

This is a far cry from the tone of Theseus' "To maken vertu of necessitee." Theseus does allude to the marriage of Emily to

Palamon, but on only one occasion does he use a word connoting
joy: "But after wo I rede us to be merye...." Theseus concludes his speech with a final word of advice:

> I rede that we make of sorwes two
> O parfit joye, lastynge everemo.

Here, he strikes an elegiac note reminiscent of the tone of
Hrothgar's speech, which is itself delivered in the midst of a
celebration:

> Bebeorh þe ðone bealonið Beowulf leofa,
> secg betsta, and þe þæt selre geceos,
> ece rædas....   (1758-1760)

The difference in purpose, form and tone between Chaucer's
version of this speech and Boccaccio's suggests Chaucer's close
ties with the tradition of Old English poetry. So too does the
general difference in style between the two passages. For many
of the stylistic features of the Chaucerian passage, especially
those which tend most to distinguish it from Boccaccio's, closely
resemble stylistic features characteristic of the older native
tradition, particularly as manifested in and filtered through
the Middle English lyrics.

A striking example is Chaucer's rendering of Boccaccio's
passage detailing the various ways in which men may meet their
end. The texts of both follow:

> Del modo ancora dico il simigliante,
> ché, come che alcuno anneghi in mare,
> alcun si muoia in sul suo letto stante,
> alcun per lo suo sangue riversare
> nelle battaglie, o in qual vuoi di quante
> maniere om pò morir.... (XII, 10, 1-6)

> This is to seyn, in youthe or elles age
> He moot be deed, the kyng as shall a page;
> Som in his bed, som in the depe see,
> Som in the large feeld, as men may see....
>   (I, 3030-3033)

Chaucer has here translated Boccaccio very closely, almost literally. Nevertheless, there is a distinct difference in the flavor
of the two passages, a difference which becomes even more apparent if we compare these passages with a quite similar one from
Beowulf. Here, too, the subject is the inevitable end confront-
ing all men:

> Nu is þines mægnes blæd
> ane hwile; eft sona bið,
> þæt þec adl oððe ecg eafoþes getwæfeð,
> oððe fyres feng, oððe flodes wylm,
> oððe gripe meces, oððe gares fliht,
> oððe atol yldo; oððe eagena bearhtm
> forsiteð ond forsworceð; semninga bið,
> þæt ðec, dryhtguma, deað oferswyðeð. (1761-1768)

Klaeber, in his note on this passage, points out, "The polysyndetic series suggests the rhetoric of a preacher (such as
Wulfstan)." The polysyndetic series, reinforced by the alliteration and the use of anaphora and strong mid-line pauses, results in a rhythmical pulsebeat that plays as a leitmotif for
the elegiac tone both of the Beowulf passage and Chaucer's, an
effect totally unlike the sonorous music produced by Boccaccio.
It is an effect perfectly suited to Hrothgar's and Theseus'
speeches, for, as we have seen, both are organized as sermons,
and we have here a splendid example of content, form and style
implying one another.

In structure, style and rhythm the Chaucerian passage more
nearly resembles the Old English passage than it does the more
grammatically complex and stylistically elaborate Boccaccian
passage. In fact, throughout his version of this speech we find
Chaucer striving for greater simplicity, directness, and clarity,
the characteristic features of an expository mcde. For example,
in stanza 12 Teseo comments upon the death of a valorous man,
referring of course to Arcite, who has died at the height of
his glory, and upon the fame that will attend such a man:

> cioè d'alcun la morte il cui valore
> fu tanto e tal, che grazioso frutto
> di fama s'ha lasciato dietro al fiore.... (2-4)

(So it is that the death of one whose valor is very great is the
delectable fruit of fame left behind after the flower has
blossomed.)

Chaucer renders these lines more simply:

> And certeinly a man hath moost honour
> To dyen in his excellence and flour.... (I, 3047-3048)

Chaucer has simplified the image and the syntax. Though he does
not achieve the same quite lovely effect Boccaccio achieves by
developing the metaphor more fully, by inverting the word order
and placing the key word "fiore" in the same emphatic position
as "frutto" at the end of the line, Chaucer's translation is
more direct and clear.

The same tendency can be observed in Chaucer's rendering of Boccaccio's passage on the mutability of all things. In stanza 7 Teseo lists examples of impermanence in nature:

> La quercie, c'han si lungo nutrimento
> e tanta vita quanta noi vedemo,
> hanno pure alcun tempo finimento;
> le dure pietre ancor, che noi calchemo,
> per accidenti varii mancamento
> ancora avere, aperto le sapemo;
> e i fiumi perenni esser seccati
> veggiamo e altri nuovi esserne nati. (XII, 7)

(The oaks, which have a capacity for living so long and which we see have so long a life, also in due time come to their end. The hard stones that we step on we know with certainty will yet be worn away by various causes. And we see old rivers becoming dried up and other new ones born.)

And in stanza 8 he makes the same point with reference to the condition of man:

> Degli uomini non cal di dir, ch'assai
> è manifesto a quel che la natura
> li tira e ha tirati sempre mai
> de' due termini a l'uno: o ad oscura
> vecchiezza piena d'infiniti quai,
> e questa poi da morte più sicura
> è terminata; overo a morte essendo
> giovani ancora e più lieti vivendo. (XII, 8)

(Concerning men there is hardly need to speak, for it is self-evident that nature draws them and has always drawn them to one of two ends--either to a gloomy old age full of infinite troubles, ultimately to be ended only by certain death; or else to death that comes when one is still young and very glad to be alive.)

Chaucer's translation of these lines is again, on the whole, more simple, more direct, and more clear. In using the example of the oak, Chaucer avoids the comparison Boccaccio makes to man's longevity. Instead, he organizes the example chronologically:

> Loo the ook, that hath so long a norisshynge
> From tyme that it first bigynneth to sprynge,
> And hath so long a lif, as we may see,
> Yet at the laste wasted is the tree. (I, 3017-3021)

Similarly, in the example of the hard stones Chaucer omits the various accidents which effect their shape and simply makes the point that is the purpose of the whole passage--they too waste away:

> Considereth eek how that the harde stoon
> Under oure feet, on which we trede and goon,
> Yet wasteth it as it lyth by the weye. (I, 3021-3023)

Again where Boccaccio refers to rivers which have long since dried and to new rivers born from them, Chaucer simply writes, "The brode ryver somtyme wexeth dreye..." (I, 3024).

After the example of the rivers Boccaccio proceeds to the passage on man. But Chaucer makes an interesting and effective addition:

> The grete tounes se we wane and wende.
> Thanne may ye se that al this thyng hath ende.
>   (I, 3025-3026)

Chaucer's addition of the example of great towns is a fine touch. For towns are the product of man, not nature, and so this last example serves to emphasize the impermanence of man's works as well and provides an effective transition from impermanence in nature to the impermanence of man, who is himself a part of that nature. Nevertheless, here too Chaucer simplifies the discussion. Boccaccio emphasizes the irony of man's condition. There are but two alternatives for man: either to live to an obscure old age, full of infinite troubles finally ended by death, or to die while still young and living happily. Chaucer, on the other hand, is conerned only with making the same point that controls his entire passage--all things, including man, must come to an end:

> Of man and womman seen we wel also
> That nedes, in oon of thise termes two,
> This is to seyn, in youthe or elles age,
> He moot be deed, the kyng as shal a page....
>   (I, 3027-3030)

Another significant feature of Chaucer's translation of this particular passage is his use of the verb "see" five times within the space of fifteen lines (3016-3030). The equivalent verb forms "vedemo" or "veggiamo" occur only twice in the corresponding sixteen lines (stanzas 7-8) of Teseo's speech, and only four times altogether in the whole speech, which consists of fourteen eight-line stanzas totalling one hundred and twelve lines. Chaucer seems determined to make these examples visually concrete for his audience. He wants them to "see" the oak, the stones, the river, the towns; he wants them to "see," both literally and metaphorically, this incontrovertible truth not only as regards the world of nature, but as regards their own lives.

Chaucer simplifies, makes more direct and concrete his source in the interest of greater clarity. To this end, as well as to emphasize and reinforce his meaning, he also employs much verbal and structural repetition, in many cases also reminiscent of the techniques of Old English poetry. Not only do we find alliterative phrases, such as "wane and wende," but also the frequent use of non-alliterative doublets, such as "trede and goon," "excellence and flour," and "duetee and honour." More significantly, we find lines where the syntactic repetition reinforces the semantic repetition and where we can observe the half-line patterning and hear echoes of the Old English four-stress measure:

> Why grucchen we, why have we hevynesse...
> (I, 3058)

> Greet was th'effect, and heigh was his entente.
> (I, 2989)

> 'That same Prince and that Moevere,' quod he...
> (I, 2994)

> What maketh this but Juppiter, the kyng,
> That is prince and cause of alle thyng...
> (I, 3035-3036)

The structure of such lines resembles the Old English technique of parallel variation and is yet another indication of the link between Chaucer's poetry and the old poetic tradition.

Chaucer's decision to recast the speech he found in his source, to put it into the form of a sermon, is characteristic of his tendency to transform his foreign models so as to make them more compatible with his own native tradition, a tradition that as early as Beowulf and as late as The Knight's Tale demanded something of morality and virtue in its poetry. But while the use of sermon structure is itself by no means unique to English poetry, it is, as a literary device, more common to the older medieval utilitarian tradition than to the new Renaissance tradition developing on the continent during the twelfth century. Nor is Chaucer's use of sermon material here an isolated case. Not only does he end The Canterbury Tales with the formal sermon delivered by the Parson, he uses sermon structure for the Pardoner's Prologue and Tale, the Wife of Bath's Prologue[20] and the Nun's Priest's Tale;[21] as Siegfried

Wenzel has shown, he makes additional use of preaching material for story-plots, images and technical terms (140-160). Chaucer's extensive use of sermon material throughout The Canterbury Tales is evidence both of the continued survival and influence of the older utilitarian tradition in England to Chaucer's day and of Chaucer's commitment to that tradition. For while Chaucer does draw on continental literature for subject matter and poetic forms, and derives much of his intellectual and philosophical quality from it, his style is at its core English, a style characterized by its "medievalism."

To a certain extent, then, we can account for the difference in form between Boccaccio's version of this speech and Chaucer's version in much the same terms that C.S. Lewis accounts for the difference between Chaucer's Troilus and Criseyde and its source, Boccaccio's Filostrato. In both cases, Chaucer, in adapting Boccaccio's poems to his own purposes, "medievalizes" them. Thus, the differences in purpose and execution, in form, tone and style between Theseus' speech in The Knight's Tale and Teseo's speech in the Teseida reflect the different traditions to which these two poems respectively belong. Boccaccio's Teseida, like the Filostrato, is a product of the Italian Renaissance; Chaucer's Knight's Tale belongs essentially to the native English poetic tradition, a tradition that remained "medieval" long after the Renaissance had dawned on continental Europe.

Professor Bennett makes a most significant point regarding Chaucer and Gower. He writes, "The ability to use English rhythms and English diction with the assurance demonstrated continually by Chaucer and Gower comes to them in part by virtue of their position in the fourteenth century. They flourished at a moment when much hard pioneer work had been done by innumerable known and unknown writers..."(11).[22] Much of this hard pioneer work was performed by the poets who composed the Middle English lyrics. Not only did the early lyric poets introduce new elements from continental traditions, they also incorporated many of the techniques developed by their English ancestors, modifying these new elements and adapting the old techniques, where necessary, to meet the exigencies of their own poetry. It was in finding ways of accommodating both the old and the new in their poetry that the early lyric poets made what was their most important contribution to the development of Middle English poetry and prepared the way for Chaucer.

Wolfgang Clemen, in his excellent study of Chaucer's early poetry, remarks, "If Chaucer was to succeed with his poetry... he had to make the style and form of French poetry come alive within the English idiom"(23). Though Clemen's point is certainly well taken, this is only one aspect of the larger problem Chaucer faced and ultimately solved. In a broader sense, it seems to me that the most significant reason Chaucer succeeds

so admirably with his poetry is that, despite his very close
affiliations with continental literatures, he never loses touch
with the native English poetic tradition. The gulf between
Beowulf and The Canterbury Tales is indeed wide and deep. Instrumental in bridging the gulf by helping keep the native
poetic tradition alive and vital were the early Middle English
lyrics.

1

"The Middle Ages in the Lineage of English Poetry," in Medieval Contributions to Modern Civilization ed. F.J.C. Hearnshaw, 2nd ed. (New York: Barnes and Noble, 1949), 181. The italics are mine.

2

The past two decades have witnessed a revival of interest in Chaucer's didacticism. See, for example, Rodney Delasanta, "Penance and Poetry in the Canterbury Tales, PMLA 93 (1978): 240-247; Edmund Reiss, who refers to didacticism as a "given" about which the court poet did not have to concern himself, in "Chaucer and His Audience," Chaucer Review 14 (1980): 390-402; Alan Gaylord, who considers the whole of Fragment VII as concerned with "the art of story telling" and concludes that at least in Harry Bailly's view, "sentence" and "solass" need not be combined in every single tale, but each tale must successfully provide one or the other, in "Sentence and Solass in Fragment VII of the Canterbury Tales: Harry Bailly as Horseback Editor," PMLA 82 (1967): 226-235. Alfred David addresses much the same issue and reaches much the same conclusion as Gaylord in "The Man of Law vs. Chaucer: A Case in Poetics," PMLA 82 (1967): 217-225. However, in his subsequent book, The Strumpet Muse: Art and Morals in Chaucer's Poetry (Bloomington: Indiana Univ. Press, 1976), David gives considerably greater weight to moral orthodoxy: "Both poet and audience...were responsive to an even more pervasive pressure, the requirement that all poetry to earn its right to exist must be moral, that the poet has an obligation to educate and uplift his audience, and that the audience, for its part, must look for instruction and edification and not only for entertainment" (5).

3

W. Meredith Thompson, based on his study of Chaucer's use of the Bible, concludes, "It was no accident that he produced his Melibeus and Parson's tale, the lost Wretched Engendering, and the Boethius. They were evidently written at such different times in his career that he must always have been a man of serious concern, with which his lighter jeux d'esprit are never really in conflict. To hold that the Parson's tale, as it comes last in the manuscripts (immediately preceded, however, by the Manciple's tale) and Retraction represent final 'repentance' on Chaucer's part is to take skeptical view of his lifelong moral integrity or accuse him, perhaps justly, of senility." "Chaucer's Translation of the Bible," in English and Medieval Studies Presented to J.R.R. Tolkien, ed. Norman Davis and C.L. Wrenn (London, 1962), 198.

4

Another of Chaucer's creations who is an astute critic of
the art of composition is Pandarus, who observes,

> How so it be that som men hem delite
> With subtyl art hire tales for to endite,
> Yet for al that, in hire entencioun,
> Hire tale is al for som conclusion.
> And sithen th'ende is every tales strengthe....
> (II, 256-260)

5

Alfred David makes much the same point in his discussion of
the role of the medieval poet: "It is his business...to give
vision and to increase the number of the blessed. This is at
least one way of looking at the role of the medieval poet, a
role from which I feel Chaucer often strayed but to which he
always returned" (Strumpet Muse, 233).

6

Margaret Honour makes the same observation about the metrical practices of the Middle English lyricists: "To use a
specific analogy, the taste of these English writers is split:
it seems in part to be like St. Bernard's, who 'neglected meter
that I might not be deficient in sense'...." "The Metrical
Derivations of the Medieval English Lyric," Diss. Yale Univ.
1949, 255.

7

The narrator's comment at the conclusion of Troilus and
Criseyde is also significant:

> And red wherso thow be or elles songe,
> That thow be understonde, God I biseche!

Chaucer's emphasis here on being understood is a further indication of his concern with conveying his meaning clearly. It is
precisely for this reason that he prays no one will "myswrite"
nor "mysmetre" the poem.

8

Commenting on Chaucer's translations of French works, Erwin
Geissman, who emphasizes the literalness of Chaucer's translations, maintains that what changes Chaucer does make can best
be explained as efforts toward greater clarity or concreteness.
Thus, Geissman accounts for Chaucer's additions in translating
Melibee as follows: "Explanations are provided for things
which need no explaining, and can be justified only in terms of
the evident determination to be clearly understood even in the
smallest detail." "The Style and Technique of Chaucer's Trans-
lations from French," Diss. Yale Univ. 1952, 82. Geissman sees
the same principle at work in Chaucer's other translations from
French, poetry as well as prose.

9

Alfred David states the matter as follows: "In retracting his works Chaucer does not deny their right to exist, but he wants to warn us about the limitations of poetry lest they be misused..." (Strumpet Muse, 239).

10

It is quite possible that Chaucer may have intended to represent this element of society by the Plowman. But this is a moot point. For besides the brief description of the Plowman in the "General Prologue," he plays no subsequent role whatsoever in any of the extant manuscripts of the Canterbury Tales.

11

Paul Strohm suggests that the bulk of Chaucer's audience was made up of what he terms "the lesser gentry." He characterizes this group as the most socially mobile of their time, uncertain of their status, but standing to benefit from the blending of class lines (30-31). Such a group has strong affinities with the Canterbury Pilgrims, and such conditions would help explain the casual atmosphere permitting the free and easy interplay among them.

12

Felix Lindner, after careful study of Chaucer's use of alliteration in the Canterbury Tales, accounts for it as follows:

> The imitation of the language of the people was
> therefore one reason for the poet Chaucer to
> revive alliteration. To this may be added a
> second,--his sympathy with the old customs and
> manners; this is visible in all his tales.
> The character of the Anglo-Saxon seems not to
> be quite lost in Chaucer's poems...So we may
> conclude, with tolerable certainty, that he
> had a strong natural inclination for the old
> alliterative forms, which was perhaps unknown
> to himself.

"The Alliteration in Chaucer's Canterbury Tales," in Essays on Chaucer (Rostock, 1876), 203. Stuart Robertson has suggested that traces of the Old English four-stress half-line pattern can be found in Chaucer's poetry, and he points to the above-mentioned passage from the Knight's Tale as a prime example. Robertson concludes his analysis with the following rhetorical question:

> Is it not significant of the other and the more
> neglected side of Chaucer's poetic background,
> that in this battle scene one may hear, surging
> through the alien iambic metre, the echoes of the
> rhythm of Maldon and Brunnanburh? Has not the
> poet, half consciously, left for the moment
> French and Italian guides behind him, to draw
> upon his English inheritance?

"Old English Verse in Chaucer," MLN 43 (1928): 236. Others who maintain that Chaucer's rhythm and meter represent developments of the Old English metrical system include: Francis B Gummere, "The Translation of Beowulf and the Relations of Ancient and Modern English Verse," American Journal of Philology 7 (1886): 46-78; C.S. Lewis, "The Fifteenth Century Heroic Line," ES 29 (1938): 28-41; Kemp Malone, "Chaucer's 'Book of the Duchess': A Metrical Study," in Chaucer und seine zeit: Symposium fur Walter Schirmer, ed. Arno Esch (Tubingen: Max Niemeyer, 1968), 71-95; Ian Robinson, Chaucer's Prosody (London: Cambridge Univ. Press, 1971).

13

The similarity between Hrothgar's and Theseus' speeches is illustrative of a narrative feature that Tripp identifies as linking Chaucer's poetry to Old English poetry--what Tripp terms "the great speech" ("On the Continuity of English Poetry," 6). In his subsequent article, Tripp establishes a similar link by comparing the Book of the Duchess to the Old English "Solomon and Saturn," both of which he characterizes as "big debates" ("The Dialectics of Debate," 41.)

14

Siegfried Wenzel describes the structure of the typical medieval sermon as consisting of five parts--Theme, Protheme, Restatement of Theme, Division, Development. "Chaucer and the Language of Contemporary Preaching," Studies in Philology 73 (1976): 138.

15

The technique is used ironically in the Wife of Bath's "Prologue" and the Pardoner's "Prologue," both of which are structured as sermons, where the instruction given the audience is inadvertent. The Pardoner, of course, represents the antithesis of Hrothgar; he is the embodiment of the evil to be avoided.

16

>   E noi che ora viviam, quando piacere
>   Sará di quel che 'l mondo circunscrisse
>   perció morremo....   (XII, 6, 4-6)

(And we who are now living, when it pleases him who circumscribed the world, will die.)

This and subsequent passages quoted from the Teseida are cited from Giovanni Boccaccio, Teseida, ed. Aurelio Roncaglia (Bari, 1941).

17

The Consolation of Philosophy: Book II, Meter 8 for the "chain of love"; Book III, Prose 10 for the origin of Nature in that which is perfect and stable; Book IV, Prose 6 and Meter 6 for the notion that mutability serves the divine will--that this constant change itself insures the survival of species according to the Creator's will.

18
    While Boethius' work purports to be a "consolation," neither
the work as a whole nor the passages in question in any way resemble the sermon structure of Theseus' speech; nor do they function in the same way. The "consolation" offered by Philosophy
is of a different order from that offered by Theseus.
    19
    (And certainly never has a valorous man not been mourned in
Greece; so, many kings and numerous people have given Arcite
proper due. He has been magnificently honored and placed upon
a splendid pyre, and all that should be done for the body has
properly been done.

And, as we can see, mourning has lasted for many days in
Athens. And for that reason all have been wearing dark clothing,
especially all those gathered here, the best from whom others
take example to follow.

Therefore, because all things that are born must die, no
matter what, and because we have given honor to him for whom we
grieve, I think it better now to remove our mourning garments
and to cease our sorrowing, which is a womanly trait and is not
manly.)
    20
    Barry Sanders, "Chaucer's Dependence on Sermon Structure in
the Wife of Bath's 'Prologue and Tale,'" Studies in Medieval
Culture 4 (1974): 437-445.
    21
    John B. Friedman, "The Nun's Priest's Tale: The Preacher
and the Mermaid's Song," Chaucer Review 7 (1973): 250-266.
    22
    No doubt Chaucer and Gower both learned much from the work
of those English poets who preceded them. On the whole, however, Gower's poetry seems considerably less characterized by
this English quality and is, in my opinion, less indebted to
the native tradition. To link Chaucer and Gower so closely
together in this regard may be somewhat misleading. Nevertheless, I would certainly agree that whatever is, in fact,
"English" about Gower's poetry derives in large part from the
native tradition.

III

CHAUCER AND THE MIDDLE ENGLISH LYRICS

On the Evolution of
the "New" Tradition

Precious few literary documents written in English have survived
from the century following the Conquest, though there is extant
an enormous bulk of Anglo-Norman and Anglo-Latin writing from
that same period. This is hardly a surprising development.
That virtually every literate person in Europe during the Middle
Ages was perfectly familiar with Latin, and that there is as
great an abundance of Latin writing in England preceding the
Conquest as during the century following need hardly be mentioned. After the Conquest French became the official language
of the court and, for all practical intents and purposes, of the
whole country. Not only was French the native tongue of the
aristocracy, but it was also, to a large extent, the native
tongue of the clergy, for William replaced many English clergy-
men with those imported from his homeland. And until the middle
of the fourteenth century French was the language of instruction
in England's schools. It is quite natural, then, that those
capable of writing would do so in French or Latin, and it follows
that these writings would be the ones most likely to be preserved.[1]
     But even though very little verse written in English sur-
vives from this period, this in itself is surely not sufficient
evidence that the native literature was totally disregarded, dis-
carded, destroyed, transformed, or driven underground. Even if
English poetry was forced to take to the highways, so to speak,
it was not necessarily overthrown. We can be reasonably certain
that all Englishmen did not stop speaking their native language
after 1066. In fact, for several hundred years after the Conquest both English and French were probably spoken throughout
the country, though perhaps at different social levels. Surely
these native speakers must have remembered and continued to sing
some of the old songs, to retell some of the old stories, to pass

on some of the bits of gnomic wisdom, some of the prayers or charms or riddles that had been part of the heritage left by their ancestors. Nor is it at all improbable that these speakers retained in their language certain of those features which conversational prose may acquire from a poetic tradition, features such as tag phrases, proverbial sayings and metaphoric expressions. These and other stylistic features must also have to some degree survived in the continuity of the prose tradition, especially in the numerous devotional treatises and in the alliterative prose sermons. These alliterative sermons, which constitute an important link between the old poetic tradition and the poetry of the Alliterative Revival, particularly <u>Piers Plowman</u>, are especially significant. For they incorporate many of the stylistic features of the old poetic tradition--not only formulaic alliterative phrases, balanced repetition, and the half-line structure, but also some of the imagery and, perhaps most important, the very rhythm of the line--and preserve these features through the period of the Conquest.[2]

We do not know, nor perhaps will we ever know, to what extent the older poetry may have survived in oral form, passed on by word of mouth from parents to their children from one generation to the next or collected and circulated by wandering minstrels. Nor can we be absolutely certain that there was no written poetry in English during this period. If English was spoken by a considerable part of the population, there would no doubt be at least some who could write it and who could have written down the verses they may have heard or themselves composed. However, it is quite likely that those who would have possessed the means to preserve this poetry, the Norman aristocracy and the Norman clergy, would not have done so, perhaps because they could not understand it, perhaps because they did not value it highly. Perhaps there were other reasons now obscured by the passing of the centuries. But whatever the reasons that so little has survived, we cannot simply conclude that the native literature ceased to exist after the Conquest, or that it did not play a role in shaping English poetry as it was to emerge in written form during the thirteenth century.

R. M. Wilson points out a very significant, though frequently overlooked, fact regarding England's literary history during the period following the Conquest: "It must be remembered that Anglo-French as a literary language was developed entirely on English soil and not imported, already flourishing, in the wake of the conquering army" (12). Along with their own customs and language the Normans must have brought to England whatever literature they may have possessed. But this literature, uprooted from its native home and transplanted in English soil, did not smother the English poetry already flourishing there. Just as the two languages existed side by side, acting upon each other and blending together, so these two literatures must have grown together, interacting with each other and, at many points, merging.

Certainly the English language and English poetry underwent enormous changes as a result of the Conquest. Even the earliest extant poetry after the Conquest is essentially a new poetry written in a new language. But this new poetry is not simply an outgrowth of the literary tradition imported from France. Rather, it is the product of many elements simultaneously at work. Not least among these elements is the old poetic tradition. The old clay is worked by many hands and placed in a variety of molds to give it its new shape; but the clay remains English clay. This new poetry forms, in a sense, a new tradition, and it is this new tradition that Chaucer inherited.

Tradition always implies some sort of unity, some common denominator, some feature or characteristic that binds a wide variety of elements together to form a single and complete whole. If this poetry does indeed form such a unit, if it does constitute a new tradition, then it must have some common centre that we need to be able to identify.

It is undeniably true that this new poetry differs in many respects from the old. Nonetheless, however much the old tradition may have been modified by foreign influences to which it was subjected after the Conquest, it was not completely overwhelmed and driven into oblivion. That these foreign influences did not completely overshadow the old tradition nor prevent it from continuing to exert a significant influence is evidenced by this new poetry itself. For the English poetry which emerges after the Conquest shows unmistakeable signs of its native ancestry, most obviously in the frequent occurrence of alliteration and in the survival of the Old English alliterative measure, somewhat modified, in heroic verse like Layamon's _Brut_ and in the alliterative romances of the following century.

Nor, as we have seen, is the survival of alliteration and the alliterative measure the only link with the past. Such features as the melancholic tone, verbal and structural repetition, and visual concreteness not only remain very much in evidence in the earliest extant Middle English poetry, but continue to be an integral part of the poetry of the new tradition and contribute much indeed to the English quality so characteristic of it. It is this English quality, deriving in part from the abiding influence of the old tradition, that is in a very real sense the "common centre" of the new poetry and distinguishes it as a unit.

By suggesting that this English quality is characteristic of the new tradition, I do not mean so much to emphasize any direct influence of the old tradition upon the new as to emphasize that quality distinguishing the poetry of this new tradition from the contemporary poetry of foreign traditions. Nor by suggesting that the English quality characteristic of Chaucer's poetry derives from a native English poetic tradition, do I mean to imply that there is a clear, unbroken continuity from Old

English poetry through Middle English poetry to Chaucer. The new tradition does not simply acquire this English quality essentially intact and unchanged from the old poetry. For the native tradition was indeed significantly affected and altered following the Conquest, and the link with the past provides only some of the features characteristic of the poetry of the new tradition.

We have already remarked that among the earliest extant examples of this new tradition are the Middle English lyrics. Concerning these lyrics Speirs comments, "Every single English song that has come down to us from before the fifteenth century has done so in a dialect and has therefore, as an essential characteristic, the speech flavour of the folk of some particular locality in England. Yet these so English lyrics have, at the same time, such resemblances to the lyrics of the rest of medieval Europe as to suggest that all medieval lyrics are, in greater or less degree, akin"(51).[3]   Speirs is, of course, right to emphasize the kinship between the English lyrics and the continental lyrics. Yet despite this kinship the Middle English lyrics differ significantly in many respects from their continental counterparts. Nor is this difference attributable solely or even primarily to the "speech flavour" which results from the various English dialects in which they were composed. Rather, the uniquely English quality of these lyrics, as well as of the later Middle English poetry, is the product of the continuing influence of the old poetic tradition and the blending of this tradition with continental traditions. For these two forces above all else, the old poetic tradition and the new continental poetry, acted upon English poetry during the centuries following the Conquest and so helped shape the new tradition that emerges in the thirteenth century and culminates in the poetry of Chaucer.

We can think of English poetry during the three centuries following the Conquest as a lake fed by many streams. Some of these streams have their source in Latin literature, others in French literature, and others still in Italian literature. But it is an English lake, formed long before 1066. As these streams converge and flow into this lake, they do in a sense transform it, not by altering its basic nature but by deepening, enlarging, and enriching it.

The vestiges of the old tradition are, then, only part of a larger whole, and we can no more look exclusively to Old English poetry than to continental poetry in attempting to account for those features of the new tradition in general, or of Chaucer's poetry in particular, which mark it as distinctively English. For the new tradition, differs as much from the one as from the other. And the particular English quality of this tradition is both new and unique, distinguishing Middle English poetry as much from Old English poetry as from the poetry of continental traditions.

Defining this English quality is not just simply a matter of showing how Middle English poetry resembles Old English poetry and differs from continental poetry. For isolating those constituent elements of the new tradition that can be traced back to Old English poetry and separating them from those that derive from continental influence is at best only a beginning, a first step towards describing the particular features of this English quality. Far more important are the ways in which elements from the older native tradition and from continental traditions combine and manifest themselves in Middle English poetry, the ways in which the Middle English poet brought such heterogeneous elements together in creating the new tradition. It is, therefore, the poetry of this new tradition itself, rather than any particular native or foreign influences, that must be our major concern if we are to define its English quality, even more so if we are to show that this same quality is characteristic of Chaucer's poetry and is not only a mark of Chaucer's indebtedness to this new tradition but a clear indication that his poetry belongs to it.[4]

Chaucer's "ABC"
     and
Its Lyric Predecessors

Commenting upon the historical development of the Middle English
lyrics, George Saintsbury writes, "The lyric of the thirteenth
century is existent and not seldom charming...that of the fourteenth is more abundant and more charming still, though, as it
happens, none of the greater poets of its closing years, neither
Chaucer, nor Gower, nor Langland, contributes to it in genuine
English kind..." (4). Certainly, by the middle of the fourteenth
century English poets like Chaucer were beginning to recognize
the limitations of earlier English poetry and turned more and
more to foreign models, especially French, in their attempts to
expand the potentialities of English poetry, to give English
poetry, as it were, the entrée to the court. But while Chaucer's
lyrics may indeed represent a fresh wave of continental influence, this does not necessarily exclude the operation of a native poetic tradition. Rather, it is in a twofold perspective--
a desire to elevate English poetry to a level equivalent to the
aristocratic poetry of other vernacular literatures against the
background of a quite different native poetic tradition still
exerting a considerable influence--that Chaucer's lyric poetry,
and his narrative poetry as well, must be viewed.
     Perhaps one of the earliest of Chaucer's extant poems is
his "ABC," a lyric prayer to the Virgin composed sometime around
1369. The "ABC" is a translation of a prayer that occurs in
Deguileville's Le Pèlerinage de la Vie Humaine and quite
naturally closely resembles Deguileville's prayer, so much so,
in fact, that Frank Allen Patterson concludes, "Chaucer, in translating his ABC poem from Deguileville's Pélérinage de la vie
humaine, managed to preserve the spirit and manner of the
original, thereby inaugurating a new school of English lyric
poetry" (44-45).[5] However, if we examine the two poems closely,
we find very significant differences. In part these differences
may be due to the difficulties of translating poetry from one
language to another. But more important, I believe, these
differences are indicative of the different poetic traditions
in which the two poets were respectively working. For when we
read Chaucer's "ABC" side by side with Deguileville's prayer
and a thirteenth century English lyric such as "Cristes Milde
Moder Seynte Marie" (Brown, XIII, 3), we find that Chaucer's
prayer, though more rigidly structured and displaying a more
elaborate and sophisticated diction and syntax than the English
prayer, seems nonetheless more closely akin to it than to
Deguileville's--this despite the fact that Chaucer's is a close

translation of the French, employing the same form and even
borrowing certain words and phrases directly from it.

Deguileville's poem, belonging essentially to the intellectual mode of medieval French lyric poetry, is an ornate, elaborately stylized, meticulously wrought artifact. In translating
this poem, Chaucer seems to follow closely the instruction
Pandarus gives Troilus regarding his letter to Criseyde, instruction in composing effective exposition:

> I woot thow nylt it dygneliche endite,
> As make it with thise argumentes tough;
> Ne scryvenyssh or craftily thow it write....
> (TC, II, 1024-1026)

As a result, Chaucer's version is more simple and direct than
Deguileville's, approximating more nearly the expository mode
of earlier Middle English lyrics, though certainly more ornate
and elaborate than most.

Chaucer's more simple and direct expression helps capture
an urgency missing from Deguileville's poem. Such a line as,
"O help yit at this neede!" stands in sharp contrast to
Deguileville's,

> A moy garder met t'entente,
> A mon besoing soiez preste.[6]

(Let your intention be to protect me and to be ready at my need.)

Both Deguileville's and Chaucer's sentences are imperative. But
Chaucer's simpler utterance, his addition of the exclamatory
"O," and especially his substitution of an active voice construc-
tion for Deguileville's passive voice construction create an
effect considerably more forceful than that created by
Deguileville's carefully balanced, perfectly controlled lines.

We can observe the same tendency in Chaucer's rendering of
Deguileville's,

> Se je fui a la poursuite
> Ou fuiray, qu'a mon refui?

(If I flee from pursuit, where would I go other than my only
refuge?)

as "Allas, I, caitif, whider may I flee?" Here again Chaucer's
more simple and direct expression and his addition of the exclamatory "Allas" create an effect more poignant than that of the
original. And though both sentences are technically interroga-
tive, Chaucer's reads more like an exclamation of grief and
bewilderment than a question.

Chaucer's poem is, on the whole, more intensely emotional
than Deguileville's, and such emotional outbursts, which do not
occur in Deguileville's poem, are only one of the techniques
Chaucer employs to intensify the emotional quality of this poem.
Another, and particularly striking, is Chaucer's use of anaphora.
Chaucer uses anaphora at moments when the speaker seems to
be in a state of reverie and breaks into uncontrolled outbursts:

> O verrey light of eyen that ben blynde,
> O verrey lust of labour and distresse,
> O tresoreere of bountee to mankynde,
> Thee whom God ches to moder, for humblesse!

When one reads this passage aloud, the craftsmanship that raises
these lines to poetic heights unequaled in English before Chaucer
is lost on the reader. This is a tribute to Chaucer's skill.
For it is precisely because the craftsmanship is servant to the
expression of intense emotion that these lines convey, and not
the master, that the passage succeeds so well.
The high point of the "ABC" comes in stanza twenty-four,
where the speaker describes the crucifixion. It is a climactic,
almost visionary moment:

> Xristus, thi sone, that in this world alighte
> Upon the cros to suffre his passioun,
> And eek that Longius his herte pighte,
> And made his herte blood to renne adoun,
> And al was this for my salvacioun;
> And I to him am fals and eek unkynde,
> And yet he wole not my dampnacioun--
> This thanke I yow, socour of al mankynde!

Chaucer's use of anaphora here imbues the passage with a kind of
incantatory power similar to ritualistic prayer. It seems to
hypnotize the reader and draw him, almost against his will, into
an identification with the speaker, who, as a result of the
coordinate structure, identifies himself, almost as if against
his will, with Longinus. For, as Longinus pierced the heart of
Christ, and this was for the speaker's salvation, so the speaker
is to Christ "fals" and "unkynde," and yet Christ does not want
his damnation. The message is hammered home by the repetition
until, with the last clause introduced by "and," the tension is
released, and the speaker breaks into an emotional outburst of
gratitude. The sense of relief is overwhelming and gratefully
shared by the reader.
This passage does not soar to the lyrical heights of the
previous one. It is considerably more subdued, but it is every
bit as effective, and, in its own way, every bit as intense.
The first passage is externally oriented, an emotional outburst
expressing delight in the Virgin. The second is internally

oriented and expresses the spiritual torment that besets man when he comes to a realization of his sinful state in light of Christ's sacrifice. But in both cases Chaucer succeeds in making it possible for the reader to share the experience, if not actually forcing him to do so. The following is the corresponding passage from the French:

> Xristus, ton filz, qui descendi,
> En terre et en la crois pendi,
> Ot pour moy le costé fendu.
> Sa grant rigour il destendi
> Quant pour moy l'esperit rendi,
> Son corps pendant et estendu;
> Pour moy son sanc fu expandu.
> Se cec j'ai bien entendu
> A mon salut bien entendi,
> Et pour ce, se l'ay offendu
> Et il ne le m'a pas rendu,
> Merci t'en rens, graces l'en di.

(Christ, your son, who came down to earth, for my sake hung on the cross and had his side pierced. His great ordeal he endured when he gave up the spirit for my sake, his body hanging and stretched out. For me his blood was shed. If I have understood correctly, he did all this for my salvation. And therefore, if I have offended him and yet he has not punished me, for this I give thanks to you and to him.)

There is nothing here quite like Chaucer's use of anaphora. This is not to say that Deguileville does not use the device, but rather that he does not use it the same way Chaucer does. In Deguileville's prayer at no point is the first word or phrase repeated in more than two successive lines. Hence, there cannot be the same kind of sustained emotional intensity that Chaucer achieves by his use of anaphora. Instead, Deguileville uses anaphora most frequently to create a clever structural contrast between two lines. For example,

> A toy pour leur medicine.
> A moy donc, virge, t'encline...

or again,

> Et de toy son salu tire,
> Et en toy seule se fonde.

Here it can only be the clever and skillful way in which the lines are arranged, in an almost playful manner, that strikes the reader.

But Chaucer's use of anaphora does closely resemble its use in the Middle English lyrics, where it functions also to intensify the emotional quality. We can observe this quite clearly in "Cristes Milde Moder Seynte Marie":

> þu ȝiuest eche reste ful of sþete blisse
> þer ðe neure deað ne come, ne herm ne sorinesse.
> Þer bloþeð inne blisse blostmen hþite & reade,
> þer ham neuer ne mei snou ne uorst iureden,
> þer ne mei non ualuþen, uor þer is eche sumer,
> ne non liuiinde þing þoc nis ne ȝeomer.

The speaker is expressing his notion of paradise, of the heavenly rewards one can expect if he puts his faith in the Virgin. As the passage reaches a crescendo in these lines, what we might call a visionary moment seems to pass before the speaker's eyes so rapidly and so powerfully that he virtually cannot control his words. It is almost as though the vision overwhelms him and takes control of his expression; he waxes eloquent despite himself. But at the same time the language is simple, and the rhythm of each individual line, natural. What imagery there is, the white and red blossoms, the snow and frost, is concrete and visual, taken from the natural world. And the association of death with winter is commonplace.

So too Chaucer's language in the passage on the crucifixion is simple, and the rhythm of the lines, quite natural. In the Chaucerian passage also, what imagery there is -- Longinus piercing Christ's heart, and the blood running down from Christ's heart -- is concrete and visual, much more so than the corresponding passage from Deguileville's prayer, where there is no reference to Longinus at all nor to Christ's "heart," but only to his side being pierced, and where the reference to Christ's bleeding is more general and abstract: "Pour moy son sanc fu expandu."

The word "þer," like Chaucer's "And," does not, in itself, attract undue attention or emphasis. But its repeated use at the beginning of the four successive lines helps create the same kind of melodically hypnotic effect created by the use of anaphora in the Chaucerian passage and further serves to introduce a subtle, complex, and intricately balanced structure from which the fullest significance of the meaning of the passage unfolds. The first line expresses the essential sense of the passage--Paradise is a place of "sþete blisse." The last line merely restates the point, for in a place of "sþete blisse" there can be no living thing either "þoc" or "ȝeomer." The meaning of the first line is reinforced by the last, and the contrast between "sþete blisse" and "þoc" and "ȝeomer" is reflected by the contrasting structure of the two lines: the first, a positive statement; the last, a negative one.

The four lines in between elaborate upon this meaning, express it in simple terms and concrete images that each individual can identify with from personal experience and respond to. And the contrasting construction of the two lines that enclose the sentence is repeated in these, where "deað," "herm," and "sorinesse" are juxtaposed and contrasted to the "blostmen hþite & reade," and the "snou" and "uorst" are juxtaposed to the "eche sumer." There is a further interrelationship in that "deað," "herm," and "sorinesse," all preceded by the negative "ne," are associated with "snou" and "uorst," also preceded by the negative "ne," while the "blostmen hþite & reade" are associated with "eche sumer." The repetitive force of "þer" completes the picture. The reader is told, or rather made to see and feel, not only what he can expect Paradise to be like, but with equal weight what he can expect it not to be like. As a result, the image of Paradise that the poet succeeds in evoking is one of complete fulfillment. It is a place not simply from which the discomforts associated with winter are absent, nor even simply a place abounding in the joys of summer--rather, it is, in the fullest sense, both at once.

What emerges from the passage is that "sþete blisse" has not only been defined, but has been translated into an experience. It has been experienced in an intensely emotional way by the speaker in the poem, just as the speaker in the Chaucerian passage intensely experiences the crucifixion. Here, just as in the Chaucerian passage, the use of anaphora helps convey this intense emotion. For the use of anaphora in both poems creates the hypnotic effect that draws the reader into the experience and makes it possible for him to share not only that experience but the emotion itself.

Anaphora is most commonly used in the early English lyrics at such visionary or intensely emotional moments, and it is used with great effect. Perhaps one of the finest passages in "Cristes Milde Moder Seynte Marie" occurs at just such a moment and illustrates the poet's skill in his use of this device:

> Mi Leoue lif urom þine luue ne schal me no þing todealen,
> Vor o þe is al ilong mi lif & eke min heale.
> Vor þine luue i spinke & sike þel ilome,
> Vor þine luue ich ham ibrouht in-to þeoudome,
> Vor þine luue ich uorsoc al þet me leof þas
> And ȝef ðe al mi suluen, looue lif, iþench þu þes.

Such a passage, which in its use of anaphora rivals the poetry of Chaucer himself, is ample evidence that this device was well-known and already highly developed in English lyric poetry of the thirteenth century. And while anaphora is by no means unique to the English poetic tradition, there is nothing in the French poetry Chaucer may have known when he composed the "ABC" that is quite like its use in this passage. It would seem then that we might reasonably conclude whatever models Chaucer may have had for his use of this device are to be found primarily in earlier English poetry.

The greater emotional intensity of Chaucer's poem is one aspect of the fundamental difference in tone between his poem and that of Deguileville. Where Chaucer's poem succeeds in con- veying a sense of the compelling urgency of a man at his prayers, Deguileville's poem is too self-consciously sophisticated to do so. The speaker of Deguileville's prayer adopts a more or less formal tone towards the Virgin, one that serves to maintain a certain distance between them. When she is addressed directly, it is almost always as "virge" or "Vierge glorieuse." Even when Deguileville employs familial terminology in depicting the relationship between the speaker, Mary, and God, she is ad- dressed as "Glorieuse vierge mere" or "douce vierge mere." On only one occasion is she addressed simply as "mere."[7]

The speaker of Chaucer's prayer adopts a more casual, even familiar tone towards the Virgin, one that tends to diminish the distance between them. Wolfgang Clemen notes this differ- ence between the two poems and comments, "Like Chaucer's ABC Deguileville's prayer, too, is always addressed to the Virgin; yet Chaucer's more urgent pleas, sometimes expressed in the 'natural idiom,' seem to bring the suppliant and the Virgin closer to one another" (178).

Though both poems are, indeed, addressed directly to the Virgin, she is addressed by a greater variety of titles in Chaucer's prayer, and these titles are used much more frequently by Chaucer, as though the Virgin were actually there in the presence of the speaker. Chaucer's poem begins formally enough as the speaker addresses the "Almighty and al merciable queene" and, a few lines later, the "Glorious virgine." But, by the next stanza she has become his "lady bright," and, in the next, his "ladi deere." In fact, "lady" is the most frequently occurring term applied to the Virgin in Chaucer's poem. Cer- tainly, the use of this term, and likewise "queene," in such a context derives from the tradition of courtly love poetry and suggests one aspect, perhaps even an erotic one, of the rela- tionship between the speaker and the Virgin. But a closer look suggests a different relationship, though equally personal and intimate, for Chaucer seems much more conscious, than does Deguileville, of Mary in her human aspect, as a mother, refer- ring to her as "Cristes blisful mooder deere," "Cristes mooder deere," and in stanza eighteen simply as "mooder."

But it is not only the variety of these terms of address nor only their frequency of occurrence that serves to create the familiar tone and, consequently, to capture the feeling of a personal and intimate relationship. Equally important is the

familiarity of the speaker's stance in respect to the Virgin, a
familiarity that permits the speaker to refer to the devil as
"oure foo," as "Thin enemy and myn" and even to offer a warning:
"ladi, tak heede!" It is a familiarity that seemingly permits
the speaker not only to take for granted the Virgin's help, but
also at times to expect or even demand it:

> Now, ladi ful of merci, I yow preye,
> Sith he his merci mesured so large,
> Be ye not skant....

The phrasing of the last line in particular reflects the attitude of the speaker implicit from the tone of the poem as a
whole, a tone totally different from that of Dequileville's
prayer. It is precisely this attitude that allows for such
emotional outbursts by the speaker as we previously remarked
upon, and these outbursts in turn reinforce the sense of the
personal and intimate relationship between the speaker and the
Virgin and contribute to the particular tone of Chaucer's
prayer we have been describing.

One final note in this regard. In Chaucer's day the plural
form of the second person pronoun ("ye," "yow," "you") was still
used as a mark of respect for addressing superiors, while the
singular ("Thou," "Thee") was the form of familiar address and
the form most commonly used in prayers. Skeat pointed out that
in the "ABC" Chaucer "mixes these usages in a remarkable way."[8]
Actually, the familiar form predominates, occurring sixty-three
times. But the plural form does occur twenty times. Here again
we observe Chaucer maintaining the delicate balance in the relationship between the speaker and the Virgin. She is always
the queen of heaven, but, at the same time, she is the mother
who gave birth to Christ, who suffered, in very human terms, the
agony of witnessing the crucifixion of her son. She is the universal symbol of motherhood, listening to the prayers of her
erring children, understanding their spiritual torment. Most
important, she is possessed of that infinite capacity for for-
giveness that marks her role as interventrix between man and
God. For, to carry the familial metaphor a step further, just
as the earthly mother frequently stands between the wrath of the
father and the erring child, so the Virgin, as mother, stands
between the wrath of God and his erring children. Such a conception of the Virgin underlies Chaucer's whole poem and helps
account for its tone and for the poignancy of passages such as
the following:

>Glorious mayde and mooder, which that nevere
>Were bitter, neither in erthe nor in see,
>But ful of swetnesse and of merci evere,
>Help that my Fader be not wroth with me.
>Spek thou, for I ne dar not him ysee,
>So have I doon in erthe, allas the while!
>That certes, but if thou my socour bee,
>To stink eterne he wol my gost exile.

A similar conception of the Virgin and of the relationship between her and man underlies "Cristes Milde Moder Seynte Marie," and the tone too of this lyric is much the same as that of Chaucer's "ABC"; it is the familiar tone of a personal and intimate relationship between the speaker and the Virgin.

In this poem too the speaker is very much aware of the Virgin in her human aspect, and the poem begins with the speaker addressing her in her role as mother of Christ. But in the very next line he addresses her as "mi leoue lefdi," and, in fact, here as in Chaucer's poem "lady" is the most frequently used term of address. She is "mi leoue lefdi," "mi spete lefdi," "mi leoue spete lefdi," or just "lefdi." She is also, of course, "spete Godes moder," but at the same time she is the "holi heouene-kþene." The dual nature of the Virgin's role that arises from such a conception accounts for a mild tension in the speaker and a charming naivete. He never seems quite sure how best to appeal to her:

>Spete Godes moder, softe meiden & þel icoren,
>þin iliche neuer nes ne neuer more ne þurð iboren,
>Moder þu ert & meiden cleane of alle laste,
>þuruhtut hei & holi in englene reste.

The speaker here also displays that kind of confident expectation that the Virgin cannot do otherwise than help those who seek her aid:

>And heo siggeð alle þet ðe ne þonteð neuer ore,
>ne no mon þet ðe þurðeð ne mei neuer beon uorloren.

But at the same time there is a kind of reticene on the part of the speaker, for he is always aware that she is a "kþene":

>þeruore ich ðe bidde, holi heouene-kþene,
>þet tu, ȝif þi þille is, iher mine bene.

At times he addresses her in a manner so familiar as to border on presumption, but his boldness is always mitigated by a qualifying word or phrase that reflects his reticence:

> Mi lif is þin, mi luue is þin, mine heorte blod is þin,
> and ȝif ich der seggen, mi leoue leafdi, þu ert min.

Here, as in Chaucer's prayer, the devil is a common foe; and here too the speaker can offer advice to the Virgin: "Nis hit ðe no perðscipe þet þe deouel me to-draþe...." What is more, he even reasons with her:

> Þu hit þost ful ȝeorne þet þe deouel hateð me,
> And nomeliche þereuore þet ich purðie þe;
> þereuore ich þe bidde þet þu me þite & þerie,
> þet þe deouel me ne drecche ne dþeolðe me ne derie.

The total effect of the tone of this poem, like that of Chaucer's "ABC," is to bring the suppliant and the Virgin closer together. Where Deguileville's speaker seems to be calling upon a distant and remote Mary, the speakers in the English poems seem instead to actually be conversing with her.

The more formal tone of Deguileville's poem tends also to maintain a certain distance between the audience and the poetic re-creation of his experience. For Deguileville's poem is his own personal offering to the Virgin, made in the hope of obtaining her aid, and as such it is internalized and individual. It is in essence a private performance that the audience can observe from a distance and admire, but they are excluded from participating in it. The more familiar tone of the English poems, on the other hand, tends to diminish this distance. For the English poets, though also re-creating a personal and private experience, strive consciously to include the audience in that experience. To that end they externalize and generalize the experience, and theirs is essentially a public performance, one that the audience is not so much invited to observe, but rather to participate and share in. Perhaps this difference is most evident in the manner in which the respective poems are concluded. Deguileville's prayer ends with a direct plea by the speaker for Mary's aid in his own behalf:

> Se tu donc as le cuer tendre
> Et m'offense n'est pas mendre
> De cil qui menga la pomme,
> Moy laver veillez entendre
> Moy garder et moy deffendre,
> Que justice ne m'asomme.

(Because you have a heart so tender and my offense is no worse than his who ate the apple, please hear my plea; cleanse me, protect me and defend me so that righteous justice does not crush me.)

Chaucer's poem, on the other hand, ends with a plea on behalf of
all mankind:

> Now lady brighte, sith thou canst and wilt
> Ben to the seed of Adam merciable,
> So bring us to that palais that is bilt
> To penitents that ben to mercy able.

So too the poet of "Cristes Milde Moder Seynte Marie" concludes
with a plea not only on his behalf, but also on behalf of his
"friends":

> And all mine ureondmen þe bet beo nu to-dai
> þet ich habbe i-sungen þe ðesne englissce lai.
> And nu ich þe biseche vor ðire holinesse
> þet þu bring þene Munuch to þire glednesse
> þet funde ðesne song bi ðe, mi looue leafdi,
> Cristes milde moder seinte marie.

It is not only at the conclusion but throughout the poem that
Chaucer consciously strives to include the audience, to diminish
the distance between them and the experience the poem re-creates,
to force them to identify with the speaker and so with his experience. One technique Chaucer employs to achieve this end is
to shift the point of view continually by slipping easily and
comfortably from the first person singular, in which the poem
is primarily written, into the first person plural. For example, "And therfor, lady bright, thou for us praye." Or again,

> As I seide erst, thou ground of our substaunce,
> Continue on us thy pitous eyen clere!

There are, in fact, stanzas where Chaucer employs the first
person plural throughout. Stanza 14, for example,

> Noble princesse, that never haddest pere,
> Certes, if any comfort in us be,
> That cometh of thee, thou Cristes moder dere,
> We han non other melodye or glee
> Us to reioyse in our adversitee,
> Ne advocat non that wol and dar so preye
> For us, and that for litel hyre as ye,
> That helpen for an Ave-Marie or tweye.

In such stanzas the speaker seems to have laid aside his individuality. It is not so much the voice of the speaker, utter-
ing his prayer on behalf of mankind, that we are here listening
to as the common voice of his whole audience; that is, all those,
including ourselves, who pray alongside of him, who share in his
experience as a result of the poetic re-creation of it.[9]

There are no such stanzas in Deguileville's poem. In fact, Deguileville uses the first person plural on only two occasions, neither of which seem intended for any special effect but seem rather almost accidental. One of these occurs in stanza 22:

> Vierge de noble et haut atour,
> Qui au chastel et a la tour
> De paradis nous atournes....

(Virgin, nobly and splendidly attired, who turns us toward the castle and tower of Paradise....)

Here the expression is almost a formulaic one--the invocation to the Virgin who leads us to paradise. The second occurs in stanza 14, Chaucer's version of which we have glanced at just above:

> Noble princesse du monde
> Qui n'as ne per ne seconde
> En royaume n'en enpire,
> De toy vient, de toy redonde
> Tout le bien qui nous abonde,
> N'avons autre tirelire.

(Noble princess of the world, who has no peer, no equal in realm nor empire, from you abounds all the good that is bestowed on us; we have no other resource.)

But where Chaucer continues in the first person plural, Deguileville shifts immediately into the more distant, more general and more objective third person:

> En toy tout povre homme espire
> Et de toy son salu tire,
> Et en toy seule se fonde.

(In you every poor man finds hope and from you draws his salvation and on you alone depends.)

Where Chaucer creates a greater rapport between the audience and the speaker by merging the speaker with the audience, Deguileville seems almost intentionally to separate the speaker from the audience. True, Mary is the source of goodness for all, but his is a special case, and he insists on his individuality. This is his own personal prayer, not anyone else's; it is on his own behalf, not anyone else's, that he himself, and not anyone else, recites it to her.

In "Cristes Milde Moder Seynte Marie," written like
Deguileville's prayer and the "ABC" primarily in the first person singular, the poet also slips easily and comfortably into
the first person plural, though not quite so often as does
Chaucer. For example,

> Þel oþe þe þe luuien, mi sþete lefdi,
> þel oþen þe uor þine luue úre heorte beien.

Or,

> Þereuore, leoue lefdi, long hit þuncheð us þrecchen
> Vort þu of þisse erme liue to ðe suluen us fecche;
> Þe ne muþen neuer habben fulle gledschipe
> er þe to þe suluen kumen to þine heie þurschipe.

And again,

> Ich ðe bidde, lefdi, uor þere gretunge
> þet Gabriel ðe brouhte urom ure heouen-kinge;
> And ek ich ðe biseche uor ihesu cristes blode,
> þet for ure note þas i-sched o ðere rode....

Of particular interest in this last example is the way the poet
switches back and forth from the first singular to the first
plural in alternate lines. Here too the poet, like Chaucer,
seems to be trying to create a sense of identification between
the audience and the speaker, to merge them, in a manner of
speaking, in a common experience.

In this poem too the poet commonly shifts into the third
person singular, even more frequently than does Deguileville.
But the effect is altogether different:

> So muchel is þi milce & þin edmodnesse
> þet no mon þet ðe 3eorne bit of helpe ne mei missen.
> Ilch mon þet to þe bisihð þu 3iuest milce & ore,
> þauh he ðe habbe sþuðe agult & idreaued sore;
> þereuore ich ðe bidde, holi heouene-kþene,
> þet tu, 3if þi þille is, iher mine bene.

Here the effect is not one of the speaker's separating himself
from the rest of mankind, but just the opposite. The poet achieves this effect by the remarkably simple expedient of employing the transitional adverb, "þereuore," to link the two parts
of the passage--Deguileville, we might note, employs no such
transition in the similar passage in his poem. It is because
the Virgin extends her mercy to all humanity, to all who need
her help and earnestly pray for it, that the speaker is himself
able to appeal to her; for the speaker is just such a man. It

is precisely as such a man, as one who is part of this common
humanity, that he utters his prayer. His is not an individual
voice. It is, rather, like that of the speaker in the "ABC,"
the collective voice of "everyman" seeking some sort of solace
and comfort in the experience of prayer.[10]

The English poets, then, employ a more casual and familiar
tone than does Deguileville and strive for a greater emotional
intensity than he does in their attempt to re-create the experience in such a way that it can be readily shared in by the
audience; that is, to make the experience as easily accessible
to the audience as possible. To this end also, the English
poets tend to be more visually concrete than their French
counterpart. For if the audience is to participate as fully
as possible in the experience, they must be able to visualize
the scene that they are to be part of.

We have already alluded to the greater visual concreteness
of Chaucer's passage on the crucifixion as compared with the
corresponding passage in Deguileville's poem. Nor is this an
isolated instance; Chaucer's poem is throughout more visually
concrete than is Deguileville's. It is not just Chaucer's
more graphic mode of expression nor his use of a greater
number of images that most distinguish his poem from
Deguileville's. It is, above all, the greater concreteness,
particularly the greater visual concreteness, of Chaucer's
poem.[11]

Chaucer does, in fact, transform rather than merely translate Deguileville's poem. Stanza 13, which relates the incident of Moses and the burning bush as prefiguring the Virgin
birth, affords an excellent example of this process, the most
apparent result of which here is to imbue the passage with a
visual concreteness lacking in the original. The passage from
Deguileville's poem follows:

> Moyses vit en figure
> Que tu, vierge, nete et pure,
> Jesu le filz Dieu conceus:
> Un bysson contre nature
> Vit qui ardoit sans arsure.

(Moses saw prefigured Jesus, the son of God, whom you conceived,
Virgin unblemished and pure; A bush which, contrary to nature,
burned without being consumed.)

Chaucer renders these lines,

> Moises, that saugh the bush with flawmes rede
> Brenninge, of which ther never a stikke brende,
> Was signe of thin unwemmed maidenhede.

Deguileville begins by referring abstractly to what Moses saw in "figure," the son of God whom Mary would conceive. He describes this incident as "contre nature," and only in the one last line are we told that the bush burned without being consumed. For Deguileville it is the exegetical significance of the burning bush episode and the paradox suggested by the phrase, "contre nature," which links this episode to the virgin birth, that is of utmost importance. Clearly, Deguileville is appealing to the reader's intellect. He assumes that the reader knows his Bible and knows the episode. There is no need to describe the experience, for Deguileville is not concerned with creating an experience for the reader to share. He is interested only in the intellectual act that recognizes the paradox common to both episodes and so links them together.

Chaucer begins with the image of the burning bush itself and, just the opposite of Deguileville, devotes more attention to this than to what it prefigures, summing up the figurative significance in one line. The image is vividly and graphically depicted, "the bush with flawmes rede"; and the use of enjambment here, in a manner rivalling Milton, is striking. For attention is focused on "Brenninge," and we are virtually forced to stop, to see the burning bush, "of which ther never a stikke brende...." By making the burning bush so visually concrete for the reader, Chaucer virtually forces him to feel as though he were actually standing there with Moses before the burning bush and so to feel the full impact of the awe and mystery of the miracle. The reader's response is then carefully and subtly transferred to the Virgin birth, and, consequently, the full impact of the second miracle, one much less tangible than the first, becomes also more keenly felt by the reader.

Patricia Kean also compares Chaucer's version of this passage with Deguileville's and concludes that Chaucer's translation here is not successful. She says of Chaucer's version, "At times it is not even syntactically clear, and the material is laid out so that, instead of a unified image, containing and illuminating the paradox, we are told first what Moses saw, then what he thought and then what we ought to think...The French, here, is less ambitious, but clearer. It begins by stating that what Moses saw was 'in figure,' then describes what he saw and then makes the application. Chaucer's attempt at a closer application is here not happy...."[12] But Kean, I believe, misses the point. She herself observes, "The ABC... reproduces the familiar, fourteenth-century mode of writing, in which imagery is discursively presented and in which there is little clear thematic development. Each image or figure, in poetry of this type, stands alone, and one image cannot take fire from another" (Art of Narrative, 197). Kean is certainly correct when she points out that the imagery in this kind of

poetry stands alone, and we have previously remarked on this
aspect of the early English lyrics. For imagery in this kind
of poetry serves primarily to make the poetic re-creation of
an experience come vividly alive for the audience, to heighten
the illusion of the audience's participation in that experience, and so to reinforce the meaning of the experience itself.
This is precisely the way the burning bush image in the "ABC"
functions. It is not, then, as Kean suggests, that Chaucer has
failed in his attempt at what she refers to as "the newer syn-
thesis of intellectual argument and illuminating image"; rather,
Chaucer, working in a different tradition, makes no such attempt here at all. He is not concerned with illuminating the
paradox, nor, as we have seen, were the earlier English lyricists, for this was not a major concern of the tradition. Instead, in translating these lines, Chaucer also transforms
them in terms compatible with his own native poetic tradition.

There are, of course, many other instances of greater
concreteness in Chaucer's poem. But enough has been said to
at least suggest the essential difference between his poem and
Deguileville's in this regard. There are, however, a number of
other features Chaucer's poem has in common with the earlier
English lyrics and which further differentiate his poem from
Deguileville's. Perhaps most obvious and most important is
Chaucer's use of alliteration.

Alliteration does occur in Deguileville's poem. For
example, in such lines as,

> Pour ma très grant transgression

> Mes pour ce que veil plait fenir

> As revivé et repeu....

There is even an instance of double alliteration:

> Et de toy son salu tire....

But alliteration in French poetry does not have the same effect
as in English poetry, where it depends not only on the repetition of an initial phoneme but also upon stress. Because French
poetry is not accentual, nor the stops aspirated, there is not
the same kind of emphatic effect produced as is produced by the
repetition of a stressed phoneme in English poetry.

Chaucer uses alliteration throughout the "ABC," and he uses
it in ways closely resembling its use in the earlier lyrics.
While alliteration in these lyrics is no longer a structural
principle, as it was in Old English poetry,[13] rhyme having
replaced it as the chief organizational and structural principle
of the verse, and there are no precise formulations for its use,
neither is it simply ornamental. Alliteration in these lyrics is
functional, though in a way different from its function in Old
English poetry.

Patricia Abel, in her discussion of the Harley lyrics, points out what may be the single most important function of alliteration in these lyrics: "Alliteration marks off for emphasis the words that the sense of the poem selects as significant, and is a genuine force in organization, as it unites word groups... groups that fit together in sense, placed together by sound..." (18).[14] That is, alliteration functions in the lyrics primarily to emphasize and reinforce meaning, and we can observe it functioning just this way in "Cristes Milde Moder Seynte Marie."

Although the most obvious observation one can make about alliteration in this poem is that it follows no particular pattern, it does most frequently occur between words that are grammatically related and so helps emphasize that relationship. The following passage affords a good example of this technique:

> Mid ham is euer more dei þið-ute nihte,
> Song þið-ute seoruþe & sib þið-ute uihte;
> Mid ham is muruhðe moniuold þið-ute teone & treie,
> Gleo-beames & gome inouh, liues þil & eche pleie.

Here, in the second line, the alliteration occurs not only between the two nouns, "song" and "sib," which introduce the parallel prepositional phrases, but also between these and "seoruþe," the noun that is the object of the first preposition. Hence, it is not only the absence of "sorrow" with respect to "song" that is emphasized, but also the absence of "sorrow" with respect to "peace." In the fourth line, the alliteration binds the compound subject, "Gleo-beames & gome"; and in the third, "teone & treie," the compound object of the preposition. In the third line too alliteration binds the noun, "muruhðe" with its modifying adjective, "moniuold," and so emphasizes the unlimited extent of joy that awaits man in heaven.

Of greater significance, however, the alliteration in this passage helps reinforce the meaning of the sentence as a whole, which is developed by the repetitive structural pattern. "Song þið-ute seoruþe" and "sib þið-ute uihte" are elaborations of "dei þið-ute nihte" and help explain the latter phrase in experiential terms. Furthermore, it is precisely "song" and "sib" that correspond to "dei" and "seoruþe," just as "uihte" corresponds to "nihte." Similarly, "Gleo-beames" and "gome" correspond to "muruhðe moniuold," and both are set up in opposition to "teone" and "treie." Here, then, the poet has skillfully blended the alliteration into the pattern of structural repetition to create a simple yet effective picture of heaven as he conceives it, a place from which all discomfort is lacking, a place of joy and peace.

Chaucer too in the "ABC" frequently employs alliteration between grammatically related words. We find alliteration occurring between nouns and their modifying adjectives: "O

fresshe flour," "sinful soule," "rightful rekeninge"; between a
verb and its subject: "any tunge telle," a variation echoing
the alliterative phrase "tunge tagen" occurring in "Cristes
Milde Moder Seynte Marie"; between a verb and its object: "as
he the lyf shal lete"; between two verbs that form a compound
predicate: "we singe and seye"; and between verbs and their
modifying adverbs: "ferther fleen," "it smert so sore." The
last is especially effective within the context of the whole
line, which reads, "That I am almost lost;--it smert so sore."
The "s" alliteration picks up the "s" sound in "almost" and
"lost." And this repetition of the dolorous "s" sound gives the
effect of the speaker heaving out the words in one great sigh
of bewilderment and pain.

Chaucer uses alliteration in more complex grammatical
structures as well. A few examples should suffice to illustrate
the point: "our foo to failen," "our bille up for to bede,"
"He hath thee maked vicaire and maistresse...." Chaucer also
uses alliteration to link words whose grammatical relationship
is not primary. However, even in such cases the alliteration is
functional, serving to create a significant semantic link between these words and often to enhance the visual quality of the
passage. For example, "Myn hele in-to thyn hand al I resigne."
This line, of course, echoes the last words of Christ on the
cross. The alliteration that binds "hele" and "hand" helps make
more vivid the image of the penitent placing his welfare into
the hands of the Virgin. Similarly, in a line such as, "And
that my soule is worthy for to sinke," the alliteration serves
to make more vivid the image of the "sinking soul" and reinforces
the sense of depression the line conveys.

Chaucer also commonly employs alliteration in lines containing a coordinate series, most frequently in lines containing
three coordinate elements where two of the elements alliterate.
In a line such as, "Haven of refut, of quiete, and of reste,"
the structural balance of the line is reinforced by the alliteration of "refut" and reste." Here again we can observe Chaucer
using alliteration as a means of enriching meaning. "Quiete"
and "reste" are, in one sense, expansions of "Haven of refut,"
describing qualities associated with such a haven. But the
alliteration of "refut" and "reste" emphasizes the relationship
of these words. Thus, a "haven of refut" is a haven of "reste,"
and the adjectival force of "quite" both refers back to the
former and points ahead to the latter and functions to reinforce
the sense that "quiete" is that quality common and vital to both.
Similarly, in the line, "To have relees of sinne, of sorwe, and
teene," the phrase "of sorwe, and teene" is an amplification of
"sinne." Here, the alliteration of "sinne" and "sorwe" emphasizes the relationship of these words, while "teene" seems to
stand off by itself. Indeed, "sorwe" bears a twofold relationship to "sinne." It is, in one sense, grief, the grief that
man feels when he becomes aware of his sins and realizes the

dire consequences. In this sense "sorwe" is also related to "teene," which carries the force of vexation, of a troubled, disturbed disposition, in this case spiritual. But in the sense of "contrition," "sorwe" is also the first step towards the absolution of sin. Thus, the "sorwe" that is the result of "sinne" and the cause of "teene" can be alleviated.

Alliteration between words in such coordinate series occurs also in "Cristes Milde Moder Seynte Marie." In the line, "Pleieð & speieð & singeð bitþeonen," the alliteration occurs between words that are virtually synonymous--"speieð" and "singeð." The alliterative pair constitutes an amplification of "Pleieð," which stands off by itself because it does not alliterate. Similarly in the line, "Al mi spinc & mi sor & mine kneoupunge," the alliteration occurs between the synonymous terms, "spinc" and "sor," and so sets them apart from the structurally parallel "kneoupunge," which, in a sense, capsulizes the meaning of the sentence. For it is the "kneoupunge" of "spinc" and "sor that leads to their being "forȝelden."

Occasionally, Chaucer uses alliteration in ways more complex and subtle than the ways it is used in the earlier lyrics. For example, in the following passage:

> Bountee so fix hath in thin herte his tente,
> That wel I wot thou wolt my sucour be;
> Thou canst not warne him that with good entente
> Axeth thin helpe, thin herte is ay so free.

Chaucer sometimes, as he does here, uses words and phrases, marked by alliteration, to create a kind of structural ambiguity that, paradoxically, expands and enriches the meaning of a line. "Bountee" not only has fixed "his tent" in the Virgin's heart, but also, because of the bond created by the alliteration, actually seems to possess ("hath") her "herte." Consequently, the meaning of the whole sentence is more forcefully driven home, for the Virgin has no choice but to help those who seek her aid "with good entente." Similarly, in the fourth line the alliteration of "helpe" and "herte" in two structurally equivalent phrases helps to create such an ambiguity. The alliteration reinforces the balanced structure and binds "helpe" and "herte" more closely together. Once again the meaning of the line is enriched, for "thin helpe" and "thin herte" are both what are being requested, and both are what is given freely. Those who ask for the Virgin's help, ask for her heart, and her heart is not only the dwelling place of "Bountee" but also possessed by "Bountee." She is at the same time both the master and the servant of "Bountee." As master, she is able to give help to those who seek it; and, as servant, she must give help to those who seek it. Finally, the alliteration of "wel," "wot," and "wolt" in the second line is an exquisite touch. It imbues the line with a melodious quality that underscores the tenderly emotional tone of the whole passage.

By and large, however, Chaucer uses alliteration in much
the same ways it is used in the earlier lyrics. This does not,
of course, necessarily mean that Chaucer was in any direct sense
imitating these lyrics in this regard. Alliteration is a quality
deeply embedded in the language Chaucer was using, and alliterative phrases are an intrinsic part of the poetic language common
to both Chaucer and the earlier English lyricists, a language
rooted in the pre-Conquest past. The fact that Chaucer's use of
alliteration closely resembles its use in the earlier English
lyrics does, however, serve as yet one more indication that both
he and these early lyricists were working in a common poetic tradition.

Another feature of Chaucer's "ABC" that distinguishes it
from Deguileville's poem is what George Saintsbury refers to as
"reduplication of synonyms" (History of English Prosody, 149).[15]
This characteristic too Chaucer's poem has in common with
"Cristes Milde Moder Seynte Marie." We have already observed
several instances of the reduplication of synonyms in the English
poems--Chaucer's "Haven of refut, of quiete, and of reste" for
example, or the line, "Pleieð & speieð & singeð bit þeonen," from
"Cristes Milde Moder Seynte Marie." Such constructions do not
occur in Deguileville's poem, and there is no need to elaborate
upon them any further here. But this technique is part of the
larger general pattern of verbal and structural repetition
characteristic of the tradition to which these English poems
belong. Thus, we find in Chaucer's poem the quite common use of
doublets--"Help and releve," "Of grace and mercy," "in wille and
dede," "melodye or glee," "vicaire and maistresse," "wisse and
counsaile," "canst and wilt." In fact, Chaucer's poem abounds
in all manner of such coordinate constructions--"Almighty and
al merciable quene," "my sinne and my confusioun," "of Iustice
and of yre," "neither in erthe nor in see," "of swetnesse and
of mercy," "wherfore and why," "Mercy axe and have," "Redresse
me, moder, and me chastyse," "thy grace and thy socour," "in
filthe and in errour," "fals and eek unkinde." So too "Cristes
Milde Moder Seynte Marie"--"To þe ich bupe & mine kneon ich
beie," "Mi lif & mi to-hope," "briht & blisful," "Karien ne
spinken," "hei & holi," "Al englene þere & all holie þing,"
"Siggeð & singeð," "þi milce & þin edmodnesse," "milce & ore,"
"agult & idreaued," "þiðuten & eke pið-innen," "mi lif & eke
min heale," "spinke & sike," and more that we need not list.

Such doublets do occasionally occur in Deguileville's poem--
"vergoigne et confusion," "Pitié et miseracion," "pes et con-
corde," "mercier et concordé," "ravivé et repeû"--as do a number
of other coordinate constructions--"nul penser ne dire," "nul
pourtraire ne escrire," "Reprens moy, mere, et chastie," "nul
bien ne foysonne," "moy garder et moy deffendre." But these do
not occur nearly so frequently in Deguileville's poem as they do

in the English poems. Nor do they seem to be nearly so integral a part of Deguileville's technique as they are in the English poems.

Another kind of repetition common to the English poems is a form of parallel variation. This is most readily apparent in certain phrases referring to the Virgin. For example, in the line, "Cristes milde moder seynte marie," "seynte marie" is a variation of "Cristes milde moder." So too in the line, "Spete Godes moder, softe meiden & pel icoren," "softe meiden" is a variation of "spete Godes moder."

In Chaucer's poem the parallel variation takes a somewhat different form. For example, in the opening stanza,

> Almighty and al merciable quene,
> To whom that al this world fleeth for socour,
> To have relees of sinne, sorwe and tene,
> Glorious virgine, of alle floures flour....

Here, not only is "Glorious virgine" a parallel variation of "quene," but the phrase "of alle floures flour" is a variation of both. The structure is very different from Deguileville's,

> A toy du monde le refui,
> Vierge glorieuse, m'en fui
> Tout confus, ne puis miex faire...

(Glorious Virgin, refuge of the world, totally bewildered I flee to you; I can do no better.)

where the Virgin is referred to only in the second line. Similarly, there is no corresponding structure in Deguileville's poem for Chaucer's,

> Lady, unto that court thou me aiourne
> that cleped is thy bench, O fresshe flour!

where "O fresshe flour" is a variation of "Lady." The same is true of Chaucer's,

> Noble princesse, that never haddest pere,
> Certes, if any comfort in us be,
> That cometh of thee, thou Cristes moder dere...

where "Cristes moder dere" is a variation of "Noble princesse."

This last example is illustrative also of another form that parallel variation takes in Chaucer's poem. The phrase, "thou Cristes moder dere," is an amplification of the pronoun "thee," and a variation of it. Chaucer on several occasions amplifies a pronoun in this manner:

Comfort is noon, but in yow, lady dere...

Nere mercy of you, blisful hevene quene...

This thanke I you, socour of al mankinde.

There is nothing that corresponds to such constructions in
Deguileville's poem. Also of interest in this regard is Chaucer's
rendering of Deguileville's "Glorieuse vierge mere" as "Glorious
mayde and moder." This last is, of course, a very minor point.
But it does seem to suggest at least that the tendency toward
amplification by repetition, here in the form of parallel variation, and the tendency toward coordinate structures is so deeply
ingrained in Chaucer's style as to be almost a matter of un-
conscious habit.

Certainly, repetition, as I have said before, is not unique
to English poetry. But its frequency of occurrence, the stylistic weight it carries, and, particularly, many of the similar
forms it takes in both the "ABC" and "Cristes Milde Moder Seynte
Marie" suggest a link between these poems, a link indicative of
a common poetic tradition.

In conception and tone, as well as certain aspects of style,
Chaucer's "ABC" more nearly resembles the thirteenth century
English lyric with which we have been comparing it than it resembles Deguileville's prayer. But such differences between
Chaucer's and Deguileville's poems as we have so far noted are
only part of the picture. By far the most outstanding difference, and the most important one, is that noted, almost in passing, by Sister Mary Madeleva.

Sister Madeleva observes that "conversational ease" is an
ideal that is rarely achieved in written poetry. But, she goes
on to suggest that it is precisely this quality that distinguishes Chaucer's prayer from that of his French model. In comparing the two poems, she asserts that Chaucer transforms a
"devout convention" into a "divine conversation."[16] The verdict
is certainly just and is borne out by a careful reading of the
two poems side by side. For when we read Chaucer's poem, we
cannot help but agree with Wolfgang Clemen's observation that,
"In some passages we seem actually to hear him speaking" (178).
We do not, however, have the same experience when reading
Deguileville's poem. In part this is due to some of the differences we have already noted. The greater simplicity and directness of Chaucer's poem, his simpler and more graphic diction,
his use of idiomatic expressions and colloquial language, the
sense of urgency created by the greater emotional intensity of
Chaucer's poem, and certainly the more casual and familiar tone--
all contribute to the conversational quality of the "ABC." And
those who have long recognized and often praised the conversational quality of Chaucer's poetry, especially of his later,
more mature works, have most commonly done so in terms of such
characteristics. But the conversational manner of Chaucer's

poetry, both here and elsewhere, is to an even greater degree than this the result of conscious technique, particularly as regards his manipulation of syntax and meter. What is more, this conversational manner, together with the techniques used to achieve it, has behind it a long and firmly established native poetic tradition.

Patricia Kean has suggested as much and attributes the conversational manner of Chaucer's poetry at least in part to the particular relationship between Chaucer and his audience. She goes on to describe this "manner" as a "plain, colloquial, sometimes blunt, conversational style," and points once again to the Middle English romances as a possible source for it (<u>Love Vision and Debate</u>, 32). But a conversational manner is characteristic of the Middle English lyrics as well and is, in my view, the single characteristic that most clearly distinguishes them from the contemporary lyrics of continental Europe.

Rosemary Woolf's excellent study of the medieval English religious lyrics helps to account in part for the conversational quality of these lyrics. She argues that the lyrics grew directly from the Latin devotional movement. And because there was no fully developed tradition of courtly poetry in the native tongue in England in the thirteenth century, no highly refined tradition of secular love poetry, as was the case in France, these lyrics developed relatively free from the forms and conventions of such a poetry. As a result the authors of the English lyrics were, of necessity, restricted to the forms and vocabulary conveniently at hand. In Woolf's words, "Only the vocabulary and rhythms of common speech were available to English writers of the thirteenth century"(23). Though Woolf addresses herself here to the religious lyrics, much the same was true of the secular lyrics as well, for these too had no such courtly models to influence their development.

The conversational manner of the Middle English lyrics is the result of other factors as well. The devotional movement from which the religious lyrics developed gave rise to poetry that did not so much reflect a spiritual experience unique to the poet as a common experience capable of being shared by "everyman." The purpose of this poetry was to arouse the proper response in the audience, occasionally fear, fear of the power of God the Father, more often love, a greater love for Christ in recognition of His sacrifice; but in either case a response generated not merely by an intellectual awareness of the Father's power or the Son's love but by the personal and intense sharing in a poetic re-creation of an experience through which that power, as in the Doomsday poems, or that love, as in the Passion lyrics, is made manifest. The Middle English lyricist's attempt to re-create the experience in such a manner was, in a broader sense, the result of his concern with teaching a lesson, a concern as much underlying the secular lyrics as the religious lyrics. And because the audience for whom this "lesson" was intended was primarily a "listening" audience, the Middle English lyricist had very much to be concerned with meeting the demands of aural comprehension. These were the two overriding concerns of the Middle English lyricist--the emphasis on teaching a lesson coupled with the demands of aural comprehension--and led to the development and exploitation of a conversational manner in the Middle English lyrics.

The Middle English lyricist adopted a conversational manner as the best means available to him to achieve the fundamental goal of his poetry, to convey his meaning through his poetry as clearly and effectively as possible to a listening audience. But in developing this conversational manner, he had also to contend with the influx of new poetic modes from the continent making their impact upon English poetry at this time. Predominant among these new modes were a rigid rhyme scheme and a perfectly regular syllabic line, both of which are, by their very nature, antithetical to a conversational manner. If the Middle English lyricist was to employ rhyme as an essential organizational principle and was to strive for greater metrical regularity, and still succeed in making his poetry acceptable to both himself and his audience, he had to find ways of incorporating such features so as to be compatible with a conversational manner and thereby consistent with the fundamental goal of his poetry. Instrumental in aiding him to solve this problem was the older English poetic tradition.

The Middle English lyricist achieves this conversational manner by employing a variety of techniques, the most important of which is his manipulation of syntax and meter. Raymond Oliver well describes this function of syntax and meter in the lyrics: "In general the syntax gives the impression of someone speaking normally, without trying for special effects through dislocated word order...or even through complicated hypotaxis...Thus, the relationship between syntax and line, like the heavy simple meter, reinforces the plain meaning of the words" (94-95).[17] In very significant respects, underlying the Middle English lyricist's particular use of syntax and meter is the older native poetic tradition.

Although the Old English metrical system is certainly more complex than might be suggested by the brief treatment afforded it below, we need only consider a few special aspects of it for the present purpose. Basically, the meter of classical Old English poetry is determined by the four strongly stressed syllables per line, two occurring in each half-line and three of the four commonly alliterating. But the number of unstressed syllables per line can and does vary considerably. Consequently, there is no regular recurrent pattern of stressed and unstressed syllables. The stressed syllables may occur at virtually any point in the line, but there is at least a strong tendency to begin the half-lines with a stressed syllable. Since these

stressed syllables frequently alliterate, both metrical stress
and semantic emphasis are distributed more or less evenly throughout the line.

The essential structural unit of Old English poetry is the
half-line. These half-lines are by and large independent syntactic units, and a number of such units combine to form a sentence.
More often than not, one sentence ends and the next begins at
some point within the verse line itself, rather than at the end
of the line. As a result Old English poetry is characterized by
run-on lines in which the sense is "variously drawn out from one
verse to another." Furthermore, the half-line patterning results in a strong internal pause, which serves to diminish the
force of the end-line pause and so not only contributes to the
distribution of stress and emphasis throughout the line but
also, in combination with a strong metrical stress at the beginning of the following line, results in the frequent occurrence
of enjambment.[18]

The total effect of such a prosodic system is quite different from that produced by Romance prosodic systems such as the
French. Not only is there the very obvious difference that results from a prosodic system that is accentual and based on
stressed syllables as opposed to one that is not accentual and
based on syllable count, but even more significant is the
difference that results in the very movement of the verse lines
and the movement from one line to another. The movement of the
Old English verse line is one of continual stop and go, and the
movement between lines is an almost continual process of going
back and forth, back and forth from one line to the next. In
contrast the movement of French verse, because of the very
regular syllabic pattern, is infinitely more smooth and even,
and the flow is always towards the end of the line, where the
rigid rhyme scheme reinforces the strong end-line pause. Thus,
even though the run-on line is not uncommon in medieval French
poetry, it is of a different order from the kind we find in Old
English poetry. Nor can it have quite the same effect. For
there is no metrical stress to reinforce the flow of one line
into another nor to force the reader to pause at and so focus
on the beginning of the subsequent line. Instead, the expectations built up in the reader by the regular syllabic pattern and
the rigid rhyme scheme draw him inexorably toward the end of
each successive line.

The Middle English lyricist did strive for greater metrical
regularity in his poetry than is characteristic of the poetry
produced by his Anglo-Saxon predecessors, and he did adopt rhyme
in place of alliteration as the organizational principle of his
verse. But it was his blending of such features derived primarily from continental traditions with newly developed techniques and those derived from the Old English poetic tradition
that resulted in the uniquely English quality of the Middle
English lyrics.

The conversational manner is the stylistic heart of the Middle English lyrics. Virtually everywhere we look in these lyrics we find the more or less familiar tone, the graphic mode of expression, the colloquial language and idiomatic usage we have previously remarked upon as important ingredients of this style. But equally important, we find the lyricist experimenting with a variety of other techniques as well, techniques such as strong internal pauses, stress distribution and variation, freedom in the use of unstressed syllables, run-on lines and enjambment. The essential models for many of these techniques that were to prove most conducive to producing a conversational manner were provided by the poetry of the old tradition.

The Old English poetic tradition proved extremely useful to the Middle English lyricist in his search for a metrical system that would meet the exigencies of his own poetry while, at the same time, allowing him to accommodate such new elements from foreign traditions as he found desirable. Patricia Abel describes well a part of the role played by the old tradition in this regard:

> It [Old English]verse differs in rhythm and feeling from Medieval verse. But the prosodic structure of Anglo-Saxon verse was not discarded, it remained as a foundation for later English poetry and exerted strong pressures on the completely different elements entering from Latin and French. For example, the emphasis on four strong beats in a line undoubtedly aided in the shift from quantitative to accentual meter, and the tradition of an indefinite number of unaccented syllables probably accounts for the roughness with which some English poets translated the stricter meters of the French. (16-17)[19]

Abel is certainly right as far as she goes, but the metrical roughness to which she alludes is not so much the result of the Middle English lyricist's lack of skill as the result of his experimentation with metrical variation in attempting to achieve a conversational manner. The lyric "Glade Us Maiden, Moder Milde" (Brown, XIII, 22) affords an interesting example of the poet's use of such variation:

> Glade us maiden, moder milde,
> þurru þin herre þu were wid childe--
> Gabriel he seide it þe--
> Glade us, ful of gode þine,
> þam þu bere buten pine
> Wid þe, lilie of chastete.

Glade us of iesu þi sone
þat þolede deit for monis loue;
  þat dehit was, quiic up aros.
Glade us maiden, crist up stey
& in heuene þe i-sey;
  He bar hin seluen into is clos.

Glade us marie, to Ioye ibrout,--
Muche wrchipe crist hau þe i-worut--
  in heuene brit in þi paleis;
Þer þat frut of þire wombe
Be i-yefin us forto fonden
  in Ioye þat is endeles.

Although it is extremely difficult to scan such a poem with
any great assurance,[20] the prevailing rhythm seems to be trochaic;
in fact, the first two lines can be scanned as perfectly regular
trochaic tetrameter. But such regularity breaks down almost
immediately, and only four of the subsequent lines seem metrically regular--lines 5, 8, 14 and 16. In every other line,
however, the poet continually varies the meter, and this metrical
variation, together with the internal pauses, helps create the
conversational quality of the poem. For the rhythm of conversation does not proceed in regular patterns; it is varied, full of
stops and goes, and uses stress to support meaning. Line 3 of
this poem, for example, is an independent syntactic and grammatical unit; it has the quality of a parenthetical aside. And the
poet's variation of the meter both contributes to this quality
by emphasizing the rather abrupt manner by which such asides are
characteristically initiated and reinforces the syntactic structure by isolating metrically the line that is also grammatically
isolated from the two surrounding it. The line begins with three
trochaic feet; however, it ends on a stressed syllable ("þe").
No unstressed syllable is provided to complete the fourth foot,
and the reader is brought up short, forced to pause in order to
satisfy the metrical expectation that has been created by the
perfectly regular trochaic tetrameter pattern to this point.
Moreover, the stress on the last syllable of "Gabriel" is not
nearly so strong as the stress on the first syllable; in fact,
it is just barely stronger, if at all, than the stresses on the
two syllables surrounding it, and the effect, when we read the
line, seems more nearly that of an initial dactylic foot followed
by two iambic feet. Even in line 1 the regular trochaic rhythm
is somewhat offset by the phrasal structure, which resembles the
half-line patterning of Old English poetry, and the resultant
strong internal pause, which is further reinforced by the
alliteration.
    Both alliteration and metrical variation, sometimes in com-
bination, are used to create internal pauses not otherwise

required by the syntax. Line 4 affords a good example of the
use of alliteration for this purpose: "þam þu bere buten
pine...." The effect of the strongly stressed alliterating "b"
syllables creates a slight but noticeable pause after "bere" in
the otherwise smooth trochaic rhythm. In line 17 we can observe
the use of metrical variation for the same purpose: "Be i-yefin
us forto fonden...." Here, the predominantly trochaic rhythm
is interrupted by the dactylic second foot, and the shift from
this dactylic second foot to the resumption of the trochaic
rhythm in the third foot again creates a slight but noticeable
pause. This pause is further reinforced by the "f" alliteration
that follows and not only emphasizes the trochaic rhythm of the
last two feet but also seems to separate this part of the line
from that which precedes.

In this poem the poet uses such internal pauses to help
achieve a run-on effect, and he also uses metrical variation
to enhance the effect. Syllabically, the norm of the poem is an
eight syllable line. But on more than one occasion the poet
deviates from this norm, as he does in line 17, a nine syllable
line. The extra syllable results from the dactylic second foot,
and the expectation created by the pattern so initiated seems
almost to require another unstressed syllable after "fonden,"
for this would complete that trochee-dactyl-trochee-dactyl
pattern. The poet provides this "missing" syllable at the
beginning of the next line, and more, he continues with a
dactylic rhythm that perfectly satisfies the metrical expectation he has created: "in Ioye þat is endeles." Even though
the line can be scanned as perfectly regular iambic tetrameter,
the effect, when we read it, is something quite different. The
stress on the last syllable of "endeles" is strong only relative to the stress on the syllable that immediately precedes it,
and the stress on "þat" is hardly noticeable at all.[21] Thus,
the movement of the line seems more nearly dactylic than iambic,
the line consisting of two dactylic feet, with the word "in"
seeming to play no significant role in its metrical structure.
The most plausible explanation for such a peculiar metrical
structure would, it seems to me, be precisely that the "in" is
meant to transform the trochaic fourth foot of the preceding
line into a dactylic foot and so satisfy the metrical expectation
created by the two lines. Thus, the metrical structure, and
also the pause following "us," diminishes whatever tendency there
may be toward a pause after "fonden" and virtually forces the
reader on to the next line. This metrical structure also supports the syntactic structure. The phrase "Be i-yefin us" completes the thought of the preceding line, "þer þat frut of þire
wombe," and the pause after "us" is syntactically valid. Similarly, the very last line completes the thought of the phrase
"forto fonden," the syntax requiring no pause after "fonden."
Consequently, the alternative, to consider the last line as a
perfectly regular iambic line, seems not only metrically

ridiculous, but also totally meaningless with reference to any
relationship between syntax and meter.

In line 10 the poet also deviates from the octosyllabic
norm, but in this case by reducing the number of syllables to
seven: "Glade us maiden, crist up stey...." Here again the
metrical expectation created by the perfectly regular first
three trochaic feet would seem to require an unstressed syllable
following "stey." Here too the "missing" syllable seems to be
provided in the next line: "& in heauene þe i-sey." The result
is once again a run-on line that supports the syntactic structure. This completes the thought of the phrase "crist up stey,"
which is itself set off from the phrase preceding it by the
strong internal pause after "maiden," and, as in the previous
example, the internal pause here serves to reduce the effect
of the end-line pause.

The chief function of the meter in this poem is to create
a conversational quality, its so-called "metrical roughness"
resulting from the poet's experimentation with meter to achieve
this quality. He seems almost determined to avoid any regularly
recurrent metrical pattern. For such a pattern, if too rigidly
imposed, would neutralize the effect of stress variation by
creating a sing-song rhythm antithetical to a conversational
manner. Furthermore, the poet uses stress to reinforce the internal pauses and so help capture the stop and go quality of
conversational rhythms. Particularly effective in this regard
is the poet's use of two successive strongly stressed syllables
in line 6 ("Wid þe, lilie of chastete") and line 9 ("þat dehit
was, quiic up aros"), where the meter emphasizes the internal
pause required by the syntax.

Finally, the poet uses metrical stress to balance the
effect of the rhyme. Rhyme, by calling attention to itself,
results in great emphasis being placed at the end of the line.
But the poet is able to offset this effect of rhyme by his use
of meter, especially his tendency to initiate a line with a
strong metrical stress and end a line with an unstressed
syllable, which may, at least in part, account for his decision
to adopt a predominantly trochaic rhythm. However, the strong
initial metrical stress is not limited to lines that begin with
a trochaic foot. On at least two occasions, line 3 ("Gabriel he
seide it þe") and line 7 ("Glade us of iseu þi sone"),[22] the
first foot is dactylic, which, of course, also provides strong
initial metrical stress. All in all, ten of the eighteen lines
begin with a strongly stressed syllable, while eleven end with
an unstressed syllable, and eight of the ten that begin with a
strongly stressed syllable end with an unstressed one. Hence,
the meter of the poem, which calls attention to these stressed
syllables, serves to distribute the emphasis more evenly throughout the line.

One final note. The poem is, on the whole, built up of a
series of phrases and clauses that, more than the number of

syllables or even the meter, determine the verse line. So too
conversation is built up primarily of such phrasal and clausal
units. And the syntax throughout the poem, of the individual
phrases or clauses, of the verse line, and of the whole sentence,
is, like the syntax of conversation, eminently straight-forward
and natural. There are virtually no unnecessarily complex grammatical constructions, and there is little if any distortion of
natural word order.[23]
  The prevailing style of this poem, as of the Middle English
lyrics in general, is one that closely approximates that of conversation. Syntax and meter are the pillars of this style. A
syntax that is eminently natural, supported by and working together with a meter that captures the rhythms of conversation,
is the most distinctive feature of this style and, more than
anything else, responsible for the conversational manner of these
lyrics.
  Perhaps nowhere in the Middle English lyrics is the conversational manner more readily apparent nor more effectively used
than in those Passion lyrics where Christ converses with His
mother. The poem, "Stond Wel, Moder, Ounder Rode" (Brown, XIII,
49), is a particularly fine example. I quote only the first
three stanzas:

> 'Stond wel, moder, ounder rode,
> Bihold þi child wiþ glade mode,
> Moder bliþe miȝt þou be.
> 'Sone, hou may ich bliþe stonde?
> Ich se þine fet and þine honde
> I-nayled to þe harde tre.'
>
> 'Moder, do wey wepinge;
> Ich þolie deþ for monnes kuinde--
> Wor mine gultes ne þolie I non.'
> 'Sone, ich fele þe deþes stounde;
> Þat swerd is at min herte grounde,
> Þat me by-heyte simeon.'
>
> 'Moder, do wei þine teres,
> Þou wip awey þe blodi teres,
> Hy doþ me worse þene mi deþ.'
> 'Sone, hou miȝtte ich teres werne?
> I se þine blodi woundes herne
> From þin herte to þi fot.'

  The setting is Calvary; Christ is on the Cross. It is a
moment of great physical and emotional pain and of spiritual torment. Yet the poem is wonderfully restrained; the tone, subdued; and there is an exquisite tenderness in Christ's words of
consolation to his mother and a touching pathos to Mary's expression of her grief. But above all, the dialogue between

Christ and Mary, between son and mother, is eminently believable, and we seem to be overhearing this conversation as we would if we were actually present and among those witnessing the scene.
The poet re-creates the scene simply and directly through the conversation itself. There is no introduction, no prelude setting the scene. Rather, the scene is vividly and immediately evoked by Christ's first words to his mother, "Stond wel, moder, ounder rode," and so we are quite unexpectedly thrust into the midst of the scene, as we find ourselves listening to Christ's words. The poet further enhances the illusion and maintains it by his use of visually concrete details, in lines 5-6 for example, where Mary "sees" her son's feet and hands "nailed" to the "hard" tree, and in lines 17-18, where she again "sees" his "bloody wounds" "running" from his "heart" to his "foot." So too the allusion to Mary's "weeping" in line 7 is further developed in the third stanza where her "tears" are specifically referred to three times. Finally, there is the constant repetition of the words "moder" and "sone," which serves not only to signal the shift in speakers, but also to keep their presence immediately before us at all times.
But most important in re-creating the experience so that the reader feels a part of it and in maintaining this illusion is the quality of the conversation itself, that is, the conversational manner of the poem.
The style of this poem differs in certain details from that of "Glade Us Maiden, Moder Milde." It is more rigidly structured; the rhyme scheme is more regular, each stanza consisting of six lines rhyming aabccb, and the rhymes themselves are more forceful; nor is there so strong a tendency toward half-line patterning. As a result the verse lines tend to be more heavily end-stopped than those of the former poem. But while such stylistic features contribute to the more restrained quality of this poem, the poem is nonetheless conversational in manner, and to achieve this conversational manner, the poet employs techniques similar to those employed in "Glade Us Maiden, Moder Milde."
In the first place, the diction of the poem is extremely simple and characterized by idiomatic expressions. The poignancy of Mary's questions, "Sone, hou miȝtte ich teres werne," is intensified by the simple, natural phrasing. It is just such a question, expressed in just such terms that a suffering mother would address to her son. What is more, the syntax, here and throughout the poem, is perfectly natural and straight-forward. There are no complex grammatical constructions, no distortions of word order for the sake of metrical regularity. In fact, the poet consciously and freely varies the meter to conform to and support the syntax rather than distorting the syntax to conform to a predetermined metrical mold, and his success in capturing the rhythms of conversation is due largely to his skillful use of metrical variation.

The metrical structure of this poem is somewhat peculiar, almost random. There is no clearly recognizable syllabic norm—there are, in the stanzas quoted, two seven-syllable lines, five eight-syllable lines, six nine-syllable lines, and five ten-syllable lines. Nor is there a single predominant meter. Occurring with equal frequency are lines that are predominantly trochaic and lines predominantly iambic, but here too there is no regularly recurrent pattern. Finally, there is metrical variation within the lines themselves. For example, the otherwise regular iambic rhythm of line 2 is broken by the final unstressed syllable, as is the otherwise regular trochaic rhythm of line 3 by the final stressed syllable.

Nevertheless, the meter of the poem, far from being rough, is quite smooth and even throughout. The rhythm of each line is natural, closely approximating the rhythm of conversation. There is no clash between syntax and meter, for in each line the meter is perfectly suited to the syntax. What the poet seems to have done is to let the meter emerge almost as if of its own accord and quite unself-consciously from the natural accentual patterns of the words themselves and the natural syntactic patterns by which they are arranged into verse lines. Never does the poet distort word accent or syntactic structure to impose a predetermined metrical pattern on a line. If word accent and syntactic structure require the substitution of a trochaic foot for an iambic one, or an iambic foot for a trochaic one, that is what we have. In line 3, for example, we have trochaic substitution in the initial foot of a line that is otherwise iambic ("Sone, hou may ich bliþe stonde"), and in line 4, an initial iambic foot in a line otherwise trochaic ("Ich se þine fet and þine honde"). In line 7 we have an initial trochaic foot followed by two dactylic feet ("Moder, do wey þi wepinge") and in line 10, two dactylic feet followed by two trochaic feet ("Sone, ich fele þe deþes stounde").

The metrical variations in this poem are so subtly and deftly handled that, in reading the poem aloud, we are virtually unaware of any metrical effect at all. But surely what we have here is a classic case of art concealed by art. For it is the poet's skill in accommodating meter to natural word accent and using meter to support syntactic structure that results in the success with which he captures the rhythms of conversation, and so the outstanding conversational quality of the poem.

Noteworthy also of the style of this poem is the splitting of each stanza between the two speakers. This too contributes to the conversational quality. There are no long-winded speeches, no lengthy moral or philosophical set-pieces. Rather, there is a mutual and almost spontaneous exchange between the speakers as one utterance leads to the next. Neither speaker is allowed to overshadow the other. Mary responds to Christ, and he to her. This continual and natural movement back and forth between speakers simulates the actual pattern that conversation most commonly takes and, at the same time, serves also to keep both speakers always clearly before us. It may well be that later poets, like Chaucer, who himself splits not only stanzas but even the verse line between speakers, found in lyrics such as this one models for the use of dialogue in their own poetry.

The fundamental style of the Middle English lyrics is the result of the poet's attempts to find a poetic form capable of satisfying the primary demands of the tradition in which he was working. The simplicity, directness, and concreteness characteristic of these lyrics were essential to the expository mode he adopted, and the natural syntax and metrical freedom were vital to producing the conversational manner he developed. By means of this combination of an expository mode with a conversational manner, the Middle English lyricist was able to achieve his goal. For the result was a poetry perfectly conducive to conveying his meaning as clearly and precisely as possible, and so to teach his lesson as effectively as possible through his poetry.

While Chaucer's audience may have differed to a certain extent in their expectations regarding poetry from the one for whom the lyrics were intended, it was still, we can be reasonably certain, an audience for whom oral recitation was more often than not their chief contact with poetry. Even if no manuscript illumination of Chaucer himself reading to an audience had survived, there could be little doubt that Chaucer was fully aware of an audience as likely to be listening to his poetry as reading it, for on more than one occasion in his works Chaucer alludes to such an audience. For example, the narrator's remark in the Miller's "Prologue":

> And therefore, whoso list it not yheere,
> Turne over the leef and chese another tale.

These lines may seem at first glance somewhat contradictory. For while the word "yheere" implies a listening audience, the phrase "Turne over the leef" implies a reading audience. While this apparent contradiction might be partially explained by Trevor Whittock's suggestion that reading in Chaucer's day was still largely an aural activity,[24] more likely these lines simply indicate that Chaucer was here thinking of both types of audience at once. That Chaucer was inclined to think in terms of both a listening and a reading audience is borne out elsewhere in his works. For example, in the passage at the conclusion of Troilus and Criseyde, where the narrator, as part of his address to his "litel bok," remarks,

> And red wherso thow be or elles songe,
> That thow be understonde, God I biseche!

158

"Songe" here, as opposed to "red," certainly seems to imply an oral recitation of the poem, and surely Chaucer is here referring both to those who might read it for themselves as well as to those who might listen to someone reciting it. Even more explicit, and perhaps best illustrating the point, is the opening of Chaucer's "Retraction": "Now preye I to hem alle that herkne this litel tretys or rede...." In the "Retraction" Chaucer is reflecting on his entire literary career, for he goes on to list all his works—those he retracts as well as those he does not. Thus, he is addressing his entire audience, one that might be acquainted with part or all of these works, early or late. That he does so in terms of those who "herkne" or those who "rede" leaves no doubt whatsoever that Chaucer was fully aware of both types of audience.

That Chaucer was, therefore, very much concerned with meeting the demands of aural comprehension and that this concern had a significant impact on his style has been recognized by Bertrand H. Bronson: "Lip service is paid from time to time to the knowledge that Chaucer wrote for oral delivery, but this primary fact is continually lost sight of or ignored...and its implications are seldom fully realized."[25] H. S. Bennett, though not primarily concerned with the question of oral delivery, nonetheless touches on one such implication in commenting upon Chaucer's style: "We shall reach no vital results...so long as we are content to examine his work in single lines, and to discuss his variations within the line or the couplet. We must escape from the line, as Chaucer did, and see the wider movement and the way in which sentences and paragraphs were built up" (89). The importance of Bennett's observation here cannot be stressed enough. For it implies one of the most fundamental differences between Chaucer's poetry and the French poetry that so strongly influenced him. The essential structural unit of this French poetry, as exemplified by Deguileville's poem, is the syllabic line. But while such a structure is capable of resulting in beautiful phrases, delicately and subtly balanced, and lends itself readily to a wide variety of rhetorical flourishes, it does not lend itself at all to producing a conversational manner. The essential unit of structure of Chaucer's poetry is the syntactic unit—the phrase, the clause, and ultimately the sentence. And this emphasis on the syntactic unit rather than on the syllabic or metrical line not only readily lends itself to a conversational manner, but is imperative to producing it. For this conversational manner depends to a great extent upon the poet's ability to use meter to support syntactic structure rather than forcing the syntax to conform to the verse line.

We can observe this difference and its effect by comparing the opening lines of Deguileville's poem with Chaucer's translation. Deguileville begins his prayer as follows:

A toy du monde le refui,
Vierge glorieuse, m'en fui
Tout confus, ne puis miex faire;
A toy me tien, a toy m'apuy.

(To you, refuge of the world, Glorious Virgin, I flee, totally
bewildered, I can do no better; I cling to you, I lean upon you.)

That these four lines form a sentence seems almost incidental.
Essentially, we have here seven phrases, almost superficially
hanging together since there are no conjunctive elements in the
sentence. Each line is carefully constructed to fit the octosyllabic pattern; each phrase is carefully molded; and there is
a beautiful balance in the two parts of the last line, both of
which are structurally and syllabically identical. Deguileville's
craftsmanship is readily apparent in the repetition of the words
"A toy" at the beginning of the first and last lines of the
sentence and in the repetition of the parallel verbal and syntactic structures they introduce--"A toy...m'en fui," "A toy me
tien," and "A toy m'apuy." Clearly, this passage is not written
in a conversational manner. This is not the language of everyday speech, nor its syntax or rhythm. Nor is the emphasis here
on the sense of the sentence, on the meaning that derives from
a particular arrangement of words; instead, the emphasis is on
the careful and self-conscious structuring of language to form
a "beautiful object."   .
    The rhetorical manner of this passage is not one with which
the reader can easily identify and so does not lend itself
readily to creating the illusion of an experience in which he
seems actually to be participating. Consequently, the effect
tends to be one of distancing the reader from the poetic re-
creation of the experience rather than inviting him to share it.
    Chaucer renders this passage as follows:

Almighty and al merciable queene,
To whom that al this world fleeth for socour,
To have relees of sinne, of sorwe, and teene,
Glorious virgine, of alle floures flour,
To thee I flee, confounded in errour.

Where Deguileville's prayer opens with an elaborately inverted
structure, a modifying phrase referring to the "Vierge glorieuse"
identified at the beginning of the next line, Chaucer's opens
more simply and naturally by addressing the "queene" to whom
the prayer is directed. This is followed by a two line modifying clause, adjectival and referring back to the "queene." Next
comes the phrase, "Glorious virgine," which stands in apposition
to the first line and serves to introduce the main clause. It
is interesting to observe that it is Mary as "queene" who is the
object of the first three lines where the subject is universal,

"this world," while it is the "Glorious virgine" who is the
object of the last two lines where the subject is "I," the
speaker. Deguileville's poem makes no such distinction. Moreover, these two parts are beautifully and harmoniously brought
together by the repetition of the verb "flee." Thus, the speaker
firmly establishes himself as a part of "this world," and he
identifies his condition with that of "this world." For the
adverbial phrase, "To have relees of sinne, of sorwe and teene,"
which expresses the condition of "this world" and explains why
"this world" flees to the "queene" for "socour," is balanced by
the adjectival phrase, "Confounded in errour," which functions
precisely the same way in regard to the "I" to which it refers.
As a result the very personal relationship between the speaker
and the Virgin becomes a reflection of the relationship between
all who are of "this world" and the "Almighty and al merciable
queene"; from the outset, the speaker's prayer is the prayer
of "everyman."

Where the repetition of a structural pattern in Deguileville's
poem is employed as a rhetorical device, the function of which is
primarily ornamental, the verbal and structural repetition in
Chaucer's poem functions essentially to define the relationship
between the constituent elements of the sentence and to convey
in the most precise manner possible the meaning of that sentence.
Where the rhetorical manner of Deguileville's sentence tends to
distance the reader, the essentially conversational manner
of Chaucer's, despite the elaborateness of the utterance, tends
to invite the reader to identify verbally as well as emotionally
with the speaker and to join in the prayer and share the experience.

Though differing considerably from the rhetorical manner of
Deguileville's sentence, the conversational manner of Chaucer's
sentence is quite similar to the conversational manner of
"Cristes Milde Moder Seynte Marie," which begins,

> Cristes milde moder seynte marie,
> Mines liues leome, mi leoue lefdi,
> To þe ich buþe & mine kneon ich beie,
> And al min heorte blod to ðe ich offrie.

Here also the poet begins simply and naturally by addressing the
Virgin directly, first in terms of her universal and spiritual
role and then, by means of the two appositive phrases of the
next line, in terms of his own personal relationship to her.
Next follow two lines composed of three main clauses, which are
the essential constituents of the sentence. The structural
repetition of the second line is nicely balanced by the structural repetition of the third line, but in neither case is there
an exact syllabic congruence nor an exact metrical congruence
between the two parts of the line. The whole passage culminates

in the last line, structurally a composite of the three preceding
lines in that it consists of a noun phrase, "And al min heorte
blod," which parallels the first two lines, and a verbal construction, "to ðe ich offrie," which parallels the third line.
Furthermore, the phrase, "min heorte blod," though closer in
structure to the second line, functions to bind the whole sentence together by referring back to the very first word,
"Cristes." For it is inescapable that "heorte blod" should
create an image that recalls Christ's suffering on the cross.
Thus, the speaker establishes an intimate and personal relationship between himself and the Virgin that in some ways reflects
the relationship between Christ and Mary. Here, as in Chaucer's
poem, the sentence is the essential unit, the structural repe-
titions not simply ornamental but functional, serving to enhance
and make clear the meaning of that sentence.

Here also the style makes it possible for the reader to
identify with the speaker, for the conversational manner seems
to invite the reader to join in the prayer. The poet who composed this prayer goes even further than Chaucer in inviting
the reader's participation. He describes the actual act of
praying--"To þe ich buþe & mine kneon ich beie...." The reader
is literally forced to visualize a familiar scene, and it is
from this scene that the emotional identification develops.
Chaucer depends more on the emotional identification, on the
common bond of those "confounded in errour," and allows the
reader to imagine the scene for himself. Nevertheless, the
over-all effect of the two poems is quite similar. It is to
break down, to the extent possible, the artificial barriers
that might arise between writer and audience when the mode of
communication assumes a poetic form; to narrow the distance
between the poet and his audience in order that they might share
in a common experience.

In Chaucer's poetry, as in the Middle English lyrics, the
syntactic unit rather than the verse line is the crucial structural unit. And in Chaucer's poetry too we find meter being
used to support and reinforce syntactic structure rather than
determining it. For Chaucer surely recognized, as did the
lyricists, that only by varying his metrical patterns and sub-
ordinating them to the syntactic patterns could he hope to capture the rhythms of conversation. As a result, even though
Chaucer's poetry tends to be more regular metrically than do
the lyrics, metrical variation is nevertheless a characteristic
and important feature of it.

H. S. Bennett remarks on Chaucer's handling of the decasyllabic line that "he seldom allows the metrical pattern to be
over-emphasized, and his ten syllables may melt to nine, or swell
to eleven or twelve at will to meet the exigencies of his
ideas" (87). Others have often pointed out the occurrence in
Chaucer's poetry of what have commonly been termed "headless"

lines and "broken-backed" lines. It is such lines that Courthope
calls "defective" and attributes to "sense being attended to
before sound." And it is such variations that Saintsbury attempts
to account for with reference to his "principle of equivalence."
But whether we consider such lines to be "defective" or "irregular," or whether we consider Chaucer's line as essentially a
syllabic one, as Bennett seems to do, or one determined by metrical feet, as does Saintsbury, one fact remains--Chaucer's poetry,
like the earlier English lyrics, is characterized by a high
degree of metrical variation, and this metrical variation, as in
the lyrics, contributes to its conversational quality.

More important still, and perhaps the strongest indication
that Chaucer did "escape from the line," is the tendency he
evinces towards run-on lines, frequently marked by enjambment,
and a number of possible foreign sources have been suggested as
models for Chaucer's use of this technique. Bennett and
Eleanor Prescott Hammond point to Boccaccio as a likely source;
Paull Baum, on the other hand, suggests French poetry as a
possible model. But while the technique is not uncommon in
medieval French or Italian poetry, we need not search for
Chaucer's models in these continental traditions; indeed, we need
search no further than the Middle English lyrics. For the use of
run-on lines and enjambment is common enough in these lyrics to
have provided a poet in Chaucer's day with sufficient models.
Moreover, in both Chaucer's poetry and in the lyrics, the use of
this technique is closely allied to and heavily dependent upon
the concomitant accommodation of meter to syntax. For in both
the subordination of meter to syntax contributes to the effect
produced by such constructions and works together with them to
enhance the conversational quality of the poetry.

In turning once again to the "ABC," we can observe Chaucer
employing techniques similar to those employed in the lyrics in
order to reproduce the essential qualities of a conversational
style. He too commonly builds up lines out of independent
syntactic units and varies the stress patterns to emphasize the
syntactic structure, which is, on the whole, quite natural; he
too employs strong internal pauses, reinforced by metrical
variation, to distribute emphasis throughout the line and capture the stop and go quality of conversation. The following
passage illustrates Chaucer at his best in this regard:

> Comfort is noon, but in yow, lady dere,
> For lo, my sinne and my confusioun,
> Which oughten not in they presence appere,
> Han take on me a grevous accioun
> Of verrey right and desperacioun;
> And, as by right, they mighten wel sustene
> That I were worthy my dampnacioun,
> Nere mercy of you, blisful heavene quene.

One could scan this passage as predominantly iambic pentameter with considerable substitution. But to impose such a reading seems to me to distort Chaucer's metrical intention here. For
there is little that resembles a pattern of stressed syllables
alternating regularly with unstressed syllables. If there is a
prosodic norm, it would seem to be a syllabic one, approximating
ten syllables per line. However, it would require that we do not
pronounce the final "e" of certain words ("dere," "appere,"
"sustene," "quene") and that we adopt the French pronunciation of
"ioun" as two syllables even to read the lines as regularly decasyllabic. But since we cannot be sure of what Chaucer's own linguistic habits might have been in these matters, it does not seem
to me valid, necessary, or even useful to impose such readings
simply to make the lines conform to a decasyllabic norm, especially
since Chaucer himself does not seem to have been overly concerned
with adhering rigidly to such a norm. For example, no matter how
we read lines like the following, we cannot arrive at ten syllables:

Glorious mayde and moder, which that never...

Who-so thee loveth he shal not love in veyn...

Continue on us thy pitous eyen clere...

That cometh of thee, thou Cristes moder dere...

Ne advocat noon that wol and dar so preye....

In any event, whatever effect the prosodic structure of the
passage may have clearly does not depend upon a regularity in the
number of syllables per line. And an effect there most definitely
is, a comfortable and smoothly flowing rhythm that, rather than
overwhelming us and controlling our reading of the passage,
emerges easily and naturally from the accentual patterns of the
words and the syntactic context in which they are placed.
The first line, for example, consists of three syntactic
units--a main clause, a mildly parenthetical prepositional phrase,
and an appositive noun phrase. The parenthetical quality of the
prepositional phrase requires that it be set off from the rest of
the line by mild pauses, and these syntactic pauses are reinforced
by metrical stress. The strong stress on the first syllable of
"comfort" together with the strong stress on "noon" encloses and
emphasizes the initial syntactic unit and helps separate it from
the prepositional phrase; the strong stress on the first syllable
of "lady" and the strong stress on "dere" enclose and emphasize
this syntactic unit and likewise separate it from the prepositional phrase. Thus, the pattern of metrical stresses enhances
the parenthetical quality of the prepositional phrase and perfectly complements the syntactic construction of the line.

Chaucer's ability to select words and place them in syntactic combinations that are perfectly natural and clear and, at the same time, to avoid any conflict between the syntax and the stress patterns that result from the accentual structure of the language itself is remarkable, as is his ability to maintain so delicate a balance over an extended number of lines. The next four lines of this passage form, for all practical intents and purposes, a single complex sentence, and the skill with which Chaucer handles these lines, both syntactically and metrically, is a sure sign that even in so early a poem as the "ABC" Chaucer was already well on the way to escaping from the verse line. The sentence begins with an exclamation, appropriately set off and emphasized by the strong stress on "lo." Next follows the compound subject, and the stresses fall on the semantically significant words "sinne" and "confusioun." The next line is a non-restrictive subordinate clause modifying the compound subject and is metrically interesting in its own right. We can consider the first part of the line as comprised of two iambic feet, with the stresses falling on the first syllable of "oughten" and on "not," emphasizing the negative construction. The second part of the line, a prepositional phrase together with the verb it modifies, consists of two anapestic feet. However, there is no abruptness in the shift from the iambic foot to the anapestic foot; unstressed syllable follows stressed syllable at the point of transition, and the line flows smoothly along.

This subordinate clause separates the compound subject of the sentence, with which the first line concludes, from its predicate. The next line, appropriately enough, begins with the main verbal construction, immediately resuming the major syntactic thread of the sentence. This line is completed by the direct object of the verb, and the whole sentence is concluded in the last line, with a prepositional phrase modifying the direct object. But what is particularly noteworthy about these last two lines is how effortlessly the one flows into the other. The prepositional phrase, "Of verrey right and desperacioun," though a complete syntactic unit, is not independent; that is, it cannot stand alone but is needed to complete the thought of the preceding line. However, the preceding line is an independent syntactic unit and can stand alone. And it is here that Chaucer uses his meter to best advantage. The metrical pattern of the line, "Han take on me a grevous accioun," is predominantly an iambic one, perfectly regular in the first four feet. But the pattern is broken in the last foot, which consists of either one or two unstressed syllables, depending upon the pronunciation of "accioun." Either way, the metrical expectation created by the iambic pattern of the line is interrupted just sufficiently to gently cajole the reader into moving on to the following line, where the iambic pattern is immediately resumed and the metrical expectation fulfilled. It is not simply that the meter here

combines with the syntactic structure to permit the reader to
move easily from one line to the next, but that, in a very
subtle way, it actually encourages him to do so, without his
ever being quite consciously aware of just what is happening.
The over-all simplicity of this passage, to which the perfectly natural and straight-forward syntactic and grammatical
constructions contribute so much, may make us overlook the
craftsmanship that has gone into it. But the use of meter in
support of syntactic structure, particularly to produce the
effect of run-on lines is a matter of conscious artistic technique and a characteristic feature of the style of the "ABC."
Throughout the poem we find such constructions. For example,

> Glorious mayde and moder, which that never
> Were bitter, neither in erthe nor in see....

Here the syntactic structure virtually demands that the lines be
read continuously, for Chaucer has split the non-restrictive
clause between them. And the meter cooperates with the syntax
to preclude a pause at the end of the first line. This first
line consists of an initial dactylic foot followed by two trochaic feet and an anapestic foot. The shift from the second
trochaic foot to the anapestic foot, resulting in an unstressed
syllable occurring in a position where we expect a stressed
syllable, corresponds precisely to the internal pause required
by the syntax, that is precisely the point at which the non-
restrictive clause is introduced, and so helps reinforce that
pause. But this metrical pattern leaves us with an extra unstressed syllable at the end of the line; thus, another syllable
seems necessary to complete the last foot, and this "missing"
syllable is provided in the next line by "Were." Furthermore,
the distribution of stresses throughout the first line, the
initial strong stress with which the line begins, the alliteration of "mayde" and "moder," reinforced again by the metrical
stress, the strong internal pause, all contribute to overcome
the inclination toward an end-line pause and combine with the
metrical pattern and syntactic structure to produce the run-on
line.
Similarly, in the following passages syntax and meter combine to create just the right rhythm so vital to the eminently
natural movement from line to line:

> We han non other melodye or glee
> Us to reioyse in our adversitee,
> Ne advocat noon that wo and dar so preye
> For us, and that for litel hyre as ye...

> Soth is, that God ne graunteth no pitee
> With-oute thee; for God, of his goodnesse,
> Foryiveth noon, but it lyke un-to thee.
>
> Now lady brighte, sith thou canst and wilt
> Ben to the seed of Adam merciable,
> So bring us to that palais that is bilt
> To penitents that ben to mercy able.

But it is where Chaucer uses syntax and meter to force the
reader's attention away from the end of one line and on to the
next and to hold the reader's attention at the beginning of that
next line, the technique I specifically refer to as enjambment,
that he achieves some of his most striking effects.

Most commonly, the effect of such constructions is to intensify and make vividly concrete some particular image that the
reader is forced to focus upon. We have already alluded to what
is perhaps the outstanding example of this technique in the
"ABC"; it occurs in the passage describing the episode of Moses
and the burning bush. The lines are well worth quoting again:

> Moises that saugh the bush with flaumes rede
> Brenninge, of which ther never a stikke brende....

Here the reader's attention is riveted to the "Brenninge," and
the image of the burning bush with its red flames is vividly and
indelibly impressed on his mind.

But this is by no means the only instance of enjambment in
the "ABC." On several occasions Chaucer uses the technique to
force the reader to focus on the cross and so to visualize the
scene on Calvary:

> Xristus, thy sone, that in this world alight
> Upon the cros to suffre his passioun....

Here it is the image of Christ on the cross that the reader is
forced to focus upon. In the following instance, it is again
the image of the cross that is the focal point and illuminates
the somewhat complex legal metaphor:

> And with his precious blood he wrot the bille
> Upon the cros, as general acquitaunce....

One more time Chaucer uses enjambment to focus on the cross, but
this time to force the reader to visualize Mary's suffering:

> Ladi, thi sorwe kan I not portreye
> Under the cros, ne his grevous penaunce....

Chaucer also uses enjambment to emphasize the extent of
Mary's influence as interventrix on behalf of mankind:

> From his ancille he made thee maistresse
> Of hevene and erthe, our bille up for to bede.

And again,

> He hath thee maked vicaire and maistresse
> Of al the world, and eek governesse
> Of hevene, and he represseth his Iustyse
> After thy wille, and therfore in witnesse
> He hath thee crouned in so ryal wyse.

In one final instance enjambment focuses attention on paradise,
the ultimate goal of the speaker and his audience, the goal that
depends so much upon the Virgin and so has inspired this poem:

> Virgine, that are so noble of apparaile,
> An ledest us in-to the hye tour
> Of Paradys, thou me wisse and counsaile....

That Chaucer did not necessarily have to depend upon French
or Italian poetry to provide him with models for the use of
enjambment is attested to by the fact that the technique is
already part of the poetic repertoire of the early Middle English lyricist. For example,

> þat þu neuer for þi sine
> vonien wid Satanasses cunne...(Brown, XIII, 19, 30-31)

> & his neb suo scene
> Wes bi-spit & al to-rend...(Brown, XIII, 24, 42-43)

> He bahit wid milde steuene
> þen suete feder of heuene
> fir-yewen hem heore mis-deden...(Brown, XIII, 24, 48-50)

> Wou þe present was ibroust
> In-to betlem þer iesus lay?(Brown, XIII, 26, 2-3)

> & þene riste wei hem taiste
> hammard in-to here owene londe.(Brown, XIII, 26, 71-72)

Nor is the technique confined to those lyrics composed in relatively short verse lines:

> & oppe þe suete rode wid stronge pine bocŏthe
> Adam & is ofspring, in helle he hem southe--
> (Brown, XIII, 28a, 22-23)

> Gooid, ye awariede, wid funden iwere,
> Into berninde fur; of blisse ye beoit scere...
> (Brown, XIII, 28a, 38-39)

> Þene latemeste dai, wenne we sulen farren
> vt of þisse worlde wid pine & wid care...
> (Brown, XIII, 29, 1-2)

Particularly striking is the following from "Cristes Milde Moder Seynte Marie,"

> Al englene þere & alle holie þing
> Siggeŏ & singeŏ þet tu ert liues þel-sprung....

Certainly here the use of enjambment, which rivets our attention to "siggeŏ & singeŏ" so that we are almost overwhelmed by the sound of the angelic choir, rivals that of Chaucer himself.

The effect produced by the use of enjambment both in the Middle English lyrics and in Chaucer's poetry contributes not only to the conversational quality of the poetry, but also, by forcing the reader to more vividly and concretely realize the experience that is being poetically re-created, contributes to the illusion of his participation in that experience. Because this effect in English poetry depends to a great extent upon the use of metrical stress to reinforce syntactic structure and so upon the accentual nature of the English language itself, it is quite unlike anything to be found in medieval French or Italian poetry. Consequently, Chaucer's use of enjambment suggests that in this regard, as in his use of anaphora and alliteration, he is again working with a technique as likely derived from his own native poetic tradition as from continental traditions.

Chaucer's "ABC," far from preserving the spirit and manner of the original and so inaugurating a new school of English poetry, belongs, in spirit and manner as well as in tone and style, firmly in the tradition established by the early Middle English lyricists. The outstanding characteristic of this tradition, its conversational manner, is deeply rooted in the older English poetry and is culminated in the poetry of Chaucer. It is, perhaps, the single most important stylistic feature that Chaucer derives from the native tradition he inherited. For in the conversational manner of this tradition Chaucer found the perfect idiom for his own poetry, poetry that has been unanimously praised for its conversational quality; for its rhythms, which seem to capture the natural rhythms of the spoken language; and for its liveliness of dialogue. To be sure, Chaucer, in exploiting this conversational manner, improved upon his English predecessors and refined their techniques. Nonetheless, in this respect, as in so many others, he was in no small measure indebted to these predecessors for providing models that paved the way for his own triumph in bringing this tradition to its greatest pitch of perfection.

1
See R.M. Wilson, The Lost Literature of Medieval England
(London: Methuen, 1952), for a more detailed discussion of this
subject.
2
Both Stuart Degginger ("The Earliest Middle English Lyrics
1150-1325") and Richard H. Osberg, "The Alliterative Lyric and
Thirteenth Century Devotional Prose," JEGP 76(1977): 40-54,
argue for the importance of the alliterative prose tradition in
preserving stylistic features of Old English poetry that subsequently were adopted by the Middle English lyricists.
3
Peter Dronke goes even a step further. In his Preface to
The Medieval Lyric (London: Hutchinson, 1968), he suggests that
all lyric poetry composed in western Europe, including England,
between 850 and 1300 comprises essentially a single tradition.
4
Patricia Kean, who argues that the Middle English romances
were a source for Chaucer's style, quite rightly points out the
difficulty of attempting to account for such an English quality
in these romances: "Most of the earlier Middle English romances
were directly translated or adapted from French, and their style
was, to a great extent, modelled on that of their sources. It
is a fascinating exercise to try to detect and describe the
peculiarly English tone of their versions; but in practice, it
is extraordinarily difficult to be precise in defining the
difference" (Love Vision and Debate, 6). Nevertheless, much of
the remainder of the present study is an attempt to undertake
just such an exercise with reference to the Middle English lyrics
and Chaucer's poetry, though here too we encounter the same
difficulty.
5
Similarly, R.H. Robbins maintains, "It should be noted that
Chaucer's hymn is a transliteration, a close copy, and not a
free adaptation" (Geoffroi Chaucier, "Poète Français," 111-112).
6
Passages from Deguileville's prayer, as well as the corresponding passages from the "ABC," are cited from W.W. Skeat, ed.,
The Complete Works of Geoffrey Chaucer, 2nd ed. (Oxford, 1952-
1961), 261-271.
7
She is also addressed once as "Dame" and once as "Noble
princesse."
8
The Oxford Chaucer (Oxford, 1894-1897), I, 453.
9
See also stanzas four and sixteen, which are similar in this
respect.

10

Anne Middleton has suggested that a new kind of public poetry makes its first appearance in the Ricardian period. This public poetry, according to Middleton, is characterized by a poetic voice that is "vernacular, practical, worldly, plain, public-spirited, and peace-loving--in a word, 'common,' rather than courtly or clerical, in its professed values and social allegiances." As regards the stance of this poetic voice, Middleton writes, "The 'I' of public poetry presents himself as, like his audience, a layman of good will, one worker among others, with a talent to be used for the common good." Thus, she concludes, "The 'voice' presented by these poets is offered not as a realization of an individual identity, but as the realization of the human condition." Middleton goes on to contrast Chaucer to both Gower and Langland, maintaining that neither his style nor his narrative stance is quite in this public tradition. "The Idea of Public Poetry in the Reign of Richard II," _Speculum_ 53(1978): 95-114.
I completely agree with Middleton that such a voice is characteristic of the poetry of the Ricardian period and that its qualities are precisely those she so well describes. However, such a public voice is a characteristic feature of the poetry of a utilitarian tradition, and, as the preceding analysis demonstrates, can be heard in Middle English poetry at least as early as the thirteenth century lyrics. Moreover, one result of the changes Chaucer makes in translating Deguileville's poem is the creation of just such a public voice. In my opinion, this poetic voice is not an innovation of Ricardian poetry but derives from the native poetic tradition, and the use of it not only by Gower and Langland but by Chaucer as well is indicative of their working in this tradition.

11

Clemen recognizes this quality and comments on it: "Concrete, tangible details are frequently woven in, their clear images appeal to the eye, the ear and the imagination, and they contribute to a transformation of Deguileville's abstract, intellectual and sometimes sophisticated mode of expression" (177).

12

Chaucer and the Making of English Poetry, Vol. II, _The Art of Narrative_ (London: Routledge & Kegan Paul, 1972), 194-195.

13

But see Richard H. Osberg, who maintains that there is a group of Middle English lyrics, including "Cristes Milde Mooder, Seynte Marie," where alliteration is a structural principle, and that the use of Old English techniques in these lyrics suggests some continuity between them and the older poetry ("The Alliterative Lyric").

14
Though Abel's remarks are here directed at certain of the
Harley lyrics, what she says is applicable to the Middle English
lyrics in general. Raymond Oliver, for example, comments, "The
most important figures of sound in the Middle English lyrics
are assonance and alliteration, especially the latter. Their
main purpose is to bind words together emphatically, not to
point out symbolic affinities between sound and sense..." (86).

15
Saintsbury, in fact, points to anaphora and the reduplication of synonyms as two significant features of Chaucer's poem
with little correspondence in the original.

16
A Lost Language and Other Essays on Chaucer (New York:
Sheed, 1951), 11-12.

17
Not only does Oliver emphasize the use of syntax and meter
to "reinforce the plain meaning of the words," he also emphasizes their function with respect to meeting the demands of
aural comprehension: "The prevailing syntactic rhythm is like-
wise conducive to a ready grasp of the sense; the structure of
the sentences, largely paratactic, lends itself to end-stopped
lines and quick aural comprehension" (99). While I do not
believe these lyrics are as heavily end-stopped as Oliver
suggests, I am in full agreement with his basic argument. And
I hope to show that the very tendency away from heavily end-
stopped lines in the lyrics contributes to "the impression of
someone speaking normally."

18
I use the term "enjambment" throughout this study to refer
to a particular form of run-on line. I consider any line where
the meter and syntax do not create a strong, natural pause at
the end of the line to be run-on. Enjambment occurs when the
meter, syntax and stress combine to actually prevent any pause
at the end of the line and so force the reader on to the next
line, where his attention is focused on the first part of that
line. For example, in the following passage the first two lines
are run-on, but only in the third line do we have enjambment:

        Oft Scyld Scefing   sceaþena þreatum,
     monegum mægþum   meodosetla ofteah,
     egsode earlas,   syððan ærest wearð
     feasceaft funden.... (Beowulf, 4-7)

In the first two lines the syntax requires the reader to move on
to the next line. But there is a somewhat artificial and not
very strong pause created at the end of each of these lines by
the meter. Hence, while the lines are run-on, there is no
enjambment. In the third line, however, the meter and syntax,

together with the strongly stressed first syllable of "feasceaft," combine to prevent any pause at the end of the line and so actually force the reader on to the next line and focus his attention on "feasceaft funden," an instance of what I refer to as enjambment.

19

Others who have pointed to the influence of Old English metrical practice on the versification techniques of the Middle English lyrics include: C.S. Lewis, "The Fifteenth Century Heroic Line," ES 29(1938): 28-41; Joseph Malof, "The Native Rhythms of English Meters," Texas Studies in Language and Literature 5(1964): 580-594; Louise Rarick, "Ten-Syllable Lines in English Poetry," Neuphilologische Mitteilungen 75(1974): 66-73; Richard Osberg, "The Alliterative Lyric and Thirteenth Century Devotional Prose"; Carolyn VanDyke Friedlander, "Early Middle English Accentual Verse," MP 76(1978): 219-230; Tauno F. Mustanoja, "Chaucer's Prosody," in Companion to Chaucer Studies, ed. Beryl Rowland, rev. ed. (Oxford: Oxford Univ. Press, 1979), 65-94.

20

The vexatious question regarding the pronunciation of final "-e," which has so long plagued the criticism of Chaucerian metrics, crops up for consideration here as well. In light of our ignorance as to what Chaucer's and the lyricists' linguistic habits might have been, it seems to me an act of futility to base our reading of their poetry on any a priori assumptions about the pronunciation of final "-e." Therefore, my discussion of metrics here and subsequently is based on no such assumptions, except for the generally accepted convention that final "-e's" elide before initial vowels and are sounded before initial consonants. However, even in this regard I have some reservations about too rigid an application. For example, while the practice of sounding the final "-e" of monosyllabic words before initial consonants seems generally valid, the sounding of the final "-e" of polysyllabic words before initial consonants seems much more doubtful. The line, "Muche wrchipe crist hou þe i-worut," is a case in point. Not only would it be extremely awkard for us to read the line sounding the "e" of wrchipe" or without sounding the "e" of "Muche," it would also be metrically ludicrous. Similarly, sounding the final "-e" of "þolede" in the line "þat þolede deit for monis loue" would give us a jingling, tongue-twisting effect totally inappropriate to the context, a context much better served by the stately, smooth-flowing, perfectly regular iambic rhythm that results when the final "-e" is not sounded.
In "Scanning the Prosodists: An Essay in Metacriticism," Chaucer Review 11(1976): 22-82, Alan Gaylord pleads eloquently for the development of a coherent and consistent methodology that will help us better understand the intricacies of Chaucer's

prosody. Certainly, no attempt to deal with Chaucer's prosody, nor for that matter with the prosody of Middle English lyrics or with Middle English poetry in general, can ignore the principles Gaylord propounds. While I am sympathetic to Gaylord's position, I also agree whole-heartedly with Ian Robinson that the test is in the reading, in what seems to sound right when we read these lines--that is, what seems to make the best sense metrically. Consequently, my own practice is to give final "-e" syllabic significance in the line when it seems natural and right to sound it; otherwise, not. Admittedly, this is a very idiosyncratic approach, perhaps overly simplistic and certainly highly subjective. But Gaylord notwithstanding, this seems to me the best we can do under the present circumstances.

For a representative sample of the range of views regarding pronunciation of final "-e," see Norman E. Eliason, The Language of Chaucer's Poetry, 30; M.L. Samuels, "Chaucerian Final -e," Notes and Queries, NS 19(1972): 445-448; Norman Davis, "Chaucer and Fourteenth-Century English," in Writers and Their Backgrounds: Geoffrey Chaucer, ed. Derek Brewer (Athens: Ohio Univ. Press, 1975), 69.

21

I prefer the term "relative stress" to "ictus." While it seems to me useful to distinguish between stresses that are relatively strong and those that are relatively weak, and we can do so with some measure of confidence, trying to distinguish precise degrees of stress as primary, secondary, tertiary, etc. seems to me largely a matter of guesswork. Nor does it seem to me particularly useful to do so, for the precise amount of stress given any syllable in performance would likely vary not only from one reader to another but also from one reading to another even by the same performer.

22

This line, like line 3, seems to make the best sense metrically if read as consisting of two dactylic feet with a concluding trochaic foot.

23

Friedlander comments on this feature of the Early Middle English lyrics: "The EME poets regarded the half-line as roughly equivalent to a spoken phrase or clause" (223).

24

A Reading of the Canterbury Tales (London: Cambridge Univ. Press, 1968), 38-39. On the basis of his study of the use of alliteration in the Middle English lyrics, Osberg makes a similar point about English readers in the Middle Ages: "Bookish Middle Englishmen read aloud to themselves" (47).

25
In Search of Chaucer (Toronto: Univ. of Toronto Press, 1960), 25-26. For discussions of the effects Chaucer's relationship to a listening audience might have had on his poetry, see Bertrand H. Bronson, "Chaucer's Art in Relation to His Audience," in Five Studies in Literature by Bertrand H. Bronson, J.R. Caldwell, J.M. Cline, Gordon McKenzie, and J.F. Ross (Berkeley: Univ. of California Press, 1940); Ruth Crosby, "Chaucer and the Custom of Oral Delivery"; Wolfgang Clemen, Chaucer's Early Poetry, especially Chapter I; Patricia Kean, Love Vision and Debate, Chapter 2, "Urbane Manner"; Percy G. Adams, "Chaucer's Assonance," JEGP 71(1972): 527-539; Norman E. Eliason, The Language of Chaucer's Poetry; Vivian Salmon, "The Representation of Colloquial Speech in The Canterbury Tales"; Paul Christianson, "Chaucer's Literacy," Chaucer Review 11(1976): 112-127; Bruce Rosenberg, "The Oral Performance of Chaucer's Poetry: Situation and Medium," Folklore Forum 13, no. 1(1980): 224-237; Beryl Rowland, "'Pronuntiatio' and Its Effect on Chaucer's Audience," Studies in the Age of Chaucer 4(1982): 33-51.

IV

CHAUCER, THE ENGLISH POET

Lyric Poetry

The simplicity, directness, clarity and concreteness characteristic of an expository mode; the natural syntactic and grammatical constructions; metrical variation; the use of run-on
lines and enjambment so vital to producing a conversational
manner--these stylistic features of so early a poem as the "ABC"
were to remain characteristic features of Chaucer's style
throughout his career and to a great extent account for the
distinctively English quality of his poetry. If we glance
briefly at some of Chaucer's other extant lyric poetry, regardless of how elaborate his utterance may become, regardless of
how rigid a rhyme scheme he adopts in emulating foreign models,
we always find present these same characteristic features of the
native tradition.

In the opening stanza of "The Complaint unto Pity," certainly one of Chaucer's earliest attempts at rhyme royal, despite the complex rhyme scheme and the predominantly iambic
meter, the conversational manner readily asserts itself as a
result of a syntactic structure that creates an easy and natural
movement from line to line and the use of strong internal pauses,
which not only contribute to this movement but help also to capture the stop and go quality of conversation:

> Pite, that I have sought so yore agoo,
> With herte soore, and ful of besy peyne,
> That in this world was never wight so woo
> Withoute deth,--and, yf I shal not feyne,
> My purpos was to Pite to compleyne
> Upon the crueltee and tirannye
> Of Love, that for my trouthe doth me dye.

So too in the following passage from "The Former Age":

> What sholde it han avayled to werreye?
> Ther lay no profit, ther was no richesse,
> But cursed was the tyme, I dare wel seye,
> That men first dide hir swety bysinesse
> To grobbe up metal, lurkinge in derknesse,
> And in the riveres first gemmes soghte.
> Allas! than sprong up al the cursednesse
> Of coveytyse, that first our sorwe broghte!

Here again, the half-line patterning and the resulting strong
internal pauses, together with metrical variation, are played
off against the iambic pentameter norm to produce the rhythms
of a conversational style. Characteristic also is Chaucer's
striving for visual concreteness in his graphic description of
the "swety bysinesse" and the metal "lurkinge in derknesse."
    But perhaps nowhere in his short poems does Chaucer exploit
the conversational style to better advantage than in his "Envoy
to Bukton":

> My maister Bukton, Whan of Crist our kyng
> Was axed what is trouthe or sothfastnesse,
> He nat a word answerde to that axing,
> As who saith, 'No man is al trewe,' I gesse.
> And therfore, though I highte to expresse
> The sorwe and wo that is in mariage,
> I dar not writen of it no wikkednesse,
> Lest I myself falle eft in swich dotage.
>
> I wol nat seyn how that yt is the cheyne
> Of Sathanas, on which he gnaweth evere;
> But I dar seyn, were he out of his peyne,
> As by his wille he wolde be bounde nevere.
> But thilke doted fool that eft hath levere
> Ycheyned be than out of prison crepe,
> God lete him never fro his wo dissevere,
> Ne no man him bewayle, though he wepe!
>
> But yet, lest thow do worse, take a wyf;
> Bet ys to wedde than brenne in worse wise.
> But thow shal have sorwe on thy flessh, thy lyf,
> And ben thy wives thral, as seyn these wise;
> And yf that hooly writ may nat suffyse,
> Experience shal the teche, so may happe,
> That the were lever to be take in Frise
> Than eft to falle of weddynge in the trappe.

Envoy

> This lytel writ, proverbes, or figure
> I sende yow, take kepe of yt, I rede;
> Unwys is he that kan no wele endure.
> If thow be siker, put the nat in drede.
> The Wyf of Bathe I pray yow that ye rede
> Of this matere that we have on honde.
> God graunte yow your lyf frely to lede
> In fredam; for ful hard is to be bonde.

This poem is composed in the expository mode characteristic of
the Middle English lyrics. Though witty and amusing, it is
also simple, direct and perfectly clear. Chaucer, the teacher,
is addressing Bukton, the pupil, and we are made to feel as
though we are privy to the scene, as though we are overhearing
the tongue-in-cheek advice Chaucer is offering to his friend.
To create this effect, Chaucer masterfully employs precisely
those techniques most likely derived from the Middle English
lyric tradition.

We are immediately drawn into the presence of this scene
by Chaucer's direct address to Bukton in the opening line. The
characteristically familiar tone Chaucer adopts heightens the
illusion, an illusion reinforced and maintained throughout the
poem by its consistently conversational manner. The diction of
the poem is simple throughout; the syntax, eminently natural;
the grammatical constructions, uncomplicated and straight-
forward. The meter, predominantly iambic pentameter, supports
the syntactic structure and combines with it to produce within
the verse lines a perfectly natural rhythm, one which never
violates the natural accentual patterns of the language itself,
and contributes to the smooth flow from line to line.

In the first line, the internal pause following "Bukton"
splits the third iambic foot, breaking up the otherwise regular
iambic rhythm, and weakens the end-line pause, thereby strength-
ening the run-on effect created by the syntax. In the fourth
line, metrical variation reinforces the internal pauses required
by the grammatical construction:

> As who saith, 'No man is al trewe,' I gesse.

Here the trochaic substitution in the second foot coincides with
the initial pause, and the anapestic substitution in the fourth
foot coincides with the second pause; together these help set
off the direct quotation, which is grammatically set off from
the rest of the line.

Chaucer also makes effective use of enjambment:

> I wol nat seyn how that yt is the cheyne
> Of Sathanas, on which he gnaweth ever....

The reader's attention is focused, by the enjambment, on Satan,
and the image is made visually concrete in the remainder of the
line where the strongest metrical stress falls on the verb
"gnaweth." In the following lines, Chaucer uses metrical variation to enhance the effect of the enjambment:

> But thilke doted fool that eft hath levere
> Ycheyned be than out of prison crepe....

The first line is perfectly regular iambic pentameter, except for the extra unstressed syllable at the end; thus, the reader's expectation of an iambic foot causes him to move on the next line, where the iambic pattern is resumed. Moreover, the strongest stress in this line falls on the second syllable of "Ycheyned," its root, and intensifies the image even more. In the last stanza, we have another instance of this technique:

> God graunte yow your lyf frely to lede
> In fredam; for ful hard is to be bonde.

Metrically, the first line here is highly irregular; it is an example of what has been referred to as a "headless" line, a line that seems to require an initial unstressed syllable that has been omitted. After the initial strong stress on "God," the remainder of the line consists of four feet--trochaic alternating with iambic. Thus, where the metrical expectation that has been created is of a ten-syllable line with five stressed syllables, we have only a nine syllable line with five stressed syllables. Nor is the solution likely to be the sounding of the final "e" of "lede," since there seems to be no reason for sounding the final "e" of any of the words rhyming with "lede" in preceding lines--to do so would result in an extra-metrical final syllable that has no function in lines that otherwise read very smoothly and naturally as regular iambic pentameter:

> I sende yow, take kepe of yt, I rede...

> If thow be siker, put the nat in drede...

> The Wyf of Bathe I pray yow that ye rede....

The metrical irregularity of the line, "God graunte yow your lyf frely to lede," seems, then, better explained as an attempt to reinforce metrically the run-on effect created by the syntax. The effect of the "missing" syllable is to urge the reader on to the next line, where the prepositional phrase, "In fredam," modifying the preceding infinitive, "to lede," completes the syntactic unit. Contributing additionally are the slight but noticeable internal pauses created by the occurrence of two strongly stressed syllables in succession, first at the beginning of the line ("God graunte") and again where an iambic foot is followed by a trochaic foot ("your lyf frely"). The strong metrical emphasis on the beginning of the line and the internal pause at the mid-point combine to diminish the tendency toward an end-line pause and allow for the smooth flow of this line into the next. Chaucer's tendency to compose in syntactic units and to use his meter to support syntactic structure is clearly evident here; for the total effect of this metrical structure is to reinforce the enjambment created by the syntax.

It is not only in these short lyric poems, but also in
many of the lyric passages one finds throughout his narrative
poetry, even those most obviously written in the "high style,"
that Chaucer employs such techniques and exploits this conversational manner. In addition to the "ABC," Chaucer composed
prayers to the Virgin for two specific occasions in The Canterbury Tales--the prologue to the Prioress's tale and the prologue
to the Second Nun's tale. While it was common practice during
the Middle Ages to preface Miracles of the Virgin and Saints'
Legends with such a prayer, Chaucer's prayers here, like the
"ABC," have a distinctively English ring to them and have in
common with his "ABC" many of the stylistic features of the
native tradition.

One such feature of the Prioress's prayer is its simplicity
and directness. The qualities of the Virgin, for example, are
enumerated without elaboration:

> Lady, thy bountee, thy magnificence,
> Thy vertu, and thy grete humylitee,
> Ther may no tonge expresse in no science....

When reference is made to the mother-maiden paradox, it is done
matter-of-factly, with no sense of wonderment or awe: "Which
that the bar, and is a mayde alway." Another feature is the
frequent occurrence of alliteration, ofttimes coinciding with
metrical stress to heighten the effect:

> Next hire Sone, and soules boote.

> O mooder Mayde! o mayde Mooder free!

The technique is most effectively used when Chaucer once again
evokes the image of the burning bush, enhancing the visual
concreteness by combining alliteration, metrical stress and
metrical variation: "O bussh unbrent, brennynge in Moyses
sighte...."

Above all, however, is the characteristic conversational
manner of the prayer. Its tone, like that of the "ABC," is a
blend of comfortable familiarity and humble respect. Similar
terms of address are employed--"mooder," "mayde," "Lady," blisful Queene"--and though there is not as free a mixture of
singular and plural forms of the second person pronoun as in the
"ABC," the more formal plural predominating, there is a switch
to the familiar singular in the concluding couplet:

> Right so fare I, and therfore I yow preye,
> Gydeth my song that I shal of you seye.

The Prioress's utterance too is marked by emotional intensity
and a sense of urgency underscored by her use of exclamatory

"O's"--"O mooder," "O mayde," "O bussh," "O blisful Queene"--
and she too shifts easily between first person singular and
plural to include her audience in her prayer:

> Thou goost biforn of thy benyngnytee,
> And getest us the lyght, of thy preyere,
> To gyden us unto thy Sone so deere.

And here once again we can observe Chaucer's composing in syntactic units, creating strong internal pauses and run-on lines,
and using metrical variation in support of syntactic structures
to produce a conversational rhythm.

The metrical norm of the prayer is iambic pentameter, and
only one of its lines cannot be read as consisting of ten
syllables: "To telle a storie I wol do my labour...." But
Chaucer varies the meter, most commonly by the device of beginning a line wih strong metrical stress: "Lady, thy bountee,
thy magnificence...." He also employs trochaic substitution
internally in a verse line, where the resulting spondaic effect
reinforces the syntactic pause: "O bussh unbrent, brennynge in
Moyses sighte...." Even in lines that can be scanned as perfectly regular iambic pentameter, Chaucer creates a variation
in tempo by placing semantically insignificant words or syllables in strong stress positions. The result is lines in
which we sometimes hear only four strong beats--"Parfourned is,
for on the brest soukynge"--and occasionally, even only three--
"That ravyshedest doun fro the Deitee."

The verse form Chaucer employs for the Prioress's prayer
is rhyme royal, a feature of which is that the last four lines
of each stanza, rhyming bbcc, form a quatrain composed of two
couplets. Particularly noteworthy is the fact that these
quatrains tend to exhibit a greater degree of metrical variation
than do the first three lines. Stanza four affords a good example:

> For somtyme, Lady, er men praye to thee,
> Thou goost biforn of thy benyngnytee,
> And getest us the lyght, of thy preyere,
> To gyden us unto thy Sone so deere.

In the first line, the occurrence of "er" in a strong stress
position and the semantically more significant "men" in a weak
stress position interrupts the iambic rhythm and results not
only in an anapestic movement in the third foot but also in a
spondaic effect emphasizing the phrase "men praye." The second
line, though perfectly regular iambic pentameter, has only three
semantically significant stresses. The third and fourth lines
have only four significant stresses each. But especially interesting here is the trochaic substitution in the last foot of
the third line, resulting in an unstressed rather than a stressed

final syllable, the effect of which is to weaken the rhyme
between "preyere" and "deere."

The last line of stanza three--"Help me to telle it in thy
reverence!"--illustrates the use of trochaic substitution in
the first foot to initiate a line with strong metrical stress,
as do each of the lines in the concluding couplet of stanza
five:

> Right so fare I, and therfore I yow preye,
> Gydeth my song that I shal of yow seye."

And the resumption of the iambic rhythm in the third foot of
the first line nicely reinforces the mid-line syntactic pause.

In such passages Chaucer seems consciously striving to
"open" the couplets, to diminish the tendency created by the
rhyme scheme toward a strong end-line pause. It is not surprising, then, that run-on lines occur most frequently in these
quatrains, nor that Chaucer's most effective use of these lines
results from similar metrical techniques to facilitate the movement from one line to the next created by the syntax. The concluding couplet of the second stanza includes a run-on line in
which the word "and" occupies the strong stress position of
the fourth foot. Not only does this result in a line with only
four significant stresses, but it also creates an anapestic
rhythm in the final foot, thus hurrying the reader along to the
next line:

> For she hirself is honour and the roote
> Of bountee, next hir Sone, and soules boote.

The quatrain of the first stanza includes two run-on lines:

> Parfourned is by men of dignitee,
> But by the mouth of children thy bountee
> Parfourned is, for on the brest soukynge
> Somtyme shewen they thyn heriynge.

The first run-on line contains only three significant stresses,
and the trochaic substitution in the last foot here results in
an unstressed syllable carrying primary responsibility for
producing the rhyme between the pair "dignitee"/"bountee." The
second contains four significant stresses, with the semantically
insignificant "on" occupying the strong stress position in the
third foot.

While no direct source has been identified for the Prioress's
prayer as a whole, several of its lines parallel passages from
the Office of the Blessed Virgin; others echo lines from
St. Bernard's prayer to the Virgin, with which Canto XXXIII of
the Paradiso opens, and this prayer is the direct source for
stanzas 2-4 of the "Invocacio ad Mariam" found in the prologue

to the Second Nun's tale. Close analysis of these three stanzas reveals precisely the same stylistic features that characterize the Prioress's prayer: from the very first line, where Chaucer replaces Dante's "Vergine Madre" with the familiar alliterative phrase "Thow Mayde and Mooder," and expands the address by providing two conventional epithets as parallel variations--"Thow welle of mercy, synful soules cure"--to the very last line, where metrical stress hammers home the bond created by the alliteration--"The Creatour of every creature."

The most dramatic changes Chaucer makes in adapting this passage from Dante are in the direction of simplifying and making more clear and precise Dante's often elliptical and complex images. For example, in the following lines Dante refers to the Incarnation:

> Tu se' colei che l' umana natura
> Nobilitasti sì, che il suo Fattore
> Non disdegnò di farsi sua fattura.

(You are she who human nature made so noble that the Maker himself disdained not to become what he had made.)

Chaucer takes five lines to render these three:

> In whom that God for bountee chees to wone,
> Thow humble, and heigh over every creature,
> Thow nobledest so forforth oure nature,
> That no desdeyn the Makere hadde of kynde
> His Sone in blood and flessh to clothe and wynde.

Chaucer's version is considerably more direct and concrete. Where Dante begins with reference to Mary's ennobling of "human" nature, which somehow makes possible the Incarnation, the Incarnation itself expressed only in the most abstract of terms, Chaucer begins by identifying Mary as God's choice for a dwelling place, proceeds to describe her virtue, which ennobled "our" nature, and then describes in explicit terms the Incarnation itself--the taking on of "blood" and "flesh." Dante describes the qualities of the Virgin in the two preceding lines:

> Umile ed alta più che creatura,
> Termine fisso d' eterno consiglio....

(Humble and heigh more than any creature; final goal of eternal counsel.)

Chaucer does not translate the vague second line at all, and he transposes the first line so that it follows the opening reference to God's choice of Mary and clearly explains the appropriateness of that choice. Dante concludes this passage with a complex metaphor:

> Nel ventre tuo si raccese l' amore,
>> Per lo cui caldo nell' eterna pace
>> Così è germinato questo fiore.

(In your womb love was kindled, through whose warmth in the
eternal peace this flower was made so to blossom.)

Chaucer's translation is again more simple and more clear, elimi-
nating the fire and flower metaphor altogether:

> Withinne the cloistre blisful of thy sydis
> Took mannes shap the eterneel love and pees....

Like the Prioress's prayer, the Second Nun's prayer is composed in rhyme royal stanzas. So too is the well-known "Canticus
Troili." This lyric outburst, which Troilus, having recently
been smitten by love, gives voice to, is a close translation of
Petrarch's Sonnet 132, "S'amor non e, che dunque e quel ch' io
sento?" The tone, the feeling, and in many respects the style of
the Chaucerian passage closely resembles that of the Petrarchan
sonnet, for both poets are attempting to poetically re-create for
their audiences the diverse and ofttimes contrary effects of love.
Nevertheless, not only does Chaucer's rendition of this passage
differ in certain technical respects from the original, it
differs also in its essential quality, Chaucer's rendition displaying an unmistakeable Englishness. The text of Petrarch's
sonnet follows:

> S'amor non è, che dunque è quel ch' io sento?
> ma s'egli è amor, per Dio, che cosa e quale?
> se bona, ond' è l'effetto aspro mortale?
> se ria, ond' è sì dolce ogni tormento?
>
> S' a mia voglia ardo, ond' è 'l pianto e lamento?
> s' a mal mio grado, il lamentar che vale?
> O viva morte, o dilettoso male,
> come puoi tanto in me, s' io nol consento?
>
> E s' io 'l consento, a gran torto mi doglio.
> Fra sì contrari venti in frale barca
> mi trovo in alto mar senza governo,
>
> sì lieve di saver, d'error sì carca,
> ch'i' modesmo non so quel ch' io mi voglio,
> e tremo a mezza state, ardendo il verno.[1]

(If it is not love, what then is it that I feel? But if it is
love, by God, what kind of thing is it? If good, from where
comes this bitter mortal feeling? If bad, why so sweet each
torment? If of my own accord I burn, why the weeping and lamenting? If it is forced on me, how can lamenting help? O living

death, O delightful anguish, how can you have such power over me unless I consent? And if I do consent, I have no cause to complain of my suffering. Amid such contrary winds in a frail bark I find myself on the high sea without a rudder, so light in knowledge, with error so laden, that I do not even know what I myself want. And I shiver in the middle of summer, burn in winter.)

The poem consists of fourteen lines, dividing into an octet and a sestet, rhyming abbaabbacdedce. The octet consists of a series of seven questions, the first six of which correspond to the first six verse lines. The last two lines make up the final question, more or less rhetorical, which is responded to in the sestet. All the lines, particularly in the octet, are heavily end-stopped, and the rhyme scheme contributes to the effect of drawing the reader inexorably toward the end of the line, not only because of the limited rhyming sounds, the "c" and "e" rhymes repeating the long "o" sound of the "a" rhymes and hardly distinguishable from them, but even more because of Petrarch's extensive use of feminine rhymes, which make the effect of the rhyme pattern all the more forceful. Even Petrarch's use of carefully balanced phrases and strong internal pauses does not overcome this effect of the rhyme and syntax.

Chaucer, in translating this sonnet, also changes its structure. He converts it into rhyme royal, first and most obviously because he incorporates it into a narrative poem written in rhyme royal, though there is no particular reason why, if he had so chosen, he could not have found some way to keep the original structure intact. But such a structure, depending so heavily on only two rhymes, is, as Chaucer must have realized and other English poets have always realized, virtually impossible in English. Not only is rhyme itself more difficult, and repeated rhyme more artificial, in English than in romance languages but because English is an analytical language, it can make only very limited use of inflectional endings for the purpose of rhyme. More important still, such a structure in English poetry would be antithetical to a conversational manner. Thus, even though Chaucer attempts a close translation of Petrarch's sonnet and strives consciously to capture its tone and feeling, and even though Chaucer's utterance is as elegant and in many ways as elaborate as Petrarch's, Chaucer makes certain significant changes. Although two stanzas of rhyme royal would be exactly equivalent to Petrarch's fourteen line sonnet, Chaucer expands these fourteen lines to twenty-one. Of the sonnet's fourteen lines, exactly half are complete, independent syntactic units terminally punctuated, the entire sonnet consisting of nine grammatical sentences—seven clustered in the octet and two forming the sestet. Of Chaucer's twenty-one lines, only one-third are complete, independent syntactic units terminally punctuated, the three stanzas consisting of eleven grammatical sentences—four each in the first two stanzas and three in the

third. Chaucer also employs a greater variety of rhymes than
does Petrarch and uses only masculine rhymes. Altogether, the
effect is to diminish considerably the emphasis on the end of
the line and the tendency toward continual, strong end-line stops
characteristic of Petrarch's sonnet. One result of Chaucer's
transformation is to imbue Troilus' "song" with a rhythm and
movement consistent with the conversational quality that is so
marked a feature of the narrative verse within which this lyric
interlude is set and quite different from the sonorous, melodic
quality of the Petrarchan sonnet:

> If no love is, O God, what fele I so?
> And if love is, what thing and which is he?
> If love be good, from whennes cometh my woo?
> If it be wikke, a wonder thynketh me,
> When every torment and adversite
> That cometh of hym, may to me savory thinke,
> For ay thurst I, the more that ich it drynke.
>
> And if that at myn owen lust I brenne,
> From whennes cometh my waillynge and my pleynte?
> If harm agree me, whereto pleyne I thenne?
> I noot, ne whi unwery that I feynte.
> O quike deth, O suete harm so queynte,
> How may of the in me swich quantite,
> But if that I consente that it be?
>
> And if that I consente, I wrongfully
> Compleyne, iwis. Thus possed to and fro,
> Al sterelees withinne a boot am I
> Amydde the see, bitwixen wyndes two,
> That in contrarie stonden evere mo.
> Allas! what is this wondre maladie?
> For hete of cold, for cold of hete, I dye.

The greater length of Chaucer's version creates a more
leisurely pace, and results, at least in part, from his amplification of certain parts to achieve greater clarity and concreteness. The first two lines of the Chaucerian passage are
virtually identical to those of the original. But in the third
and fourth lines, Chaucer expands Petrarch's elliptical constructions, "se bona" and "se ria," to full clauses—"If love be
good" and "If it be wikke." While this is but a minor change,
it reflects Chaucer's tendency throughout his translation of
the sonnet both to be more explicit and to expand Petrarch's
highly compressed style and adopt a style more conversationally
natural. But at this point Chaucer deviates much further from
the original. Petrarch is content simply to raise another question: "se ria, ond' è sì dolce ogni tormento?" This question,
like the three that precede it, is intended to express the

paradoxical effects of love, and Petrarch sees no need to elaborate upon the paradox. Not so Chaucer, who raises the same question but then elaborates considerably upon it:

> If it be wikke, a wonder thynketh me,
> When every torment and adversite
> That cometh of hym, may to me savory thinke,
> For ay thurst I, the more that ich it drynke.

Chaucer transforms Petrarch's oxymoron into a complex sentence
that elucidates the meaning. As if to drive the point home,
Chaucer adds a metaphoric sentence that, though itself paradoxical, nevertheless translates the paradox into more concrete
and experiential terms. The lover is like a man who is perpetu-
ally thirsty. For such a man each drink is "savory" as it
momentarily quenches his thirst. But after each drink, his
thirst is renewed, and it seems as though the more he drinks,
the more he thirsts. It is a constant cycle of discomfort
followed by gratification, of pain followed by pleasure, until
the two become virtually indistinct. So too the lover; the more
he loves, the more he suffers, but the more he suffers, the more
his love seems to soothe him and so seems pleasing to him. For
the lover too the cycle of pain followed by delight followed by
pain is continual.

Also of particular interest here is Chaucer's use of run-on
constructions and of metrical variation to enhance their effect.
For example,

> When every torment and adversite
> That cometh of hym, may to me savory thinke....

The metrical norm of the "Canticus Troili" is iambic pentameter,
and the first of these lines can be scanned as a perfectly regular one. However, this would require a strong stress on "and,"
which is not only semantically unjustifiable but which seems to
violate the natural stress pattern of the line as we read it.
The stress on "and" is, in fact, hardly any stronger than the
stress on the last syllable of "torment" or the first syllable of
"adversite," and in reading the line, we are hardly aware of it.
Rather, there is a crescendoing effect as the coordinate conjunction brings together the two most semantically significant words
in the line--"torment" and "adversite." Thus, the reader's
expectation of five _strong_ beats per line built up in the four
preceding lines is just sufficiently thwarted to encourage him
on to the next line as meter and syntax combine to produce the
run-on effect. This next line begins with an iambic foot, resuming the metrical pattern to which the reader has become
accustomed, and satisfying his metrical expectation. But here
again Chaucer varies his meter to support the syntax. The
second foot is anapestic, and this foot is followed in turn by

a trochaic foot, an iambic foot, and a final anapestic foot.
Significantly, the shift from the anapestic second foot to the
trochaic third foot, resulting in a spondaic effect, coincides
with and reinforces the strong internal pause between "him" and
"may" required by the syntax.

Chaucer uses such run-on constructions to good effect on
several occasions, particularly in the last stanza:

> And if that I consente, I wrongfully
> Compleyne, iwis. Thus possed to and fro,
> Al sterelees withinne a boot am I
> Amydde the see, bitwixen wyndes two,
> That in contrarie stonden evere mo.

The metrical pattern of the first line hinges upon whether or
not we pronounce the final "e" of "consente." If we do not
pronounce this final "e," the line is perfectly regular iambic
pentameter. But that Chaucer himself intended it to be pronounced seems likely from his use of the same word in the preceding line--"But if that I consente that it be?" Here, the
pronunciation of the "e" is necessary to the iambic rhythm and
results in a perfectly regular iambic pentameter line. That
Chaucer so intended it is supported by the fact that the entire
stanza that concludes with this line, except for a slight variation in the second line, is perfectly regular iambic pentameter.
Of course it is possible that Chaucer intended the first "e" to
be pronounced and the second one not, but such an explanation
seems unnecessary to account for the metrics of the line in
question. It seems on the whole better to consider this line
as another example of Chaucer's use of metrical variation than
to try to force it into the iambic pentameter mold by arbi-
trarily not pronouncing the "e." Thus, I would read the line
as consisting of five iambic feet with a strong caesura separating the first three from the last two. The final syllable of
"consente," seemingly extra-metrical in this pattern, nonetheless
has a significant effect on the rhythm. The phrase "I wrongfully" can, in isolation, be scanned as two perfectly regular
iambs; however, the preceding extra-metrical "e" results in a
greater stress on "I" than it would otherwise receive. The
effect is that of a "broken-backed" line, with two relatively
strong stresses following the caesura. As a result, five relatively strong stresses occur in the line before the final
syllable of "wrongfully," and the relatively strong stress this
final syllable would usually receive is significantly diminished.
The total effect of the extra syllable and of this diminished
stress is to cause a spilling over of the line into the next,
where the word "Compleyne" completes the syntactic unit. Moreover, the resumption of the iambic pattern, resulting in a
strong stress only after three relatively weak stresses, nicely

supports the syntactic structure by reinforcing the pause required after "Compleyne" and underscoring the parenthetical
quality of "iwis."

The third line too flows smoothly and naturally into the
fourth. For although both lines are perfectly regular iambic
pentameter, there is a definite run-on effect created by the
syntax, the fourth line beginning with the prepositional phrase
"Amydde the see," which modifies the last word of the preceding
line, the pronoun "I."

Noteworthy also here is Chaucer's expansion of Petrarch's
highly compressed image as well as the change Chaucer makes in
the manner in which the significance of the image is summed up.
As elsewhere, Chaucer's changes seem intended to simplify the
passage and make it more concrete. Where Petrarch begins by
stating that amid contrary winds in a frail bark he finds himself, in a high sea without means of control, Chaucer begins by
immediately locating Troilus in a "stereless" boat that is amid
the sea. The syntax of Petrarch's expression is ambiguous, no
doubt intentionally so. "Mi trovo" can refer either to "Fra sì
contrari venti in frale barca" or to "in alto mar senza governo"
and indeed refers to both. For he finds himself in a boat on
the storm-tossed sea. Chaucer's syntax is simpler and more
straight-forward. Troilus is within the boat amid the sea,
between two winds that are ever in opposition--"that in con-
trarie stonden evere mo." The syntactic relationship, and so
the image itself, is perfectly clear. He is within the boat,
which is tossed about by these contrary winds and so is himself
tossed about, unlike Petrarch, who seems tossed about by the
winds themselves.

Petrarch continues by referring to himself as laden with
error and lacking the knowledge to rectify the situation, and
this leads him to another metaphor that is somewhat confusing in
that it evolves directly from the metaphor of the storm-tossed
lover but seems to bear no readily apparent relationship to it:

> sì lieve di saver, d'error sì carca,
> ch'i' medesmo non so quel ch' io mi voglio,
> e tremo a mezza state, ardendo il verno.

Chaucer, on the other hand, omits the vague reference to being
laden with error and not having the necessary knowledge of where
to turn. Instead, he lets the image of the storm-tossed lover
stand by itself, for it has served its purpose and needs no
further elaboration. Thus, he concludes with a second image,
that of love's "wondre maladie," which in no way conflicts with
or confuses the preceding one and which serves to just rightly
introduce the oxymoronic last line, "For hete of cold, for cold
of hete, I dye." Clearly, the feverish condition described in
this last line is that of an illness, love's "wondre maladie."
Just as the preceding image stands by itself, so too this final
metaphor stands by itself and is perfectly clear, more concrete

and less ambiguous than Petrarch's shivering in summer and burning in winter.

Patricia Thomson comments on Chaucer's rendition of this
passage, "Petrarch, no less than Troilus, is tossed to and fro
by conflicting winds of feeling; but he gives reasons for this
emotional floundering...The Petrarchan image is a means of
analyzing why, as well as describing what, the lover suffers.
The Chaucerian image is merely descriptive and suggestive."[2]
Thomson goes on to suggest that Chaucer's seafaring metaphor is
"light in weight" in comparison with Petrarch's, and though she
is right about the difference between Petrarch's metaphor and
Chaucer's, she seems to miss the reason for this difference.
Petrarch's use of the metaphor to "analyze" what the lover
suffers is, as we have previously seen, firmly in the tradition
of continental love poetry. Chaucer's use of a more simple,
clear, and concrete image that stands by itself is, on the other
hand, in the poetic tradition established by the early English
lyricists.

In conclusion, then, despite the similarities between the
"Canticus Troili" and Petrarch's sonnet, Chaucer's tendency
towards greater simplicity, clarity, and concreteness, his use
of meter to support syntactic structure, his use of run-on lines
and metrical variation to make his poem more conversationally
natural, are indications that Chaucer has characteristically
transformed rather than simply translated his source in order
to make it compatible with his own native poetic tradition.[3]

Narrative Poetry

E. K. Chambers, remarking upon Chaucer's influence on the
English poetry of the fifteenth century, writes, "What Chaucer
really did was to divert the fifteenth century from lyric to
narrative..." ("Some Aspects of Medieval Lyric," 280). Certainly, Chaucer's reputation does not rest primarily upon his
lyric poetry but rather upon his achievements in narrative
poetry.

In turning to narrative poetry, Chaucer was confronted by
numerous new and difficult problems, problems concerning structure and organization and characterization. That Chaucer
successfully solved these problems is readily attested to by
such works as Troilus and Criseyde and The Canterbury Tales,
works which far surpass anything appearing in English poetry
before or during, and for a long time after, Chaucer's day. But
the style of Chaucer's narrative poetry, at the most rudimentary
level, is essentially the same, though increasingly more polished
and refined, as the style of the lyrics we have been discussing,
a style rooted in the native English poetic tradition. For it
is a conversational style, eminently suited to a teller of tales,
and one that Chaucer cultivates from his earliest work, both
lyric and narrative, to his final masterpiece.

In his discussion of the "Prologue" to The Legend of Good
Women, H. S. Bennett describes the essential qualities of this
style:

> In the Prologue...Chaucer is the complete master:
> the verse moves without effort from line to line,
> carrying on the ideas without any feeling of con-
> straint, or of the exigencies of rhyme or verse-
> ending impeding its progress. And at the same
> time it is all so good-mannered: there is no
> apparent striving for effect--the limpid flow of
> the lines serves just sufficiently to clothe but
> not to obscure the thought.   (65)

Bennett has gotten here to the core of Chaucer's style at its
very best. When we read the Prologue to The Legend of Good
Women, it seems almost as though we are in the presence of the
narrator, listening to him recount his dream for us. To achieve
this effect, Chaucer employs many of the same techniques he
employs in his lyric poems.

From the very beginning of the Prologue[4] Chaucer endeavors
to establish a casual and comfortable relationship with his
audience, an audience he has constantly before him and one with
whom he seems to be conversing. The passage is marked by
authorial interjections that are clearly directed at this audience:

> A thousand tymes have I herd men telle
> That ther ys joy in hevene and peyne in helle,
> And I acorde wel that it ys so;
> But, natheles, yet wot I wel also
> That ther nis noon dwellyng in this contree,
> That eyther hath in hevene or helle ybe,
> Ne may of hit noon other weyes witen,
> But as he hath herd seyd, or founde it writen;
> For by assay ther may no man it preve.
> But God forbede but men shulde leve
> Wel more thing then men han seen with ye!(1-11)

The effect of such authorial interjections as, "And I acorde wel
that it ys so," "Yet wot I wel also," together with such idiomatic expressions as, "A thousand tymes have I herd men telle,"
and "But God forbede," is to diminish the distance between the
audience and the speaker, and so between the audience and the
poetic re-creation of the experience that he is about to undertake. Though this experience is a most private and individual
one, and one that turns out to be highly unusual, Chaucer, in
the opening lines, carefully prepares the way for the audience's
ready acceptance of it. The hyperbolic opening line, "A thousand tymes have I herd men telle," emphasizes that it is commonplace for people to be aware of and to believe in things not
always demonstrable within their own experiential frame of
reference. And just as they accept that there is joy in heaven
and pain in hell, so should they accept the dream he is about
to relate to them.

The tone of this passage is the characteristically familiar
one of a conversational style, to which the authorial interjections and idiomatic expressions, as well as the diction,
which is simplicity itself, contribute greatly. But here again
it is the clear and straight-forward grammatical constructions
and, above all, Chaucer's use of meter to support the eminently
natural syntactic structure that more than anything else account
for the conversational manner of the passage.

The Legend of Good Women is perhaps Chaucer's earliest
attempt at the sustained use of iambic pentameter couplets. But
throughout this opening passage, and throughout the whole poem,
Chaucer consciously strives, in a variety of ways, to avoid the
strong end-line pause and to overcome the sing-song effect that
would result from a too rigid adherence to this or any other
verse form.

The first line is perfectly regular iambic pentameter, but
the alliteration of "tymes" and "telle" and of "have" and "herd,"
reinforced by the metrical stress, are played off against the
iambic rhythm and help distribute the emphasis throughout the
line. Moreover, the grammar and syntax of the line create a
mildly run-on effect. The line introduces an indirect statement

and ends with the verbal construction that requires an object to
complete it--this object is the indirect statement itself, the
clause that follows in the next line and completes the syntactic
unit. Thus, this first line flows easily and unobtrusively into
the second. In the second line, Chaucer varies the rhythm ever
so slightly, substituting an anapest for an iamb in the fourth
foot and creating a crescendoing effect that results in a strong
metrical stress on "peyne," the strongest stress in the whole
line. The falling off effect that follows with the shift back
to an iamb in the last foot serves also to off-set somewhat the
emphasis on the end of the line created by the strong rhyme of
"helle" with "telle."

In the fourth and fifth lines we observe Chaucer doing much
the same thing. The fourth line is again perfectly regular
iambic pentameter, and because it completes the couplet, we
would expect a strong end-line pause following the rhyming word
"also." But Chaucer uses not only the alliteration of "wot"
with "wel," reinforced by the metrical stress on these words, to
help off-set the effect of the couplet, but also grammatical
construction and syntax to create, instead, another mildly run-
on effect. Like the first line, line four introduces an indirect
statement that is completed in the following line. The strong
internal pauses required by the grammatical construction to set
off "natheless" serve not only to break up the otherwise regular
metrical stress pattern of the line, but also to diminish the
end-line pause, thereby allowing the reader, if not actually
encouraging him, to proceed to the next line with little if any
pause. In line five Chaucer employs metrical variation to excellent effect in capturing the stop and go quality of conversational rhythms. The line begins with two iambic feet, followed
in turn by a trochaic foot, another iambic foot, and a final
trochaic foot. The shift from an iambic to a trochaic foot,
resulting in two strongly stressed syllables in succession,
creates two slight but noticeable pauses occurring precisely at
the two most semantically significant points in the line--the
first syllable of "dwellyng" and the first syllable of "contree."
These internal pauses, emphasized by the metrical variation,
together with the extra unstressed syllable at the end of the
line, contribute to the run-on effect, again very mild, created
by the syntax; for the next line, a subordinate clause modifying
"noon," completes the syntactic unit. The first three feet of
this sixth line are iambic, thereby resuming the rhythmical
pattern to which the reader has become accustomed. But in the
fourth foot Chaucer again substitutes an anapest, again creating
a crescendoing movement, peaking as the strongest stress falls
on "helle." The total effect is precisely the same as the one
created by the anapestic substitution in line two. Not only is
there a subtle variation in the rhythm and a more even distribution of emphasis throughout the line, but the falling off
effect in the last foot once more helps off-set the tendency

toward a strong end-line pause following "ybe," the rhyming word that completes the couplet.

Finally, in the last two lines Chaucer's syntax again creates a run-on effect:

> But God forbede but men shulde leve
> Wel more thing then men han seen with ye!

But what is particularly interesting here is that this last line is almost perfectly regular trochaic pentameter, with the exception of the last foot, which lacks an unstressed syllable to complete the pattern. The effect is to bring the reader up short, a halting effect that seems to just rightly underscore the exclamatory nature of the utterance.

Throughout the poem Chaucer uses syntax, supported by meter, to create run-on lines, to capture the rhythms of conversation, to achieve a conversational manner. A few additional examples should illustrate the point sufficiently:

> The smale foules, of the sesoun fayn,
> That from the panter and the net ben scaped,
> Upon the foweler, that hem made awhaped
> In wynter, and distroyed hadde hire brood,
> In his dispit hem thoghte yt did hem good
> To synge of hym, and in hir song despise
> The foule cherl that, for his coveytise,
> Had hem betrayed with his sophistrye. (130-137)

Even where Chaucer's expression is more elaborate still and his diction more ornate, such as in the following passage where he describes his first view of the God of Love and Alceste, the natural rhythm of the lines, the easy flow from line to line, and, we might also add, the authorial interjection, serve to maintain the conversational style:

> And from afer com walkyng in the mede
> The god of Love, and in his hand a quene,
> And she was clad in real habit grene.
> A fret of gold she hadde next her heer,
> And upon that a whit corowne she beer
> With flourouns smale, and I shal nat lye;
> For al the world, ryght as a dayesye
> Ycorouned ys with white leves lyte,
> So were the flowrouns of hire coroune white. (212-220)

So too in the following passage, where the poet expresses his devotion to the daisy:

The hert in-with my sorwfull brest yow dredeth
And loveth so sore that ye ben verrayly
The maistresse of my wit, and nothing I.
My word, my werk ys knyt so in youre bond
That, as an harpe obeieth to the hond
And maketh it soune after his fyngerynge,
Right so mowe ye oute of myn herte bringe
Swich vois, ryght as yow lyst, to laughe or pleyne.

(86-93)

Chaucer's source for this passage is Boccaccio's invocation
to his lady at the beginning of the _Filostrato_, particularly
stanzas two, four, and five. In this invocation Boccaccio
employs all the resources at his command to sound a note of the
highest lyric intensity. For example, stanza five:

Tu se' nel tristo petto effigiata
Con forza tal, che tu vi puoi più ch' io;
Pingine fuor la voce sconsolata
In guisa tal, che mostri il dolor mio
Nell' altrui doglie, e rendila sì grata,
Che chi l' ascolta ne divenga pio;
Tuo sia l' onore, e mio si sia l' affanno,
Se i detti alcuna laude acquisteranno.[5]

(Your image is in my sad breast so strongly that you have more
power than I do. Force out from me my disconsolate voice in
such a way that my sorrow may be seen in another's grief, and
make it so pleasing that whoever hears it be moved to pity.
Yours be the honor, and mine be the labor should these words
receive any praise.)

The intensity of the expression is controlled by the smooth and
regular rhythm, which, together with the strong and sonorous
rhymes, imbues the passage with an exquisitely melodious quality.
We might expect to hear such a passage sung as part of a religious service, and Boccaccio is in a sense engaged here in such
a service as a practitioner of the religion of courtly love,
worshipping his divinity. Chaucer too is a worshipper. He
worships the daisy, associated with Alcest, who represents the
feminine principle as the object of man's love. But the
Chaucerian passage, though quite ornate in its own right, is
considerably more subdued than the Italian. Chaucer does not
strive for the same kind of intensity. His passage is more
simple and direct, more explicit and more natural than
Boccaccio's. It is also more concrete. Especially interesting
in this regard is the image of the harp, which Chaucer himself
adds.[6] Not only does the image of the harp create a concrete
experiential frame of reference for the reader, but the particular way that Chaucer develops the simile renders the experience

visual. It is not just that the harp "obeys" the hand, but more
particularly it is the "fingering," the movement of the fingers
plucking the strings and producing the "sound" that provides
this close-up, detailed view of the playing of a harp and makes
it so visually concrete.

In this passage we again observe Chaucer working with forms
and conventions from continental poetry, adapting his source
and transforming it where necessary in such a way as to make it
compatible with his own native poetic tradition. The result
reflects the characteristic difference that most often distinguishes Chaucer's poetry from his continental models. For here
again Chaucer's poetry is more visually concrete and more conversational in manner than is his source.

But nowhere is the conversational manner employed to better
effect in this poem than in the passages of dialogue. For
example, in this first exchange between the dreamer-narrator and
the God of Love:

> This god of Love on me hys eyen caste,
> And seyde, 'Who kneleth there?' and I answerde
> Unto his askynge, whan that I it herde,
> And seyde, 'Sir, it am I,' and com him ner,
> And salwed him. Quod he, 'What dostow her
> So nygh myn oune floure, so boldely?
> Yt were better worthy, trewely,
> A worm to neghen ner my flour than Thow.'
> 'And why, sire,' quod I, 'and yt lyke yow?'
> 'For thow,' quod he, 'art thereto nothing able.'
>   (311-320)

What we have here is a reported conversation, a conversation that
the narrator makes come vividly alive for us. The exchanges are
brief, and each piece of reported speech depends upon some formal
construction such as, "I answerde...and seyde," "quod he," "quod
I," which serve to separate them from one another and to keep
the dramatis personae distinct and always clearly before our eyes
and ears, as it were. Chaucer varies the pattern of these constructions and the pieces of reported speech. In one case the
reported speech is surrounded by two such constructions; in
another, the formal construction occurs in the middle of the
line, after a period, and so introduces not only the reported
speech but also a new sentence within the same verse line; and
twice, formal constructions break up a single piece of reported
speech, the narrator's in the first case and the God of Love's
in the second. These variations help create a sense of movement
that together with such descriptive clauses as, "Whan that I it
herde," and "and com him ner,/ And salwed him," intensifies the
dramatic quality of the scene. Not only do we seem to be listening to the narrator's account of this conversation, but we seem

to be overhearing it as we view the scene, a scene Chaucer makes
come alive not simply by describing it but rather by having it
acted out.

The entire passage sounds so perfectly natural, so perfectly
conversational in manner, both with respect to the narrator's
account of the scene and the reported dialogue itself. The God
of Love's mode of expression is no more elevated nor artificial
than the narrator's. Because the language the God of Love uses and
the form it takes are much the same as the narrator's, his mode
of expression neither more elevated nor artificial, he becomes
as "real" as the narrator himself. Throughout the passage,
whether the narrator is speaking directly to us, reporting his
own words or those of the God of Love, we are almost totally
unaware of any conscious striving for special effects. Throughout Chaucer uses syntax to create strong internal pauses and
just sufficiently varies his meter in support of the syntactic
structure to produce a conversational rhythm that he skillfully
plays off against the predominant iambic pentameter norm.
Furthermore, these strong internal pauses, supported by metrical
stress, help neutralize the emphasis on the end of the line that
would otherwise result from the use of couplets and contribute
a great deal to the run-on effect created by the syntax. The
following is perhaps the best example of Chaucer's skill in
this regard:

> And seyde, 'Sir, it am I,' and com him ner,
> And salwed him. Quod he, 'What dostow her
> So nygh myn oune floure, so boldely?'

The first line consists of an iambic foot, followed by two trochaic feet, followed by two iambic feet. The shift from the
initial iambic foot to the first trochaic foot and the one from
the second trochaic foot back to an iambic foot coincide precisely with the pauses required by the syntax. The meter
further reinforces the syntactic structure in that the two
trochaic feet make up the piece of reported speech, thereby
setting off metrically that part of the verse line that is also
syntactically set off from the rest of the line.

Noteworthy also is the fact that Chaucer not only ends the
first sentence and begins the next in the middle of a verse
line, but that he splits the couplet between the two speakers,
a technique he was to employ to good effect in later works, such
as Troilus and Criseyde and The Canterbury Tales. The strong
internal pause required at the end of this first sentence is
reinforced by metrical variation, by a shift from an iambic to
a trochaic foot, which brings two strongly stressed syllables
together. There is a second strong internal pause in this line
following "he," which is also reinforced by metrical variation,
in this case by a shift from a trochaic foot back to an iambic
foot. These two strong internal pauses contribute to the run-on

effect of the line by diminishing the end-line pause. As a
result of Chaucer's splitting the couplet between the two
speakers and using syntax, supported by metrical stress, to
create strong internal pauses and a run-on line, the rhyme
between "her" and "ner" becomes unobtrusive, so unobtrusive,
in fact, that we are hardly even conscious of it, and this
rhyming couplet detracts little from the illusion of our overhearing a conversation taking place in a scene we are witnessing.

Chaucer's successful exploitation of the conversational
manner in passages such as these is amply attested to by the
fact that, although his language is so many centuries removed
from our own and in many ways different from ours, the present
day reader cannot help but feel that he is surely in the presence of his own native language as it must have been commonly
used in Chaucer's day. The key to Chaucer's triumph is that,
while the splendid effects he achieves depend so much upon his
conscious manipulation of syntax and meter, he is most careful
not to allow his manipulations to distort the natural syntactic
patterns nor the natural accentual patterns of the language
itself. The effects Chaucer achieves through his manipulation
of syntax and meter are, for the most part, quite subtle and
unobtrusive, and for this very reason enhance the illusion of
our being part of an audience that seems to be listening to a
pleasant and casual recitation.

Chaucer, in fact, seems consciously to strive to create
and maintain this illusion. His repeated use of the phrase,
"As I seyde erst," seems not only to be a recognition of the
limits of a listening audience, but serves also to keep the
raconteur continually before our eyes and ears. By shifting
easily and comfortably from the first person singular, in which
the poem is primarily written, to the first person plural or to
the second person pronoun of direct address, Chaucer intensifies the audience's involvement in the experience:[7]

     Than mote we to bokes that we fynde...(17)

     Wel ought us thanne honouren and beleve
     These bokes, there we han noon other preve.(27-28)

     But helpeth, ye that han konnyng and myght,
     Ye lovers that kan make of sentement;
     In this cas oghte ye be diligent
     To forthren me somwhat in my labour,
     Whethir ye ben with the leef or with the flour.(68-72)

In this poem Chaucer also makes use of more elaborate
effects; for example, anaphora:

> That tellen of these olde appreved stories
> Of holynesse, of regnes, of victories,
> Of love, of hate, of other sondry thynges,
> Of whiche I may not maken rehersynges. (21-24)

But the anaphora here is unostentatious. It does not call undue
attention to itself, nor does it detract from the conversational
manner. The phrases, "Of holynesse" and "Of love," are part of
the asyndetic series and so blend easily into the syntactic
structure that produces the run-on effect. The coincidence of
strong metrical stress with the semantically significant words
serves to clearly and forcefully hammer home the meaning of the
passage. Nowhere does the rhythm seem artificial, for Chaucer
is careful, as always, not to distort his syntax or the natural
accentual patterns of the words to conform to the predominant
metrical pattern. In the first line, for example, which is
otherwise regularly iambic, there is an extra unstressed syllable
at the end; in the last line, an extra unstressed syllable that
results in an anapestic fourth foot, which nicely varies the
effect of the heavily iambic rhythm of the two previous lines.
Much the same is true of the following passage, where
Chaucer again makes use of anaphora:

> As she that is of alle floures flour,
> Fulfilled of al vertu and honour,
> And evere ilyke faire, and fressh of hewe;
> And I love it, and ever ylike newe,
> And evere shal, til that myn herte dye. (53-57)

The poet is describing his love for the daisy, a love the recollection of which seems almost to send him into an ecstatic rap-
ture. He seems, for the moment, to have forgotten his surround-
ings, his audience, and everything else, and waxes rhapsodic.
The use of anaphora, together with the repetition of the word
"evere" and the repetitious syntactic structure, imbues the
passage with an incantatory quality reminiscent of similar
passages in the "ABC" as well as in the earlier English lyrics.
Here it is the perfect mode of expression for the narrator's
adoration of this flower. But again there is, on the surface,
no overt striving for a special effect. The language is simple;
the syntactic structure, though somewhat complicated by the
repetition, quite clear; and the rhythm, perfectly natural. It
is the kind of expression that a person engaged in a conversation
might just slip into upon recalling a moment that sounds an
intense and vibrant chord somewhere deep within his being. And
as a result of the power with which Chaucer here poetically re-
creates this particular experience, we are drawn into an intense
emotional identification with him and come not only to understand
but to share his love for this flower.

The Legend of Good Women is of a quite different order from anything we find in the early Middle English lyrics. But in the posture that Chaucer, as poet, assumes, that of addressing a listening audience, in his attempts to include that audience in the experience he is poetically re-creating for them, in his adoption of a conversational manner, which heightens and maintains this illusion of the audience's participation in the experience, and in his use of techniques similar to those used by the English lyric poets who preceded him, Chaucer establishes himself as working essentially in the same tradition as these earlier English poets. And it is, on the most fundamental level, Chaucer's style itself that most clearly marks his place in that tradition.

There is good reason for agreeing with Bennett that in the Prologue to The Legend of Good Women Chaucer is the "complete master" of the style Bennett describes, the style that I have referred to, in the most general and comprehensive sense, as conversational, though like so many other aspects of Chaucer's art this conversational style is culminated in The Canterbury Tales. Nor is it surprising that by the time Chaucer came to write The Legend of Good Women he had succeeded so well in mastering this style. For Chaucer had been cultivating this conversational style, experimenting with it, polishing and refining it, from his earliest period of poetic activity. We have already observed manifestations of this style in Chaucer's early lyric poetry, and if we turn to his early attempts at narrative poetry, we again find him working in the same direction, consciously striving to develop a conversational manner.

Certainly one of Chaucer's earliest attempts at a sustained narrative poem is his translation of the Roman de la Rose. Perhaps one of the reasons that Chaucer undertook this translation is that in the part of the Roman composed by Guillaume De Lorris, Chaucer found a model for the kind of poetry he was himself trying to write. Guillaume's poem is a courtly poem, addressed to a courtly audience, and, at the same time, written in a style that is in many respects readily adaptable to the English poetic tradition in which Chaucer was working. It is a leisurely, easy-going style, marked by the frequent use of run-on lines, and very nearly conversational in manner. Guillaume adopts a posture that Chaucer was to find particularly amenable. He consciously strives to keep himself constantly before his audience and to establish a comfortable relationship with them. His tone is casual and familiar, and he frequently addresses remarks directly to his audience:

> Or ueil cel songe rimeer,
> Por uos cuers plus feire agaeer....[8]

(Now I'll set this dream to rhyme to make your hearts more gay.)

More important still, Guillaume employs the kind of tongue-in-cheek, self-deprecatory humor that Chaucer was to exploit to such excellent effect in his later works: "Qui se uoudra, por fol m'en tiegne" (Whoever wishes may call me a fool.). It is not at all surprising, then, that Chaucer's translation of the Roman is, as Erwin Geissman points out, a close and careful one.

Yet, if we carefully compare Chaucer's translation with the original, we find certain significant differences, differences that reflect the influence of the native English poetic tradition upon Chaucer's treatment of his source.[9]

In the first place, Chaucer strives for greater simplicity and directness. As an example we can take Chaucer's rendition of Guillaume's opening passage on the beauties of May. The texts of both passages follow:

> Qu' en may estoie, ce sonioie,
> El tens enmoreus, plain de ioie,
> El tens ou toute rien s'esgaie,
> Que l'en ne uoit buisson ne haie
> Qui en may parer ne se ueille
> E courir de nouele fuelle. (47-52)

> That it was May, thus dremed me,
> In tyme of love and jolite,
> That al thing gynneth waxen gay,
> For ther is neither busk nor hay
> In May, that it nyl shrouded ben,
> And it with newe leves wren. (51-56)

Chaucer simplifies Guillaume's syntax. In the second line, where Guillaume has a noun, "tens," modified first by an adjective, "enmoreus," then by a prepositional phrase, "plain de ioie," Chaucer simply uses a prepositional phrase with a compound object, "of love and jolite," to modify the noun, "tyme." In the fifth line Chaucer not only simplifies and makes more precise the syntax of the original by shifting the prepositional phrase, "In May," to the beginning of the line, thereby keeping the two subordinate clauses separate and distinct, but also, in so doing, creates a run-on effect.

In the fourth line Chaucer translates the French third person general and abstract "l'en ne uoit" with a simple, direct, though also impersonal, "ther is." This last is, of course, due primarily to the differing linguistic necessities of the two languages. So too, in the preceding line, where Chaucer translates Guillaume's passively reflexive construction, "s'esgaie," with the more active, more direct, "gynneth waxen gay." Many of the stylistic differences between Chaucer's translation and the original, not just here but throughout the poem, are no doubt dictated by such linguistic considerations. But it is Chaucer's

ability to find precisely the right English idiom for French
constructions that have no exact English equivalent that results
in the eminent naturalness of his translation and contributes so
much to its "Englishness."

We can observe these same tendencies in Chaucer's translation of Guillaume's passage on time. The French follows:

> Li tens qui s'en uet nuit e ior,
> Sanz repox prendre e sanz seior,
> E qui de nos se part e emble
> Si celeement qu'il nos semble
> Qu'el s'areste adès en .i. point,
> E il ne s'i areste point,
> Ainz ne fine de trespasser,
> Que l'en ne peut neïs penser
> Quel tens ce est qui est presenz.... (361-369)

Chaucer renders these lines:

> The tyme, that passeth nyght and day,
> And resteles travayleth ay,
> And steleth from us so prively
> That to us semeth sykerly
> That it in oon poynt dwelleth ever,
> And certes, it ne resteth never,
> But goth so faste, and passeth ay,
> That ther nys man that thynke may
> What tyme that now present is.... (369-377)

Here again Chaucer simplifies the syntax of the original.
Guillaume begins with the subject, "Li tens," which is followed
by a modifying subordinate clause. So too Chaucer. But at
this point Guillaume introduces a highly elaborate syntactic
structure. The next line consists of two prepositional phrases,
beautifully balanced by the repetitive verbal structure and the
repetition of the preposition, "sanz," which modify the verb of
the preceding subordinate clause. In the next line, Guillaume
introduces another subordinate clause that refers back to and
also modifies "Li tens." Chaucer's syntax is much simpler, and
his expression, more direct. He combines the major elements of
these three lines into one single subordinate clause with a
compound predicate--"The tyme, that passeth...and resteles
travayleth...and steleth...." Here too Chaucer's active verb
forms are more forceful and direct than the reflexive verbs and
verbal constructions of the original.

Chaucer also simplifies the concluding lines of the passage
and makes the rather complex point they express more clear. Both
poets begin with a simple statement. Guillaume writes, "E il ne
s'i areste point," which Chaucer translates literally--"And
certes, it ne resteth never." In the next line, Guillaume

repeats the statement in slightly different terms, "Ainz ne fine de trespasser." Chaucer, however, introduces a subtle variation--"But goth so faste, and passeth ay." Chaucer's use of the adverbs "faste" and "ay" prepare the way for the result clause introduced by "so" and establishes much more clearly the cause-effect relationship developed through the two concluding lines than does the original. In Chaucer's version, it is precisely because time goes <u>so</u> <u>fast</u> and passes <u>continually</u> that one can never know the exact moment. The French is here more abstract and ambiguous. It is only the negative aspect regarding the movement of time, that it <u>never</u> ceases moving, that accounts for the complex idea expressed in the following two lines--that even in one's thoughts one cannot precisely pinpoint any given moment in time, for even as he thinks of that moment, the moment has passed.

One of the effects of Chaucer's tendency toward greater simplicity and directness is greater clarity. Chaucer makes considerably more frequent use of doublets than does Guillaume, of extended coordinate series, and of structural repetition, which Guillaume also uses but primarily for rhetorical flourish rather than in the interest of clarity--for example, in the line, "sanz repox prendre e sanz seior" (without taking rest and without sojourning). While it would be tedious to list every such occurrence in Chaucer's translation, a few examples should suffice to illustrate the point adequately.

Doublets do occur in the <u>Roman</u>, and Chaucer invariably incorporates them into his translation. But quite frequently Chaucer also uses a doublet where there is none in the original, sometimes, no doubt, unconsciously, from force of habit, and at other times, simply as metrical fillers. For example, in the following instances (in each case the original French is followed by Chaucer's rendition):

> Por uos cuers plus feire agaeer
> To make your hertes gaye and lyght
>
> Qu'el doit estre Rose clamee
> That she wel ought, of pris and ryght,
> Be cleped Rose of every wight
>
> Qu'ele ne porte leauté
> A compaignon ne a compaigne
> That feith ne trouthe holdith she
> To freend ne felawe, bad or good
>
> Sa malice trop malement
> Hir malice and hir maltalent
>
> E s'il iere tant bien apris
> And if he were so hende and wis

> Toz celz qui mielz font a amer
> That best deserven love and name

> E por ce la fist Dex estable
> Therfore God held it ferme and stable

Chaucer also frequently uses a series of three coordinate elements where the original has a doublet:

> As demoisaus e au puceles
> Doon maydens, children, and eek gromes

> El ne fu gae ne ioliue
> Ne she was gay, fresh, ne jolyf

> Car tel ioie ne tel deduit
> For sich solas, sich joie, and play

> Mès sage e antre, sanz outrage
> But wys, and war, and vertuous

More often than not, when Chaucer makes such changes, he
does so for a specific reason; sometimes, to achieve a particular
effect, as in the following instance, where the repetitious
structure, supported by metrical stress, strikingly hammers home
the particularly odious quality of hate:

> Amydde saugh I Hate stonde,
> That for hir wrathe, yre, and onde....

The effect is quite different from Guillaume's,

> Enz en le mileu ui Haïne,
> Qui de corroz e d'ataïne....

So too in the following instances, where Chaucer's use of doublets renders the translation more emphatic than the original:

> E qu'el nooit si durement
> And that she hidde and bond so stronge

> Lorent les genz li losengier
> These losengeris hem preyse, and smylen

> Mes lor losenges les gen poignent
> And aftirward they prikke and poynten

Sometimes, Chaucer renders Guillaume's more complex syntactic structure by a more simple coordinate series, again, apparently, in the interest of greater explicitness and clarity:

> Qu'il ne sera ia bien peůz,
> Ne bien uestuz, ne bien chauciez;
> N'il n'est amez ne essauciez

> Is ony povere man wel yfed,
> Or wel araied or wel cled,
> Of wel biloved, in sich wise

Chaucer's simpler structure here makes his translation more easily comprehensible than the original.

But the most frequent changes that Chaucer makes are in the direction of greater concreteness. On occasion, he simply adds a descriptive adjective:

> De chanter e de feire noise
> To make noyse and syngen blythe

> D'arbres ne d'oiselons chantanz
> Of briddes song, and braunches grene

> Son uis, son nés e sa bouchete
> His nose, his mouth, his yen sheene

At other times, he uses a more concrete adjective than he finds in the original:

> E le tens diuers e frarin
> In wedres gryl and derk to sighte

Sometimes, he uses a doublet where there is none in the original:

> A une perche greilleite
> Upon a perche, weik and small

> Front reluisant, soreix uotis
> With bente browis smothe and slyke

And sometimes he uses a triplet where the original has a doublet:

> La praierie grant e bele
> The medewe softe, swote and grene
>
> Si n'i ot bube ne malem
> Withoute bleyne, scabbe, or royne

Geissman is, generally speaking, right in observing with
reference to Chaucer's translation of the Roman, "Where the
French is general and commonplace, the English is often more concrete and arresting" (178). But this does not necessarily mean
that Guillaume's poem is totally lacking in concreteness. In
fact, quite the opposite is true. Concreteness is a characteristic feature of Guillaume' style, particularly in the many
descriptive passages, and this may well be another reason that
the poem so much appealed to Chaucer. Rather, the difference is
one of degree. Where Guillaume's work is concrete, Chaucer's is
still more so, especially in these very same descriptive passages,
where Chaucer's subtle changes, often only a touch here and a
touch there, are a sure indication of his conscious striving for
greater visual concreteness, of his determination to make a scene
or a character come visually alive for his audience. Chaucer's
translation of Guillaume's description of Hate is a good example:

> Enz en le mileu ui Haîne,
> Qui de corroz e d'ataîne
> Sembla bien estre meneresse;
> Corroceuse e tançoneresse,
> Et plaine de grant cuuertage
> Estoit par semblant cele ymage;
> Si n' estoit pas bien atornee,
> Ainz sembloit fame forsenee.
> Rechinié auoit e froncié
> Le uis, e le nés secorcié;
> Hisdeuse estoit e roillie;
> E si sa teste entorteillie
> Hisdeusement d'une toaille. (139-151)

> Amydde saugh I Hate stonde,
> That for hir wrathe, yre, and onde,
> Semede to ben a moveresse,
> An angry wight, a chideresse;
> And ful of gyle and fel corage,
> By semblaunt, was that ilk ymage.
> And she was nothyng wel arraied,
> But lyk a wod womman afraied.
> Yfrounced foule was hir visage,

And grennyng for dispitous rage;
Hir nose snorted up for tene.
Ful hidous was she for to sene,
Ful foul and rusty was she, this.
Hir heed ywrithen was, ywis,
Ful grymly with a greet towayle. (147-161)

We have already observed the greater emphasis Chaucer
achieves in the second line by rendering the French doublet, "de
corroz e d'ataïne," as a triplet, "wrathe, yre, and onde," and
might only add that the extra detail contributes also to the
greater concreteness of Chaucer's translation. Similarly,
Chaucer's fourth line, "And ful of gyle and fel corage," is, as
a result of the added detail, more explicit and concrete than
the French, "Et plaine de grant cuuertage." But it is in the
description of Hate's face that Chaucer does most to heighten
the concreteness. Guillaume tells us that her face was "dark"
and "frowning"; Chaucer, that it was "Yfrounced foule," and he
describes the frown, "grennyng for dispitous rage." Guillaume
tells us that her nose was "turned up"; Chaucer, that it was
"snorted up for tene." And finally, where Guillaume tells us
that her head was "hideously wrapped in a towel," Chaucer tells
us it was "ywrithen...ful grymly" with a "greet" towel.

Chaucer never seems to miss an opportunity to add such
touches. For example, as part of the description of Covetous-
ness, Guillaume tells us that those whom she enflames are, in
the end, often hanged ("Qu'en la fin maint en couient pendre").
Chaucer makes the same point, but adds that they are hanged "by
her throtes." In another instance, the description of Elde,
Guillaume tells us that her ears "quivered" ("Les orelles auoit
uelues"); Chaucer, that "Her eeres shoken faste withalle,/ As
from her heed they wolde falle."

Chaucer adds such touches in his translation of passages
describing scenery as well. One of the more exquisite of these
is in the description of the garden where Narcissus' pool is
found. Guillaume describes the grass in this garden as "fresh"
and "thick," and adds that one can lie on it with his sweetheart
as on a "couch":

> Entor les ruisiaus e les riues
> Des fontaines cleres e uiues
> Poignoit l'erbe freschete e drue,
> Ausi i pooit l'en sa drue,
> Couchier come sus une coute.... (1391-1395)

Chaucer renders this passage as follows:

>   About the brinkes of these welles,
>   And by the stremes overal elles,
>   Sprang up the grass, as thicke yset
>   And softe as any veluët,
>   On which men myght his lemman leye,
>   As on a fetherbed, to pleye.... (1417-1422)

Chaucer's comparison of the grass to velvet, though commonplace
enough in itself, when combined with his substitution of a
"fetherbed" for a couch, nicely enhances the visual quality of
the scene and makes it that much more concrete than Guillaume's.
And Chaucer's addition of the verb "to pleye" is a most delightful touch in the same direction.

Such individual touches are, in themselves, little enough.
But when taken together, their cumulative effect is to make
Chaucer's translation significantly more vivid, significantly
more concrete, than the original. Admittedly, the difference is
one of degree rather than kind. But Chaucer's efforts towards
greater concreteness are only part of a larger concern, his
greater concern with clarity than literalness. As a result, his
translation is not only more concrete than the original, but
also more simple, more direct, and more explicit. That the style
of Chaucer's translation of the Roman is characterized by the
very same qualities fundamental to the style of the early
Middle English lyrics would seem to suggest, then, that even at
this so very early stage of his literary career, at a time when
he was most deeply immersed in and so strongly influenced by
French poetry, he had already committed himself to following in
the tradition of his English predecessors.[10]

In the final analysis, however, it is once again the particular combination of syntax and meter resulting in the conversational manner of Chaucer's translation that is its most
distinctive feature and most distinguishes it from the original.
In translating the Roman, Chaucer attempted to duplicate the
octosyllabic norm of the original. But because Chaucer was
working with an accentual language, he had also to be concerned
with the stress pattern of the verse line, and the predominant
meter of his translation is iambic tetrameter. But Chaucer binds
himself neither to a perfectly rigid syllabic norm nor to a
perfectly regular metrical one, for the poetic tradition in
which he worked allowed him considerable freedom in this regard
and allowed him to take metrical licenses impossible to
Guillaume. Moreover, because the language in which Guillaume
composed his poem is non-accentual, he is not able to produce
the kinds of effects that Chaucer is able to produce by the use
of stress variation. Thus, where Chaucer is able to capture the
rhythm of conversation by varying the rhythm of a line, where
Chaucer is able to simulate the stop and go quality characteristic of conversation by varying the stress patterns, where

Chaucer is able to use stress, as we do in conversation, to
create semantic emphasis, Guillaume is not.

Both Guillaume and Chaucer make considerable use of run-on
lines, and such constructions contribute to the conversational
quality of both the original and the translation. However,
there is a marked difference between the effect produced by
Guillaume's use of such constructions and that by Chaucer's,
even where Chaucer translates the original nearly literally. To
create run-on lines, Guillaume must depend entirely upon his
manipulation of syntax. And while he is capable of achieving
excellent effects by playing off the syntactic structure against
the octosyllabic verse line, he does not have available to him,
as Chaucer does, the use of metrical stress to support the
syntactic structure. In each of the following examples, Chaucer's
translation follows the original:

> D'un tertre qui près d'ilec iere
> Descendoit l'eue fort e roide.
> Clere estoit l'eue e ausi froide
> Come puis ou come fontaine...

> For from an hill that stood ther ner,
> Cam doun the strem ful stif and bold.
> Cleer was the water, and as cold
> as any welle is, soth to seyne...

> Priuee sui mout a acointe
> De Deduit le mignot, le cointe...

> Aqueynted am I and pryve
> With Myrthe, lord of this gardyn...

> A chanter furent ententif
> Li oiselet, qui aprentif
> Ne furent pas ne non sachant...

> Ententif weren for to synge
> These briddis, that nought unkunnynge
> Were of her craft, and apprentys...

> Icil bachelers regardoit
> Les queroles, e si gardoit...

> This bacheler stod biholdyng
> The daunce, and in his hond holdyng....

In the first example the run-on effect of both passages
depends primarily upon the syntactic structure, which creates a
comparison between the stream's water and that of a well. However, in Chaucer's lines metrical variation reinforces the run-on

construction. The particular technique Chaucer uses here is one
he resorts to on frequent occasions. He places a semantically
insignificant, monosyllabic word, one that would not usually be
heavily accented in normal speech patterns, at a point in the
verse line where the reader has been led by the established meter
to expect strong metrical stress. Technically, Chaucer's third
line is iambic tetrameter with trochaic substitution in the
first foot. But the stress falling on "and," which such a metrical pattern would require to be relatively strong, is hardly
noticeable. The line reads more like dactylic trimeter, with
two initial dactylic feet followed by an iambic foot. Thus, the
metrical expectation of four _strong_ beats to a line is somewhat
thwarted, and the reader is encouraged by the meter to move on
to the next line where the regular iambic pattern is resumed.
Both in this line and in the preceding line, the succession of
unstressed syllables resulting from the trochaic substitution
in the first foot gives the lines a hurried movement, which not
only contributes to the run-on effect, but also simulates the
rippling, hurried movement of the stream as it flows down the
hill.

In the second example too the run-on effect of both the
French and the English depends primarily upon the syntax; that
is, the movement from the one line to the next is insisted upon
by the need for the prepositional phrase to complete the verbal
structure of the first line. Measured against a tetrameter norm,
Chaucer's first line would read as iambic tetrameter with trochaic substitution in the last foot. But when we read the line,
the stress on "and," which such a metrical pattern would require
to be relatively strong, is hardly noticeable, and so this line
too reads more like trimeter, consisting of two iambic feet,
followed by an anapestic foot and one extra unstressed syllable.
Once again the expectation of four strong beats to a line encourages the reader on to the next line. There is also an
interesting secondary effect that results from the metrical
pattern of Chaucer's lines. The first foot of the second line
is iambic, but when combined with the extra unstressed syllable
at the end of the preceding line, it forms, as it were, an anapestic foot. Thus, the metrical expectation of four strong
beats is satisfied at this point in the second line, which coincides precisely with the completion of the syntactic unit.
It is almost as though the first line and the first part of the
second line make up a single verse unit consisting of two iambic
feet followed by two anapestic feet, a metrical structure that
perfectly supports the syntactic structure to enhance the run-on
effect.

The same technique is clearly evident in the third example
as well, where the stress on the word "to" in the first line,
which the tetrameter norm would require to be relatively strong,
is hardly noticeable; in fact, the word "for" seems to receive

equal or even stronger stress. But it is the second line that
is of more interest. For no matter how we scan this line, unless
we distort the natural accentual patterns of the words completely,
there are only three strong stresses, with the "missing" strongly
stressed syllable provided at the beginning of the next line by
the word "Were." Here, as before, the metrical variations contribute to the effect of the run-on constructions, greatly enhancing the smooth and natural flow from line to line.

In the final example Chaucer uses his syntax and meter to
create the effect I have specifically referred to as enjambment.
In the first line the shift from the iambic second foot to the
trochaic third foot, resulting in two successive strongly
stressed syllables, creates a slight but noticeable pause after
"stod," which is further reinforced by the "b" alliteration.
This slight internal pause, combined with the syntactic structure, which requires the direct object of the following line to
complete the grammatical construction, and the reader's expectation of an iambic norm, which is resumed in the following line,
create the run-on effect. In the second line the strong internal
pause required by the syntax following "daunce," upon which also
falls the strongest metrical stress in the line, forces the
reader to stop and focus on the dance. And the reader seems
almost to join the narrator and the "bachelor" in "beholding"
this dance; that is, he is virtually forced by the poetic re-
creation of the scene to become part of that scene.

In fact, Chaucer quite frequently uses enjambment to create
a special emphasis; for example, to evoke more powerfully than
does Guillaume the season:

> For ther is neither busk nor hay
> In May, that it nyl shrouded ben....

These lines are a close translation of Guillaume's,

> Que l'en ne uoit buisson ne haie
> Qui en may parer ne se ueille....

However, the structure of Chaucer's lines seems specifically
designed to rivet the reader's attention on "May." Chaucer
achieves this effect by making a subtle syntactic change. Where
Guillaume's entire second line is a subordinate clause introduced
by "Qui," Chaucer shifts the prepositional phrase "In May" to the
beginning of the line and introduces the subordinate clause after
it. As a result not only has the prepositional phrase been
placed in a more emphatic position in the line, it has also been
made a grammatical part of the preceding line. Moreover,
Chaucer's syntax requires a strong internal pause preceding the
subordinate clause. This internal pause, which helps focus the
reader's attention on the prepositional phrase, is further reinforced by the strong rhyme between "May" and "hay," which in

itself calls attention to and underscores the season. The rhyme
occurs in Guillaume's lines, but is made considerably more emphatic in Chaucer's, where the rhyming words are closer to one
another, belong to the same syntactic unit, and receive heavy
metrical stress.[11]

On several occasions Chaucer uses enjambment to focus on
a character, particularly when he is describing the characters
he encounters in the garden of Mirth. First, there is Sir Mirth
himself:

> That I ne wente inne for to see
> Sir Myrthe; for my desiryng....

The reader is just as anxious as the narrator to "see" this lord.
The French here does not produce the same effect, for there is
not the same emphasis created by the structure:

> Qu'adonc Deduit uoair n'alase;
> Car a uoair mout desirasse....

The same is true a few lines later, where Chaucer first introduces us to "Gladnesse":

> A lady karolede hem that hyghte
> Gladnesse, [the] blissful and the lighte....

Again, Guillaume's lines do not create the same kind of emphasis:

> E une dame lor chantoit,
> Qui Leesce apelee estoit.

So too, in one final instance, when Chaucer introduces us to
"Largesse":

> And after on the daunce wente
> Largesse, that sette al hir entente....

Once again the effect of the French is quite different:

> Apres se fu Largesce prise,
> Qui bien fu fete e bien aprise....[12]

The technique that Chaucer employs here is closely related
to another characteristic feature of his style--the tendency
to begin a line with a semantically significant and strongly
stressed word, a tendency we have previously observed as characteristic also of the Middle English lyrics. Guillaume too
occasionally begins a line with a semantically significant word,
though considerably less often than does Chaucer. But of course,

there is, in the French, no metrical stress to underscore the semantic significance. Most often, these words are, in the French, verb forms:

Portret de hors e entaillié...

Pestri a lessu fort e aigre...

Parlé en remanz e en liure....

In each of these cases, Chaucer's translation is marked by a strongly stressed initial syllable:

Portraied without and wel entailled...

Kneden with eisel strong and egre...

Spoken in bookis dyversely.

Occasionally, these are, in the French, more or less significant adjectives:

Iolis e gais, pleins de leesce...

Hauz fu li murs e toz quarez....

Here again we find in Chaucer's translation strong initial metrical stress underscoring such adjectives:

Jolif and gay, ful of gladnesse...

Square was the wall, and high sumdell....

Sometimes Guillaume even begins a line with a noun, though the grammatical structure and idiomatic expression of French, requiring the article much more frequently than does English, precludes him from doing so with any regularity:

Lais d'amors e sonoiz cortois...

Flors i auoit de maintes guises...

Rubiz i ot, saphirs, iagonces....

In these instances too Chaucer's use of metrical stress underscores the semantic significance:

Layes of love, ful wel sownyng...

Floures there were of many gise...

Rubyes there were, saphires, jagounces....13

But rarely if ever does Guillaume begin a line with a parti-
cipial construction, as Chaucer does in the following examples
from the description of Avarice, where the reader's attention is
drawn by the syntactic structure, supported by metrical stress,
to the particular quality of the item Chaucer is describing:

Clouted was she beggarly...

Furred with no menyver....

In every one of these examples Chaucer has employed metrical
variation, most commonly trochaic substitution in the first foot,
to create a line with strong initial metrical stress, to create
the emphasis on the semantically significant word. And it might
be noted here that this metrical variation results also in a
pleasant variation of the rhythm of the individual lines, which
further enhances the conversational quality of his translation.
But the most important aspect of Chaucer's technique in such
lines is the use of meter to support syntactic structure, to
emphasize the meaning of the words themselves, and also, quite
often, to intensify concreteness, to make an object more visually
concrete by focusing the reader's attention directly upon it or
by focusing upon a particularly significant quality of it.

In commenting upon Chaucer's attempts to emulate the French
octosyllabic couplet, H. S. Bennett alludes to some of the problems Chaucer may have encountered and, more important still, to
some of the differences between Chaucer's use of this verse form
and its use by French poets:

> The merits of octosyllabics had been well-tested:
> it is an excellent verse for a quick-moving,
> conversational type of poem. It is not so well
> adapted to convey emotion as it is to convey in-
> formation or description, and the line nowhere
> seems long enough to allow much freedom to the
> writer, or any undue elaboration. The rhyme-
> words seem to bustle along, and a tendency for
> the verse to break into a jog-trot, or even a
> gallop, is not easily restrained. Chaucer uses
> this verse with considerable skill, and essays
> with some success to overcome its difficulties.
> Thus he employs run-on lines, at times only
> within the couplet, but sometimes over-stepping
> even this. He ends a paragraph on the first

> half of the couplet, and gets welcome variation
> by a reversal of the first foot...or by omit-
> ting the first syllable of the line altogether.
> He splits a couplet between two speakers and
> occasionally splits a line between them. By
> these devices, and some skill at varying the
> pause in the line, throwing it very early...or
> ignoring it and running on to an early pause
> in the next line...Chaucer made a lively
> measure of octosyllabics.   (86-87)[14]

Bennett is here referring to Chaucer's handling of the octosyllabic couplet in The Book of the Duchess and The House of Fame.
But the techniques Bennett describes Chaucer as employing to
make "a lively measure of octosyllabics" are essentially the
same as those Chaucer employs in his translation of the Roman.
Furthermore, they are the same as those he employs to achieve
the same kinds of effects in those poems written in decasyllabic
lines as well, whether these are in rhyme royal, as is Troilus
and Criseyde, or in couplets, as is The Legend of Good Women.
     In a sense it is somewhat ironic that Chaucer's first major
poetic undertaking is the translation of the Roman, for in many
respects the Roman is the culmination of the analytical mode of
the medieval French poetic tradition and fundamentally at the
opposite pole from the native English poetic tradition. But it
is altogether significant that in this very early work Chaucer's
style clearly exhibits an affinity with the style of the early
Middle English lyrics--a style characterized by its simplicity,
directness, explicitness, and clarity; a style visually concrete
and conversational in manner. It is this style, inherited from
the native English poetic tradition that Chaucer cultivates from
his earliest poetic undertakings and continues to develop and
exploit throughout his literary career. But even if, as Bennett
suggests, Chaucer is in many respects the complete master of
this style in The Legend of Good Women, it is in Chaucer's
final masterpiece, The Canterbury Tales, that he brings this
style to its greatest pitch of perfection and so achieves full
poetic maturity.
     Certainly nowhere in Chaucer's own poetry, in medieval
English poetry in general, or for that matter in the whole of
English poetry, is the conversational manner more successfully
exploited than in the little vignettes that constitute the
internal framework of The Canterbury Tales. This framework is
primarily responsible for creating and maintaining the illusion
of our participation in the poetic re-creation of the experience,
for creating the illusion that we are actually a part of the
company journeying to Canterbury. And this illusion is so
powerfully created that not only do we seem to be listening to
the pilgrims, overhearing their squabbles and bickerings, when
we are reading The Canterbury Tales, but long after, when we

can still hear the words of the Host to the narrator, "Thy drasty rymyng is nat worth a toord," or the heated exchange between the Host and the Pardoner:

> 'Com forth, sire Hoost, and offre first anon,
> And thou shalt kisse the relikes everychon,
> Ye, for a grote! Unbokele anon thy purs.'
> 'Nay, nay!' quod he, 'thanne have I Cristes curs!
> Lat be,' quod he, 'it shal nat be, so theech!
> Thou woldest make me kisse thyn olde breech,
> And swere it were a relyk of a seint,
> Though it were with thy fundement depeint!
> But, by the croys which that Seint Eleyne fond,
> I wolde I hadde thy coillons in myn hond
> In stide of relikes or of seintuarie.
> Lat kutte hem of, I wol thee helpe hem carie;
> They shul be shryned in an hogges toord!'

Or again the restrained but malevolent tone of the Reeve's reply to the Miller's tale:

> 'This dronke Millere hath ytoold us heer
> How that bigyled was a carpenteer,
> Peraventure in scorn, for I am oon.
> And, by youre leve, I shal hym quite anoon;
> Right in his cherles termes wol I speke.
> I pray to God his nekke mote to-breke....'

Neither Chaucer's graphic and colloquial language nor his idiomatic expression alone is totally responsible for the conversational quality of such passages; contributing equally are the simplicity, directness, and explicitness of the expression, the simplicity of the syntactic structure, everywhere supported by the meter, and the use of meter and syntax not only to create the easy and natural flow from line to line but, above all, to capture the rhythm of conversational exchanges.

Nor is it this conversational manner alone that is responsible for so powerfully creating the illusion of our participation in this adventure. Equally important are the characteristically concrete details Chaucer everywhere includes to make these little vignettes come visually alive for us. Thus, not only do we seem to be hearing the pilgrims, we seem also to see them: we see them drawing straws for who shall tell the first tale; we see the drunken, pale Miller sitting unsteadily upon his horse; we see the Cook congratulating the Reeve for his tale by "clawing" him on his back; we see the Summoner standing high in his stirrups and shaking like a leaf at the conclusion of the Friar's tale; we see the Cook, in a drunken stupor "napping" in his saddle, becoming so angry at the Manciple that he falls from his

horse, the pilgrims struggling to get him back in the saddle, and
the reconciliation of the Cook with the Manciple as the latter
offers him a drink from his own "gourd," which the Cook readily
accepts.

Such visually concrete details are an extremely important
part of Chaucer's descriptive technique in the "General Prologue"
as well.[15] Who can ever forget the Monk's shiny, bald head; the
Merchant's forked beard; the "mormal" on the Cook's shin; the
Miller's red beard; the "gat-toothed" Wife of Bath in her scarlet
hose; the fire-red face of the Summoner, which frightened children; the matted down, yellowish hair of the Pardoner; and many,
many more such details! But the outstanding feature of the
"General Prologue" is its conversational manner.

Among the best-known and best-loved passages in English
poetry is the one with which The Canterbury Tales opens:

> Whan that Aprill with his shoures soote
> The droghte of March hath perced to the roote,
> And bathed every veyne in swich licour
> Of which vertu engendred is the flour;
> Whan Zephirus eek with his sweete breeth
> Inspired hath in every holt and heeth
> The tendre croppes, and the yonge sonne
> Hath in the Ram his halve cours yronne,
> And smale foweles maken melodye,
> That slepen al the nyght with open ye
> (So priketh hem nature in hir corages);
> Thanne longen folk to goon on pilgrimages,
> And palmeres for to seken straunge strondes,
> To ferne halwes, kowthe in sondry londes;
> And specially from every shires ende
> Of Engelond to Caunterbury they wende,
> The hooly blisful martir for to seke,
> That hem hath holpen whan that they were seeke.

The passage consists of eighteen lines forming one complete
sentence. Yet, there is no obscurity or ambiguity whatsoever;
the reader, or listener, has absolutely no difficulty following
the train of thought. For Chaucer is in perfect control of the
syntax throughout. And the very structure of the sentence itself,
its slow, easy progress, its leisurely unfolding, its intricate
winding from thought to thought, is a perfect reflection of the
content--the intricate chain of interrelated events set in motion
by the approach of spring, when all things in the world of nature
slowly awaken from their long winter's sleep. The rain falls
and waters the roots; flowers are "engendred" and begin their
leisurely process of growing and unfolding; the sweet breeze
"inspires" the young and "tendre" crops; the birds once again
sing; so too man seems to awaken from the doldrums of winter and

is "inspired" with a yearning for activity, in this case, "to goon on pilgrimages."

The sentence is composed in two major movements. The opening movement, developed in the first eleven lines, sets the scene and establishes the atmosphere, thus providing the background against which the subsequent movement will be acted out. Most appropriately, this opening movement is cast in a subordinate construction made up of two subordinate clauses, each introduced by "Whan." The first of these is a simple subordinate clause consisting of a simple subject, "Aprill," and a compound predicate, "hath perced...and bathed"; the second, a compound subordinate clause dependent upon the "Whan" at the beginning of line five and comprised of three simple subjects with three simple predicates--"Zephirus...hath inspired," "sonne...hath yronne," and "foweles maken" respectively. The second movement, beginning at line twelve, introduces the central action of the entire framework, the pilgrimage, and is appropriately developed in two main clauses, the first of which consists of a compound subject, "folk...and palmeres," with a simple predicate, "longen," and the second of which consists of a simple subject and predicate, "they wende." The sentence is further complicated by a number of other subordinate modifying clauses: "Of which vertu engendred is the flour," modifying "licour"; "That slepen al the nyght with open ye," modifying "foweles"; "That hem hath holpen," modifying "martir"; "whan that they were seeke," modifying "holpen."

The idea Chaucer expresses here is a complex one, requiring a complex structure to be satisfactorily expressed. But the subordination is so skillfully handled, the grammatical constructions so straight-forward, the syntax so clear that, despite the elaborate and complex construction of this sentence, we are at no point confused by it nor ever in doubt as to Chaucer's meaning. Moreover, there is no apparent overt striving for effect. Rather, the whole passage seems quite unostentatious, and the remarkable naturalness of it all would seem to belie the craftsmanship that has been lavished upon it.

This illusion of perfect naturalness, of an almost spontaneous utterance, is enhanced by the over-all simplicity of the diction, the reference to "Zephirus" constituting the only significant exception. In this regard we might also note that Chaucer seems intentionally to avoid, wherever possible, words of romance origin and to use instead words of native origin, particularly words such as "holt," "heeth," "priketh," "longen," and "kowthe," where words of French origin would have been readily available. To be sure, Chaucer's vocabulary includes words of French origin, "corages" and "melodye" for example. But these words and others, like "inspired" and "engendred," which may have come into English from French or Latin, were already naturalized and commonplace by Chaucer's day.[16] In short,

Chaucer's audience would no doubt have found his vocabulary comfortably familiar and would have experienced little if any difficulty listening to him recite passages such as this.

But without question the single most significant factor contributing to the conversational quality of the passage is Chaucer's ability to capture the rhythms of conversation within the verse line and to create the easy and natural flow from line to line. To this end he employs a variety of devices, in particular metrical variation. For while the entire prologue is written primarily in decasyllabic couplets, the metrical norm being iambic pentameter, Chaucer neither in this opening passage nor elsewhere ever allows the syllabic or the metrical norm to constrain him, and he freely deviates from both to meet the syntactic demands of natural word order and to avoid monotonously regular rhythms antithetical to a conversational style.

In the opening lines of the passage a mildly run-on effect is created by the syntactic structure, the subject of the clause, "Aprill," being introduced in line one and the verb, "hath perced," delayed until line two. Contributing to this run-on effect is the succession of "s" sounds in the phrase "his shoures soote." The sound is drawn out and seems almost continuous, like the exhalation of a single breath, thus compressing the phrase itself and speeding up the movement of the last part of the line, in a sense hurrying us along to the next line. The run-on effect is further enhanced by the meter. The initial foot of line one is iambic, but Chaucer then shifts to a trochaic pattern, creating a slight pause where the two stressed syllables come together and a very strong emphasis on the first syllable of "Aprill," semantically the most significant word in the line. The next three feet are trochaic, but the line ends somewhat abruptly with a strong stress on "soote." The result is a seemingly incomplete last foot that urges the reader on to the next line, where, with the resumption of the iambic pattern, the "missing" syllable needed to complete the foot is provided and the metrical expectation, satisfied. That Chaucer intended "soote" to be heard as monosyllabic, the final "e" not being sounded, can be inferred from the evidence in the second line that strongly suggests Chaucer intended the rhyme word, "roote," to be heard as monosyllabic. For this second line is perfectly regular iambic pentameter, with no internal pauses; it flows smoothly toward the end-line pause that coincides with the completion of the syntactic unit, and a sounded final "e" would make no sense metrically or otherwise.

In the lines that follow we can again observe Chaucer varying the metrical pattern and employing subsidiary sound effects to achieve a conversational rhythm:

> Thanne longen folk to goon on pilgrimages,
> And palmeres for to seken straunge strondes,
> To ferne halwes, kowthe in sondry londes;
> And specially from every shires ende
> Of Engelond to Caunterbury they wende,
> The hooly blisful martir for to seke....

The first line is regular iambic pentameter, except that there is an extra unstressed syllable at the end. The first four feet of the next line are also iambic, but if "straunge" is read as monosyllabic, the last foot is trochaic. Such a reading results not only in an interruption of the reader's metrical expectation but also in a slight pause where the two unstressed syllables come together just before the end of the line, a pause reinforced by the "s" alliteration. The effect is to diminish the tendency toward the end-line pause sufficiently enough so that the reader is gently coerced into moving on to the next line, where the initial foot resumes the iambic pattern. But the second foot is again trochaic, as is the remainder of the line, and this shift again brings two strongly stressed syllables together, creating a stop and go movement that emphasizes the strong internal pause following "halwes."

The run-on effect created in the fourth line is more forceful, the movement more insistent because of the strong grammatical relationship between the last word of the line, the noun "ende," and the prepositional phrase modifying it, "Of Engelond," with which the next line begins. While this fourth line can be scanned as perfectly regular iambic pentameter, there are only four significantly strong stresses, the stress on the last syllable of "specially" only slightly more pronounced than on the preceding syllable or on "from," and the effect is more nearly dactyllic than iambic. The result is a line the movement of which is ever so slightly speeded up, a smoothly flowing line in which the repetition of the "sh" sound in "specially" and "shires" contributes to the movement, a line in which sound and meter combine to enhance the run-on effect.[17]

However, the conversational rhythms of this passage are not achieved entirely by such overt devices as subsidiary sound effects and the substitution of one kind of metrical foot for another. For Chaucer has also mastered the technique of subtly playing off the natural accentual patterns of the words themselves, as well as the linguistic stress patterns of the spoken language, against the metrical norm to enhance the conversational quality of the passage, even where the metrical pattern is perfectly regular. The following lines afford an excellent example of Chaucer's consummate skill in this regard:

Whan Zephirus eek with his sweete breeth
Inspired hath in every holt and heeth
The tendre croppes, and the yonge sonne
Hath in the Ram his halve cours yronne....

The first three lines are perfectly regular iambic pentameter;[18] the fourth, iambic pentameter with trochaic substitution
in the initial foot. Yet, the total effect is not an artifi-
cially rigid, monotonous rhythm played to the beat of a metro-
nome, but a rhythm much more conversationally natural. For the
iambic meter is not heavy-handed; it is more like a gentle under-
current, a leit-motif serving as a background against which the
linguistic and semantic stress patterns are played. In the
first line, there are only three significant strong stresses,
falling on the three most semantically significant points in the
line--on the first syllable of "Zephirus," on "sweete," and on
"breeth." Though placed at points within the verse line where
the iambic pentameter norm creates the expectation of a relatively strong stress, the last syllable of "Zephirus" and the
semantically insignificant "with" receive stresses that are,
when we read the line, just barely noticeable. And the line,
like a gust of April wind, seems to rush along, the hurried
movement contributing to the run-on effect created by the
syntactic structure.
Chaucer's manipulation of syntax here is also noteworthy.
Unlike the fourth line, where Chaucer's placing of the auxiliary
verb "hath" at the beginning of the line results in an initial
trochaic foot and a strong metrical stress on the auxiliary
verb, the second line has an inverted verbal construction,
Chaucer having placed the main verb first. The effect is to
reduce the metrical emphasis on the auxiliary verb, which,
though placed in a strong stress position within the iambic
pattern, does not carry the same weight as it does in the fourth
line. Consequently, this second line has only four significant
stresses--on the second syllable of "inspired," on the first
syllable of "every," and on "holt" and "heeth," where the metrical emphasis is reinforced by the alliteration. The effect is
to carry on the hurried movement, begun in the previous line,
which so nicely reflects the April wind. And here again this
hurried movement reinforces the run-on effect created by the
syntax. Chaucer begins the third line with the direct object
of the verb at the beginning of the second line, separating the
direct object from the verb by a prepositional phrase that fills
out the initial line. The direct object completes the syntactic
unit, and at this point in the line there is a strong internal
pause required by the syntax, a pause that coincides precisely
with the point at which we seem almost to run out of breath.
The movement from the first line to the mid-point of the third
line is almost continuous, like the gust of wind that "inspires"
the "tendre croppes." And just as this gust of wind dies down,

just as Zephirus has, so to speak, expended his breath, so the reader has expended his breath and comes to a pause, a pause that allows the reader to take a fresh breath before continuing on to the next syntactic unit, which introduces a new thought.

The true test of Chaucer's poetry is, indeed, in the reading. In the final analysis it is really necessary to read such a passage aloud to appreciate how effectively Chaucer has re-created here the qualities of a conversational style. For despite the complex structure of the sentence, despite the pre-dominantly regular metrical pattern, despite the effect of the rhyme scheme, the rhythm of each line and the movement from line to line is eminently natural; indeed, the progress of the entire sentence is eminently natural and, equally important, at all times perfectly clear.

In this opening passage of The Canterbury Tales Chaucer shows what a poet working in the native English poetic tradition is ultimately capable of achieving. The quality I have referred to as "English," which is so distinctive a mark of The Canterbury Tales as a whole, and of this opening passage as well, is largely a matter of conscientious stylistic techniques. The use of a largely native vocabulary including its most graphic and idiomatic expressions; the use of subsidiary sound effects, especially alliteration, and other patterns of verbal and structural repetition; the emphasis on the syntactic unit and the concomitant accommodation of meter to syntax; the use of metrical stress to reinforce semantic emphasis and of metrical variation to capture the rhythms of conversation; the use of run-on lines--these are the techniques that Chaucer employs so effectively to create a conversational style, eminently natural and, at the same time, visually concrete, a style marked by its directness, explicitness, and clarity. These stylistic tech-niques, so instrumental in the development of Chaucer's mature style, are in some part or other rooted in and derived from the English poetic tradition that emerged after the Conquest, the native tradition to which Chaucer was heir and which he brought to fullest fruition in The Canterbury Tales. Stylistically, this native tradition leads to a poetry in Chaucer that is, above all else, conversational in manner and visually concrete. And so at least with regard to its style, Chaucer's poetry in gen-eral, and The Canterbury Tales in particular, does not so much represent the beginning of a new tradition in English poetry as the culmination of the native tradition that Chaucer inherited, a tradition itself rooted in pre-Conquest English poetic soil and, in many respects, already highly developed and refined by Chaucer's day as the result of the work of the many poets, them-selves largely unknown, who preceded him, not least among whom were the composers of the early Middle English lyrics.

1
Quoted from Francesco Petrarca, Opere, ed. Giovanni Ponte (Milan, 1968).

2
"The 'Canticus Troili': Chaucer and Petrarch," Comparative Literature 11(1959): 318.

3
For an interesting discussion of how Chaucer draws on native material to transform his source for Troilus' letter to Criseyde (V, 1317-1421), see Norman Davis, "The Litera Troili and English Letters," Review of English Studies 16(1965): 233-244.

4
Discussion of the "Prologue" is based on the F Text.

5
Quoted from Nathaniel Edward Griffin and Arthur Beckwith Myrick, The Filostrato of Giovanni Boccaccio (Oxford: Oxford Univ. Press, 1929), 134.

6
In his notes on this passage F. N. Robinson remarks that the simile of the harp suggests the title of Machaut's Dit de la Harpe. But he also points out that there is not evidence for Chaucer's use of the French (842).

7
Noteworthy also in this regard is Chaucer's reference to "oure toun" in line 43 as he begins his exquisite passage on the daisy.

8
All passages from the Roman are cited from Ronald Sutherland, The Romaunt of the Rose and Le Roman de la Rose (Oxford: Blackwell, 1967).

9
Geissman alludes to one such difference in passing. Referring to Mersand's study of the vocabulary of the Romaunt of the Rose, Geissman remarks, "These figures are interesting as indicative of the predominantly native character of Chaucer's vocabulary even when he is translating closely from a Romance Source" (159).

10
For a careful and detailed study of Chaucer's descriptive techniques, see Claes Schaar, The Golden Mirror (Denmark, 1967). Schaar's basic argument is that Chaucer's descriptive technique derives essentially from a common medieval continental tradition, though he is careful to point out that certain features of his descriptive technique, particularly his use of concreteness in

certain special situations, seems more closely related to native English practice than to continental practice. Though Schaar draws most of his parallels with earlier English narrative poetry, particularly the romances, and with <u>Piers Plowman</u>, his argument in this respect coincides with my own sense that this quality is, indeed, characteristic of the native tradition in general. For we have seen that it is characteristic of the lyrics as well. However, Schaar's suggestion that such con- creteness is a fairly late development in Chaucer's art seems to me highly doubtful. And I would take issue with his observa- tion that, "We may notice, on the whole, a slight tendency in the works previous to the <u>Canterbury Tales</u> to represent people described in a more abstract and vague and less concrete manner than is found in the originals..." (245). As I hope to have shown in this examination of Chaucer's translation of the Roman, as well as in the earlier discussion of the "ABC," this tendency toward greater concreteness is already clearly marked in Chaucer's earliest work and signifies his indebtedness to the native poetic tradition even in these early poetic ventures.

11
Chaucer achieves the same effect a few lines later:

> Hard is the hert that loveth nought
> In May, whan al this mirth is wrought....(85-86)

Here, however, the second line is Chaucer's own addition; it does not occur in the original.

12
While run-on constructions are characteristic of Guillaume's style and occur with great frequency in his poem, Chaucer throughout his translation outdoes his source in the use of this device. For additional examples of Chaucer's particularly effec- tive use of run-on constructions where the original is end- stopped, see lines 11-12, 33-34, 45-46, 88-89, 137-138, 324-325, 433-434, 496-497, 543-544, 621-622.

13
While Chaucer occasionally begins a line with a semantically insignificant word where the original has a semantically signifi- cant one, his over-all tendency by far is in the opposite direc- tion. Throughout his translation he places semantically signifi- cant words, accompanied by strong metrical stress, at beginnings of lines where the French has a semantically insignificant word. These may be verbs (lines 129, 138, 282, 771, 1004, 1575), adjectives (lines 861, 923, 942), or nouns (lines 508, 680, 764, 1186, 1467).

14
Elbert Thompson also describes Chaucer's handling of the octo- syllabic couplet in his analysis of the measure as it is used in

The House of Fame. And the features of Chaucer's style that Thompson emphasizes, like those pointed out by Bennet, are, as we have seen, characteristic of the style of the early Middle English lyrics:

> Chaucer, of course, despite his professions
> to the contrary, knew the principles of
> medieval rhetoric, yet his expression is
> never bound by rule. And even though his
> verse seems limpid in its simplicity, he
> all the while practiced modulations that
> have been constant features of easy-flowing
> octosyllabic poetry. Run-on lines are frequent,
> little heed is given to balance of phrase, and
> the thought is never forced into the mold of
> the couplet. Indeed, the couplets often lose
> their identity in the syntax....

"The Octosyllabic Couplet," _PQ_ 18(1939): 258.

15
Commenting upon J.V. Cunningham's well-known argument that the portraits in the _Roman de la Rose_ provide models for Chaucer's portraits in the "General Prologue," (_Tradition and Poetic Structure_. Denver: 1960), Claes Schaar remarks, "If we want to find closer parallels to these we will find it fruitful to turn from continental literature to vernacular Middle English Poetry" (314).

16
Nor does it seem likely that even more recent additions, like "veyne" and "licour" would be unfamiliar to Chaucer's sophisticated audience.

17
My own impression that more of Chaucer's verse lines are run-on than has heretofore been recognized has been reinforced by the publication of Professor John H. Fisher's edition of Chaucer's works (_The Complete Poetry and Prose of Geoffrey Chaucer_. New York: Holt, Rinehart and Winston, 1977). Professor Fisher, who also evidently reads more of Chaucer's lines as run-on than have previous editors, places no commas at the end of lines 13 and 16 of the "General Prologue," the lines presently under discussion, nor at the end of line 17. In F. N. Robinson's edition, commas are placed at the end of each of these lines.

18
Here it seems right and natural, and makes sense metrically, to slightly sound the final "e" of "sweete" and "yonge."

CONCLUSION

Commenting upon Chaucer's <u>The House of Fame</u>, Patricia Kean writes, "It is perhaps not going too far to suggest that one of the underlying problems which Chaucer tries to thrash out in this strange poem is the exact relation of a poet of his day, with all France and Italy to draw on in addition to the Classical language of Virgil and Ovid, to his own roots in his own language" (<u>Love Vision and Debate</u>, III). But the implications here are much more far-reaching than her tentative suggestion about Chaucer's intention in this one poem. For, in a broader sense, this was Chaucer's problem throughout his poetic career; even more, this was perhaps the most fundamental problem of English poets from the time of the Conquest to Chaucer. In their attempts to solve this problem, to find ways of bringing harmoniously together their own pre-Conquest poetic inheritance with continental traditions, Chaucer's predecessors laid the foundation of a new English poetic tradition and prepared the way for Chaucer's ultimate triumphs.

Chaucer himself seems to have understood fully the implications of the fact that he was an English poet and, even more, that he had to be an English poet if he was to succeed with his poetry. For Chaucer this meant more than simply writing in English; it meant, from the very beginning of his literary career, committing himself to and drawing upon the vital poetic tradition left him by his English predecessors. George Saintsbury puts it well:

> It was by using to the very utmost what already
> existed, by getting the last pound of work out
> of the actual conditions of English poetry, by
> doing everything that was possible at the moment,
> with the materials accumulated and the methods
> left him by his predecessors, that Chaucer is
> Chaucer. (<u>History of English Prosody</u>, 197)

And, we might add, that Chaucer is English!

Chaucer's poetry does not represent so much the beginning of a new tradition that we can credit him with fathering as the culmination of the tradition he inherited, not exclusively nor even primarily the Romance tradition of continental Europe but a native poetic tradition that had been evolving for three centuries. Nor did Chaucer find this native tradition a barren wasteland; rather, he found it a fertile garden. And like a skillful gardener he not only cultivated the natural beauties of the garden, but added to them. He introduced beautiful flowers from France and Italy; he planted new seeds, some of which blossomed immediately, others which would burst into exquisite bloom in future generations. Where Chaucer had found a fertile

garden, he left a veritable cornucopia, a bountiful garden of
Nature,

> ful of blosmy bowes
> Upon a ryver, in a grene mede,
> There as swetnesse everemore inow is,
> With floures white, blewe, yelwe, and rede....

SELECTED BIBLIOGRAPHY

History and Development of English Poetry

Adams, Percy G. "The Historical Importance of Assonance to
    Poets." PMLA 88(1973): 8-18.
Andrew, S.O. Syntax and Style in Old English. London:
    Cambridge UP, 1940.
Baugh, Albert C., ed. A Literary History of England. New York:
    Appleton-Century-Crofts, 1948.
Baum, Paull F. The Principles of English Versification. 1922.
    Hampden, Ct.: Shoe String, 1969.
Bloomfield, Morton. "Understanding Old English Poetry." Annuale
    Mediaevale 9(1968): 5-25.
Chambers, E.K. English Literature at the Close of the Middle
    Ages. Oxford: Clarendon, 1945.
Chambers, R.W. On the Continuity of English Prose from Alfred
    to More and His School. Oxford: Oxford UP, 1932.
Chatman, Seymour. A Theory of Meter. The Hague, 1965.
Chaytor, H.J. The Troubadours and England. London: Cambridge
    UP, 1923.
------------. From Script to Print. London: Cambridge UP, 1945.
Clark, Donald L. "Rhetoric and the Literature of the English
    Middle Ages." Quarterly Journal of Speech 45(1959): 19-28.
Courthope, W.J. A History of English Poetry. New York:
    Macmillan, 1895.
Ford, Boris, ed. The Age of Chaucer. Vol. I of A Guide to
    English Literature. Baltimore: Penguin, 1954.
Friedlander, Carolynn VanDyke. "Early Middle English Accentual
    Verse." MP 76(1978): 219-230.
Gollancz, Sir Israel. "The Middle Ages in the Lineage of English
    Literature." Medieval Contributions to Modern Civilization.
    Ed. F.J.C. Hearnshaw. 2nd ed. New York: Barnes and Noble,
    1949.
Grierson, J.C. and J.C. Smith. A Critical History of English
    Poetry. New York: Oxford UP, 1946.
Gruber, L.C. "The Wanderer and Arcite: Isolation and the Con-
    tinuity of the English Elegiac Mode." Four Papers for
    Michio Masui. Denver: The Society for New Language Study,
    1972. 1-10.
Gummere, Francis B. "The Translation of Beowulf and the Rela-
    tions of Ancient and Modern English Verse." American
    Journal of Philology 7(1886): 46-78.
Halle, Morris and Samuel J. Keyser. English Stress: Its Form,
    Its Growth, and Its Role in Verse. New York: Harper &
    Row, 1971.
Hamer, Enid. The Metres of English Poetry. London, 1961.
Kaluza, Max. A Short History of English Versification. Tr.
    A.C. Dunstan. London: Geo. Allen and Co., 1911.

232

Kane, George. _Middle English Literature_. London: Methuen, 1951.

Ker, W.P. _Medieval English Literature_. London: Oxford UP, 1912.

Lewis, C.S. "The Fifteenth Century Heroic Line." _ES_ 29(1938): 28-41.

Malof, Joseph. "The Native Rhythm of English Meters." _Texas Studies in Language and Literature_ 5(1964): 580-594.

Medary, Margaret P. and Carleton Brown. "Stanza-Linking in Middle English Verse." _Romanic Review_ 7(1916): 243-270.

Oakden, J.P. _Alliterative Poetry in Middle English_. 2 vols. Manchester: Manchester UP, 1935.

Owen, Lewis J. and Nancy H. Owen, eds. _Middle English Poetry_. New York: Bobbs-Merrill, 1971.

Pearsall, Derek. _Old English and Middle English Poetry_. London: Routledge & Kegan Paul, 1977.

Rarick, Louise. "Ten Syllable Lines in English Poetry." _Neuphilologische Mitteilungen_ 75(1974): 66-73.

Saintsbury, George. _A History of English Prosody_. 2nd ed. London: Macmillan, 1923.

Salter, Elizabeth. "The Alliterative Revival." _MP_ 64(1967): 146-150, 233-237.

Sandison, Helen. _The Chanson D'Aventure in Middle English_. Bryn Mawr College Monographs. Bryn Mawr, 1913.

Schipper, Jakob. _A History of English Versification_. Oxford: Oxford UP, 1910.

Schofield, W.H. _English Literature from the Norman Conquest to Chaucer_. New York: Macmillan, 1906.

Speirs, John. _Medieval English Poetry: The Non-Chaucerian Tradition_. London: Faber, 1957.

Stone, Brian, ed. _Medieval English Verse_. Baltimore: Penguin, 1964.

Sykes, F.H. _French Elements in Middle English_. Oxford: Oxford UP, 1899.

Tarlinskaya, Marina. "The Syllabic Structure and Meter of English Verse from the Thirteenth through the Nineteenth Century." _Language and Style_ 6(1973): 249-272.

Thompson, John. _The Founding of English Meter_. London, 1961.

Trager, G.L. and H.L. Smith, Jr. _An Outline of English Structure_. Washington: American Council of Learned Societies, 1957.

Tripp, Raymond P. "On the Continuity of English Poetry between _Beowulf_ and Chaucer." _Poetica_ (Fall, 1976): 1-21.

----------. "The Dialectics of Debate and the Continuity of English Poetry." _Massachusetts Studies in English_ 7(1978): 41-51.

Waldron, Ronald A. "Oral Formulaic Technique and Middle English Alliterative Poetry." _Speculum_ 32(1957): 792-804.

Wilson, R.M. _Early Middle English Literature_. London: Methuen, 1939.

----------. _The Lost Literature of Medieval England_. London: Methuen, 1952.

------------. "On the Continuity of English Prose." Mélanges
de linguistique de philologie. Fernand Mossé in Memorium.
Paris, 1959.
Wimsatt, W.K. The Verbal Icon. Lexington: U of Kentucky P,
1954.
------------ and Monroe C. Beardsley. "The Concept of Meter:
An Exercise in Abstraction." PMLA 74(1959); rpt. in
W.K. Wimsatt. Hateful Contraries. Lexington: U of
Kentucky P, 1965.
Wrenn, C.L. "On the Continuity of English Poetry." Anglia
76(1958): 41-59.
Wyld, C. "Diction and Imagery in Anglo-Saxon Poetry." ES
11(1925): 49-91.
------------. "Laymon as an English Poet." RES 6(1930): 1-30.

Medieval Poetry

Baldwin, Charles Sears. Medieval Rhetoric and Poetic.
Gloucester, Mass.: Peter Smith, 1959.
Bowra, Sir Maurice. Medieval Love-Song. The John Coffin
Memorial Lecture. London, 1961.
Chaytor, H.J. The Troubadours. London: Cambridge UP, 1912.
Crosby, Ruth. "Oral Delivery in the Middle Ages." Speculum
11(1936): 88-110.
Curtius, Ernst R. European Literature and the Latin Middle
Ages. Tr. Willard R. Trask. New York: Routledge and
Kegan Paul, 1953.
Dronke, Peter. Medieval Latin and the Rise of the European Love-
Lyric. 2 vols. Oxford: Oxford UP, 1965.
------------. The Medieval Lyric. London: Hutchinson, 1968.
Faral, Edmond. Les Arts Poétiques du XIIe e du XIIIe Siecle.
Paris: É Champion, 1924.
Gaselee, Stephen. The Transition from the Late Latin Lyric to
the Medieval Love Poem. Cambridge, Mass.: Harvard UP,
1931.
Goldin, Frederick. German and Italian Lyrics of the Middle
Ages. New York: Doubleday, 1973.
------------. Lyrics of the Troubadours and Trouveres. New
York: Doubleday, 1973.
Hill, R.T. and T.G. Bergin. Anthology of the Provençal
Troubadours. 2nd ed. 2 vols. New York: Yale UP, 1973.
Jeanroy, A. Les origines de la poésie lyrique en France au moyen
âge. Paris: Champion, 1889.
------------. La poésie lyrique des troubadours. 2 vols. Paris:
Didier, 1934.
Ker, W.P. Epic and Romance. London: Constable, 1896.
Meyer, P. "Le couplet de deux vers." Romania 23(1894): 1-35.
Myrick, A.B. and N.E. Griffin, eds. The Filostrato of Giovanni
Boccaccio. Oxford: Oxford UP, 1929.

234

Nichols, Stephen G., Jr. "The Medieval Lyric and Its Public."
     Medievalia et Humanistica, NS 3(1972): 133-153.
Paris, Gaston. _La poésie du moyen âge_. Paris: Champion, 1895.
Raby, F.J.E. _A History of Christian-Latin Poetry_. Oxford:
     Clarendon, 1927.
----------. _A History of Secular Latin Poetry in the Middle
     Ages_. 2 vol. Oxford: Clarendon, 1934.
Smalley, Beryl. _The Study of the Bible in the Middle Ages_.
     Notre Dame: U of Notre Dame P, 1964.
Voretzsch, Carl. _Introduction to the Study of Old French
     Literature_. Tr. Francis M. DuMont. 3rd ed. Halle:
     Max Niemeyer, 1931.
Wilhelm, James J., ed. _Medieval Song_. New York: Dutton, 1971.

Middle English Lyrics

Abel, Patricia Anna. "Imagery in the English Medieval Secular
     Lyric in the Thirteenth and Fourteenth Centuries." Diss.
     U of Missouri, 1957.
Baskerville, C.R. "English Songs on the Night Visit." _PMLA_
     36(1921): 594-621.
Brook, G.L. "The Original Dialects of the Harley Lyrics." _Leeds
     Studies in English and Kindred Languages_ 2(1933): 38-61.
----------, ed. _The Harley Lyrics_. Manchester: Manchester
     UP, 1948.
Brown, Carleton, ed. _Religious Lyrics of the XIVth Century_.
     Oxford: Clarendon, 1924.
----------, ed. _English Lyrics of the XIIIth Century_. Oxford:
     Clarendon, 1932.
----------, ed. _Religious Lyrics of the XVth Century_. Oxford:
     Clarendon, 1939.
Davies, R.T., ed. _Medieval English Lyrics_. London: Nelson,
     1963.
Degginger, Stuart H. Lewis. "The Earliest Middle English Lyrics
     1150-1325; An Investigation of the Influence of Latin,
     Provençal and French." Diss. Columbia U, 1953.
Evans, Robert. "A Neglected Fourteenth-Century Religious Lyric."
     Studies in Medieval Culture 4(1974): 368-373.
Fifield, Merle Jane. "Alliteration in the Middle English Lyric."
     Diss. U of Illinois, 1960.
----------. "Thirteenth-Century Lyrics and the Alliterative
     Tradition." _JEGP_ 62(1963): 111-118.
Gibinska, Marta. "Some Observations on the Themes and Techniques
     of the Medieval Religious Love Lyrics." _ES_ 57(1976): 103-
     114.
Gray, Douglas. "The Five Wounds of Our Lord." _NQ_ 208(1963):
     50-51, 82-89, 127-134, 163-168.
Greene, Richard Leighton, ed. _The Early English Carols_. Oxford:
     Clarendon, 1935.

Hall, Joseph, ed. The Poems of Laurence Minot. Oxford:
    Clarendon, 1914.
Hogan, Sister Theresa Clare. "A Critical Study of the Middle
    English Lyrics of British Museum MS. Harley 2253." Diss.
    U of Notre Dame, 1962.
Honour, Margaret C. "The Metrical Derivation of the Medieval
    English Lyric." Diss. Yale U, 1949.
Kinney, Thomas Leroy. "English Verse of Complaint, 1250-1400."
    Diss. U of Michigan, 1959.
Malone, Kemp. "Notes on Middle English Lyrics." ELH 2(1935):
    58-65.
Manning, Stephen. Wisdom and Number: Toward A Critical Appraisal
    of the Middle English Relgious Lyric. Lincoln: U of
    Nebraska P, 1962.
Matonis, A.T.E. "An Investigation of Celtic Influences on MS.
    Harley 2253." MP 70(1972): 91-108.
Menner, Robert J. "Notes on Middle English Lyrics." MLN
    55(1940): 243-249.
Meroney, Howard. "Line-Notes on the Early English Lyrics." MLN
    62(1947): 61-64.
Moore, Arthur K. The Secular Lyric in Middle English. Lexington:
    U of Kentucky P, 1951.
Oliver, Raymond. Poems Without Names: The English Lyric,
    1200-1500. Berkeley: U of California P, 1970.
Osberg, Richard H. "The Alliterative Lyric and Thirteenth
    Century Devotional Prose." JEGP 76(1977): 40-54.
Patterson, Frank Allen. The Middle English Penitential Lyric.
    New York: Columbia UP, 1911.
Person, Henry A. Cambridge Middle English Lyrics. Seattle: U
    of Washington P, 1953.
Reed, E.B. English Lyrical Poetry. London: Oxford UP, 1916.
Rees, Elinor. "A Study of the Portrayal of Moods and Emotions in
    Early English Vernacular Lyrical Poetry." Stanford Univer-
    sity Bulletin, Abstracts of Dissertations 11(1935-36):
    57-63.
----------. "Provençal Elements in the English Vernacular Lyrics
    of Manuscript Harley 2253." Stanford Studies in Language
    and Literature. Ed. Hardin Craig. Stanford, 1941.
Reiss, Edmund. "A Critical Approach to the Middle English Lyric."
    CE 27(1966): 273-279.
Revard, Carter. "Sulch Sorw I Walke With." NQ, NS 25(1978): 200.
----------. "The Lecher, the Legal Eagle, and the Papelard Priest:
    Middle English Confessional Satires in MS. Harley 2253 and
    Elsewhere." His Firm Estate: Essays Presented to Franklin
    James Eckenberry. U of Tulsa Monograph Series No. 2(1967):
    54-71.
Robbins, Rossell Hope. "The Earliest Carols and the Franciscans."
    MLN 53(1938): 39-45.
----------. "Popular Prayers in Middle English Verse." MP
    36(1938-39): 337-350.

----------. "Private Prayers in Middle English Verse." Speculum 36(1939): 466-475.

----------. "The Authors of the Middle English Religious Lyrics." JEGP 39(1940): 230-238.

----------. "A Highly Critical Approach to the Middle English Lyrics." CE 30(1968): 74-75.

----------. "The Lyrics." Companion to Chaucer Studies. Ed. Beryl Rowland. Rev. ed. Oxford: Oxford UP, 1979. 380-402.

----------. "The Middle English Court Love Lyric." The Interpretation of Medieval Lyric Poetry. Ed. W.T.H. Jackson. New York: Columbia UP, 1980. 205-232.

----------, ed. Secular Lyrics of the XIVth and XVth Centuries. Oxford: Clarendon, 1952.

----------, ed. Historical Poems of the XIVth and XVth Centuries. New York: Columbia UP, 1959.

Ross, Thomas W. "Five Fifteenth Century 'Emblem' Verses from Brit. Mus. Addit. Ms. 37049." Speculum 32(1957): 274-282.

Saintsbury, George. The Historical Character of English Lyric. Warton Lecture on English Poetry. Proceedings of the British Academy. Vol. V. London, 1912.

Schelling, Felix E. The English Lyric. Boston: Houghton Mifflin, 1913.

Schoeck, R.J. "Alliterative Assonance in Harley MS. 2253." ES 32(1951): 68-70.

Sikora, Ruta. "Structural Simplicity of the Early Middle English Lyrics: Three Examples." Kwartalnik Neofilologiczny 11(1964): 233-242.

Spitzer, Leo. "Explication de Texte Applied to Three Great Middle English Poems." Archivum Linguisticum 3(1951): 1-22, 137-165.

Stevick, Robert D. "The Criticism of Middle English Lyrics." MP 64(1966): 103-117.

Taylor, G.C. "The English Planctus Mariae." MP 4(1906): 605-637.

Weber, Sarah A. Theology and Poetry in the Middle English Lyric. Columbus: Ohio State UP, 1969.

White, Natalie E. "The English Liturgical Refrain Lyric before 1450 with Special Reference to the Fourteenth Century." Diss. Stanford U, 1945.

Woolf, Rosemary. The English Religious Lyric in the Middle Ages. Oxford: Oxford UP, 1968.

Chaucer: Poetry and Poetics

Adams, Percy G. "Chaucer's Assonance." JEGP 71(1972): 527-539.

Baum, Paull F. Chaucer's Verse. Durham: Duke UP, 1961.

Bennett, H.S. Chaucer and the Fifteenth Century. Oxford: Oxford UP, 1947.

Benson, L.D. "A Reader's Guide to Writings on Chaucer." Writers and Their Backgrounds: Geoffrey Chaucer. Ed. Derek Brewer. Athens: Ohio UP, 1975. 321-351.

Blake, N.F. "Chaucer and the Alliterative Romances." Chaucer Review 3(1969): 163-169.

Bland, D.S. "Chaucer and the Art of Narrative Verse." English 7(1949): 216-220.

Braddy, Haldeen. Chaucer and the French Poet, Graunson. Baton Rouge: Louisiana State UP, 1947.

Brewer, D.S. "The Ideal of Feminine Beauty in Medieval Literature, Especially 'Harley Lyrics,' Chaucer, and Some Elizabethans." MLR 50(1955): 257-269.

------------. Chaucer in His Time. London: Nelson, 1963.

------------, ed. Chaucer and Chaucerians. London: Nelson, 1966.

------------. "Toward a Chaucerian Poetic." Proceedings of the British Academy 60(1974): 219-252.

Bronson, Bertrand H. In Search of Chaucer. Toronto: U of Toronto P, 1960.

------------, et. al. Five Studies in Literature. Berkeley: U of California P, 1940.

Brown, Emerson. "Chaucer and the European Literary Tradition." Geoffrey Chaucer: A Collection of Original Articles. Ed. George D. Economou. New York: McGraw Hill, 1975. 37-54.

Brusendorf, Aage. The Chaucer Tradition. London: Oxford UP, 1925.

Bryan, William and G.C. Dempster, eds. Sources and Analogues of Chaucer's Canterbury Tales. Chicago: U of Chicago P, 1941.

Burrow, J.A. Ricardian Poetry. New Haven: Yale UP, 1971.

Chesterton, G.K. "Chaucer as an Englishman." Chaucer. New York: Greenwood, 1956. Ch. VI, 176-204.

Christianson, Paul. "Chaucer's Literacy." Chaucer Review 11(1976): 112-127.

Clemen, Wolfgang. Chaucer's Early Poetry. Tr. C.A.M. Sym. London: Methuen, 1963.

Coffman, G.R. "Old Age from Horace to Chaucer." Speculum 9(1934): 249-277.

Coghill, Neville. The Poet Chaucer. London: Oxford UP, 1947.

Coulton, G.G. Chaucer and His England. London: Methuen, 1921.

Cowling, G.H. "A Note on Chaucer's Stanza." RES 2(1926): 311-317.

Crosby, Ruth. "Chaucer and the Custom of Oral Delivery." Speculum 13(1938): 413-432.

Cummings, Hubertis M. The Idebtedness of Chaucer's Works to the Italian Works of Boccaccio. U of Cincinnati Studies, Series II, Vol. X, 1944.

Cunningham, J.V. Tradition and Poetic Structure. Denver: Swallow, 1960.

D'Ardenne, S.R.T.O. "Chaucer, the Englishman." *Chaucer und seine Zeit: Symposion fur Walter Schirmer*. Ed. Arno Esch. Tubingen: Max Niemeyer, 1968. 47-54.

David, Alfred. "The Man of Law vs. Chaucer: A Case in Poetics." *PMLA* 82(1967): 217-225.

----------. *The Strumpet Muse: Art and Morals in Chaucer's Poetry*. Bloomington: Indiana UP, 1976.

Davis, Norman. "The Litera Troili and English Letters." *RES* 16(1965): 233-244.

----------. "Chaucer and Fourteenth-Century English." *Writers and Their Backgrounds: Geoffrey Chaucer*. Ed. Derek Brewer. Athens: Ohio UP, 1975. 58-84.

Delasanta, Rodney. "Penance and Poetry in the *Canterbury Tales*." *PMLA* 93(1978): 240-247.

Dempster, Germaine. "Chaucer at Work on the Complaint in the Franklin's Tale." *MLN* 52(1937): 16-32.

Donaldson, E.T. "Idiom of Popular Poetry in the *Miller's Tale*. *English Institute Essays*. New York: Columbia UP, 1950.

----------. "Chaucer and the Elusion of Clarity." *Essays and Studies in Honour of Beatrice White*. Ed. T.S. Dorsch. London, 1972.

----------. "Gallic Flies in Chaucer's English Word Web." *New Perspectives in Chaucer Criticism*. Ed. Donald M. Rose. Norman: Pilgrim Books, 1981. 193-202.

Donner, Morton. "Derived Words in Chaucer's Language." *Chaucer Review* 13(1978): 1-15.

Economou, George D. "Introduction: Chaucer the Innovator." *Geoffrey Chaucer: A Collection of Original Articles*. Ed. George D. Economou. New York: McGraw Hill, 1975. 1-14.

Eliason, Norman E. *The Language of Chaucer's Poetry*. *Anglistica*. Vol. XVII. Copenhagen: Rosenkilde and Bagger, 1972.

Elliott, Ralph W.V. *Chaucer's English*. London: Deutsch, 1974.

Emerson, Oliver Farrar. "English or French in the Time of Edward III." *Chaucer: Essays and Studies*. 1929. Freeport: Books for Libraries, 1970. 271-297.

Everett, Dorothy. "Chaucer's Good Ear." *RES* 23(1947): 201-208.

Fansler, D.S. *Chaucer and the Roman de la Rose*. *Columbia Studies in English and Comparative Literature*. Vol. 7. New York, 1914.

Fichte, Joerg O. *Chaucer's Art Poetical: A Study in Chaucerian Poetics*. Tubingen: Gunter Narr Verlag, 1980.

Finnie, Bruce W. "On Chaucer's Stressed Vowel Phonemes." *Chaucer Review* 9(1975): 337-341.

Fisher, John H. "Chaucer and the French Influence." *New Perspectives in Chaucer Criticism*. Ed. Donald M. Rose, Norman: Pilgrim Books, 1981. 177-191.

Fox, Denton. "The Scottish Chaucerians." Chaucer and Chaucerians. Ed. D.S. Brewer. London: Nelson, 1966.

Friedman, John B. "The Nun's Priest's Tale: The Preacher and the Mermaid's Song." Chaucer Review 7(1973): 250-266.

Fyler, John. Chaucer and Ovid. New Haven: Yale UP, 1979.

Gaylord, Alan T. "Sentence and Solaas in Fragment VII of the Canterbury Tales: Harry Bailly as Horseback Editor." PMLA 82(1967): 226-235.

------------. "Scanning the Prosodists: An Essay in Meta-criticism." Chaucer Review 11(1976): 22-82.

Geissman, Erwin W. "The Style and Technique of Chaucer's Trans-lations from French." Diss. Yale U, 1952.

Halle, Morris, and S.J. Keyser. "Chaucer and the Study of Prosody." CE 28(1966): 187-219.

Haskell, Ann S. "Lyrics and Lyrical in the Works of Chaucer: The Poet in His Literary Context." English Symposium Papers, III. Ed. Douglas Shepard. Fredonia: SUNY College at Fredonia, 1972. 1-45.

Hussey, M., A.C. Spearing and J. Winny. An Introduction to Chaucer. London: Cambridge UP, 1965.

Jefferson, Bernard L. Chaucer and the Consolation of Philosophy of Boethius. Princeton: Princeton UP, 1917.

Kean, Patricia M. Chaucer and the Making of English Poetry. 2 vols. London: Routledge and Kegan Paul, 1972.

Kirk, Elizabeth D. "Chaucer and His English Contemporaries." Geoffrey Chaucer: A Collection of Original Articles. Ed. George D. Economou. New York: McGraw Hill, 1975. 112-127.

Kitchel, A.T. "Chaucer and Machaut's Dit de la Fontaine Amoureuse." Vassar Medieval Studies, 1923.

Kittredge, G.L. Chaucer and His Poetry. Cambridge, Mass.: Harvard UP, 1915.

------------. "Guillaume de Machaut and the Book of the Duchess." PMLA 30(1915): 1-22.

Landrum, Grace W. "Chaucer's Use of the Vulgate." PMLA 39(1924): 75-100.

Licklider, Albert H. Chapters on the Metrics of the Chaucerian Tradition. Baltimore: J.H. Furst Co., 1910.

Lindner, Felix. "The Alliteration in Chaucer's Canterbury Tales." Chaucer Society Publications, 2nd series, no. 2 Rostock, 1878.

Loomis, L.H. "Chaucer and the Auchinleck MS." Essays and Studies in Honor of Carleton Brown. New York, 1940.

Lowes, J.L. "The Chaucerian 'Merciles Beaute' and Three Poems of Deschamps." MLR 5(1910): 33-39.

------------. "Chaucer and the Miroir de Mariage." MP 8(1910-11): 165ff. and 305ff.

------------. "Chaucer and Dante." MP 14(1916-17): 705ff.

------------. The Art of Geoffrey Chaucer. London: Oxford UP, 1930.

------------. Geoffrey Chaucer and the Development of His Genius. Boston: Houghton Mifflin, 1934.

240

Lynn, Karen. "Chaucer's Decasyllabic Line: The Myth of the Hundred-Year Hibernation." Chaucer Review 13(1978): 116-127.

Madeleva, Sister Mary. A Lost Language and Other Essays on Chaucer. New York: Sheed, 1951.

Malone, Kemp. "Chaucer's 'Book of the Duchess': A Metrical Study." Chaucer und seine Zeite: Symposion fur Walter Schirmer. Ed. Arno Esch. Tubingen: Max Niemeyer, 1968. 71-95.

Manly, J.M. Chaucer and the Rhetoricians. Warton Lecture on English Poetry. Proceedings of the British Academy. London, 1962.

Maynard, Theodore. "The Connection between the Ballade, Chaucer's Modification of It, Rime Royal, and the Spenserian Stanza." Diss. Catholic U, 1934.

Mersand, Joseph. Chaucer's Romance Vocabulary. Port Washington, N.Y.: Kennikat, 1968.

Middleton, Anne. "The Idea of Public Poetry in the Reign of Richard II." Speculum 53(1978): 95-114.

Murphy, James Jerome. "Chaucer, Gower, and the English Rhetorical Tradition." Diss. Stanford U, 1957.

Muscatine, Charles. Chaucer and the French Tradition. Berkeley: U of California P, 1957.

Mustanoja, Tauno F. "Chaucer's Prosody." Companion to Chaucer Studies. Ed. Beryl Rowland. Rev. ed. Oxford: Oxford UP, 1979. 65-94.

Payne, Robert O. The Key of Remembrance. New Haven: Yale UP, 1963.

Pearsall, Derek. "The English Chaucerians." Chaucer and Chaucerians. Ed. D.S. Brewer. London: Nelson, 1966. 201-239.

Poirion, Daniel. Le Poète et le Prince. Paris: Presses Universitaires de France, 1965.

Pratt, Robert A. "Chaucer's Use of the Teseida." PMLA. 62(1947): 598-621.

Praz, Mario. "Chaucer and the Great Italian Writers of the Trecento." The Monthly Criterion 6(1927): 18-39, 131-157.

Preston, Raymond. "Chaucer and the Ballades Notées of Guillaume de Machaut." Speculum 26(1951): 615-623.

Reiss, Edmund. "Dusting off the Cobwebs: A Look at Chaucer's Lyrics." Chaucer Review 1(1966): 55-65.

------------. "Chaucer and His Audience." Chaucer Review 14 (1980): 390-402.

Robbins, Rossell Hope. "The Vintner's Son: French Wine in English Bottles." Eleanor of Aquitaine: Patron and Politician. Ed. William W. Kibler. Austin: U of Texas P, 1976. 147-172.

------------. "Geoffroi Chaucier, Poète Français, Father of English Poetry." Chaucer Review 13(1978): 93-115.

Robertson, D.W., JR. A Preface to Chaucer. Princeton: Princeton UP, 1963.

Robertson, Stuart. "Old English Verse in Chaucer." MLN 43(1928): 234-236.

Robinson, Ian. Chaucer's Prosody. London: Cambridge UP, 1971.

------------. Chaucer and the English Tradition. London: Cambridge UP, 1972.

Root, Robert K. The Poetry of Chaucer. Boston: Houghton Mifflin, 1922.

Rosenberg, Bruce. "The Oral Performance of Chaucer's Poetry: Situation and Medium." Folklore Forum 13.1(1980): 224-237.

Rossetti, W.M. Chaucer's Troylus and Cryseyde Compared with Boccaccio's Filostrato. London, 1873.

Rowland, Beryl. "'Pronuntiatio' and Its Effect on Chaucer's Audience." Studies in the Age of Chaucer 4(1982): 33-51.

Salmon, Vivian. "The Representation of Colloquial Speech in The Canterbury Tales." Style and Text: Studies Presented to Nils Enkvist. Ed. Hakan Ringbom, et. al. Stockholm: Sprakforlaget Skriptor AB, 1975. 263-277.

Samuels, M.L. "Chaucerian Final -e." NQ, NS 19(1972): 445-448.

Sanders, Barry. "Chaucer's Dependence on Sermon Structure in the Wife of Bath's 'Prologue' and 'Tale.'" Studies in Medieval Culture 4(1974): 437-445.

Schaar, Claes. "Troilus' Elegy and Criseyde's." Studia Neophilogica 24(1952): 185-191.

------------. The Golden Mirror. Denmark, 1967.

Schlauch, Margaret. "Chaucer's Colloquial English: Its Structural Traits." PMLA 67(1952): 1103-1116.

Schofield, W.H. "The Sea-Battle in Chaucer's 'Legend of Cleopatra.'" Kittredge Anniversary Papers. Boston, 1913.

Shannon, Edgar F. "Chaucer's Use of Octosyllabic Verse in the Book of the Duchess and the House of Fame." JEGP 12(1913): 277-294.

Shoaf, R.A. "Notes Toward Chaucer's Poetics of Translation." Studies in the Age of Chaucer 1(1979): 55-66.

Sledd, James. "Dorigen's Complaint." MP 45(1947): 36-45.

Smith, Roland M. "Three Notes on the Knight's Tale." MLN 51(1936): 318-322.

Southworth, James G. Verses of Cadence. Oxford: Blackwell, 1954.

------------. The Prosody of Chaucer and His Followers. Oxford: Blackwell, 1962.

Speirs, John. Chaucer the Maker. London: Faber, 1951.

Spurgeon, Caroline. Five Hundred Years of Chaucer Criticism and Allusion, 1357-1900. 3 vols. London: Cambridge UP, 1925.

Stone, E.W. "Chaucer's Prosody Based on a New Method." Diss. U of Denver, 1960.

Strohm, Paul. "Chaucer's Audience." Literature and History 5(1977): 26-41.

242

Strong, Caroline. "Sir Thopas and Sir Guy." MLN 23(1908): 73-77, 102-106.

Sutherland, Ronald, ed. The Romaunt of the Rose and Le Roman de la Rose. Oxford: Blackwell, 1968.

Tatlock, J.S.P. and A.G. Kennedy. Concordance to the Complete Works of Geoffrey Chaucer and to the Romaunt of the Rose. 2 vols. Washington: The Carnegie Foundation, 1927.

Ten Brink, Bernhard. The Language and Metre of Chaucer. Tr. M. Bentnick Smith. 2nd ed. London: Macmillan, 1921.

Thomas, W. Meredith. "Chaucer's Translation of the Bible." English and Medieval Studies Presented to J.R.R. Tolkien. Ed. Norman Davis and C.L. Wrenn. London, 1962.

Thompson, Elbert. "The Octosyllabic Couplet." PQ 18(1939): 257-268.

Thomson, Patricia. "The 'Canticus Troili': Chaucer and Petrarch." Comparative Literature 11(1959): 313-328.

Townsend, James. "Chaucer's Lyricism." Diss. U of California, Berkeley, 1962.

Tuve, Rosemond. "Spring in Chaucer and before Him." MLN 52 (1937): 9-16.

Walcutt, Charles Child. "The Pronoun of Address in Troilus and Criseyde." PQ 14(1935): 282-287.

Wenzel, Siegfried. "Chaucer and the Language of Contemporary Preaching." Studies in Philology 73(1976): 138-161.

Whittock, Trevor. A Reading of the Canterbury Tales. London: Cambridge UP, 1968.

Wilkins, Ernest H. "Canticus Troili." ELH 16(1949): 167-173.

Wimsatt, W.K. "The Rule and the Norm: Halle and Keyser on Chaucer's Meter." Literary Style: A Symposium. Ed. Seymour Chatman. New York, 1971.

INDEX

II

(Titles and First Lines of Medieval Lyrics)